HIKING KENTUCKY

HELP US KEEP THIS GUIDE UP TO DATE

Every effort has been made by the authors and editors to make this guide as accurate and useful as possible. However, many things can change after a guide is published—trails are rerouted, regulations change, techniques evolve, facilities come under new management, etc.

We appreciate hearing from you concerning your experiences with this guide and how you feel it could be improved and kept up to date. While we may not be able to respond to all comments and suggestions, we'll take them to heart and we'll also make certain to share them with the author. Please send your comments and suggestions to the following address:

> FalconGuides
> Reader Response/Editorial Department
> Falconeditorial@rowman.com

Thanks for your input, and happy trails!

HIKING KENTUCKY

A GUIDE TO THE STATE'S GREATEST HIKING ADVENTURES

4TH EDITION

Carrie Stambaugh

Revised by Johnny Molloy

ESSEX. CONNECTICUT

This book is for all who have made and hiked the trails of the one and only Bluegrass State.
Thanks to my wife, Keri Anne, for her help, as well as the folks
at Falcon for making this edition come to be.

FALCONGUIDES®

An imprint of Globe Pequot, the trade division of The Rowman & Littlefield Publishing Group, Inc.
4501 Forbes Blvd., Ste. 200
Lanham, MD 20706
www.rowman.com
Falcon and FalconGuides are registered trademarks and Make Adventure Your Story is a
trademark of The Rowman & Littlefield Publishing Group, Inc.

Distributed by NATIONAL BOOK NETWORK

Photos by Johnny Molloy unless otherwise noted
Maps by Melissa Baker and The Rowman & Littlefield Publishing Group, Inc.

Library of Congress Cataloging-in-Publication Data

Names: Molloy, Johnny, 1961- author. | Stambaugh, Carrie L., author.
Title: Hiking Kentucky: a guide to the state's greatest hiking adventures / Carrie Stambaugh;
    revised by Johnny Molloy.
Description: Fourth edition. | Guilford, Connecticut: FalconGuides, 2023. | Series: Falcon guide |
    Includes index. |
Summary: "From old country roads to dense forest paths, Kentucky boasts more than 1,500 miles
    of marked and maintained trails. In this fully updated and revised guide, author Johnny Molloy
    describes some of the best hikes in the state, from 1-mile nature trails to multiday backpacks"—
    Provided by publisher.
Identifiers: LCCN 2022023475 (print) | LCCN 2022023476 (ebook) | ISBN 9781493065608
    (paperback) | ISBN 9781493065615 (epub)
Subjects: LCSH: Hiking—Kentucky—Guidebooks. | Kentucky—Guidebooks.
Classification: LCC GV199.42.K4 M658 2023 (print) | LCC GV199.42.K4 (ebook) | DDC
    796.5109769--dc23/eng/20220525
LC record available at https://lccn.loc.gov/2022023475
LC ebook record available at https://lccn.loc.gov/2022023476

CONTENTS

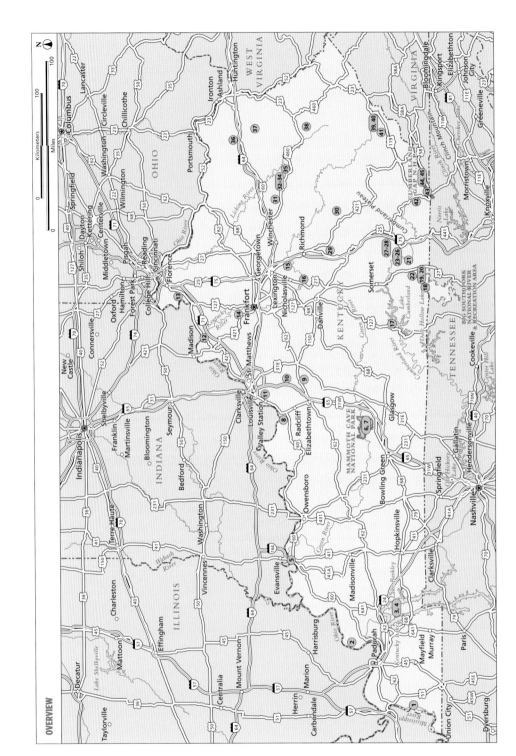

Big South Fork and Rockcastle Valley

Greater Eastern Kentucky

Southeastern Kentucky

MEET YOUR GUIDES

Johnny Molloy is a writer and adventurer based in Johnson City, Tennessee. His outdoor passion ignited on a backpacking trip in Great Smoky Mountains National Park. That first foray unleashed a love of the outdoors that led Johnny to spend over 4,000 nights backpacking, canoe camping, and tent camping throughout North America over the past four decades.

Friends enjoyed his outdoor adventure stories; one even suggested he write a book. He pursued his friend's idea and soon parlayed his love of the outdoors into an occupation. The results of his efforts are over eighty books and guides, most of them in multiple editions, written for six different publishers. His writings include how-to outdoor guides and true adventure stories, as well as hiking, camping, and paddling books covering all or parts of twenty-eight states.

Though primarily involved with book publications, Molloy also writes for varied magazines and websites. To this day, he continues writing and traveling extensively throughout the United States, endeavoring in a variety of outdoor pursuits.

A Christian, Johnny is an active member of Christ Community Church and Gideons International. His non-outdoor interests include reading, American history, and University of Tennessee sports. He lives in Johnson City, Tennessee. For the latest on Johnny, please visit JohnnyMolloy.com.

Carrie Stambaugh is the author of *Hiking Kentucky* (3rd edition). A journalist and photographer, her work has appeared in *The Independent, Ironton Tribune, Greater Ashland Beacon, Bridges, Huntington Quarterly, Portsmouth Metro,* and *Tri-State Living.* She lives in Ashland, Kentucky. Visit her at CarrieStambaugh.com.

INTRODUCTION

From the Big Sandy River in the east to the mighty Mississippi River in the west, from the rolling Ohio River in the north to the Tennessee line in the south, Kentucky encompasses 40,395 square miles of scenic lands and waters. Within the Bluegrass State are two national parks; two major federal recreation areas; the Daniel Boone National Forest, stretching almost the width of the state; more than a dozen large US Army Corps of Engineers reservoirs with significant amounts of adjacent land; more than 160 state parks, forests, wildlife areas, and nature preserves; as well as scores of additional parcels owned by private groups and local governments and open to public use.

This book is a guide to the most scenic of these areas and to forty-five specific hikes within them, presenting a mosaic of trail experiences for the hiker. Kentucky boasts more than 2,000 miles of maintained, marked trails. I certainly haven't been on all of them, but these forty-five hikes offer a range of experiences and scenery from overnight backpacks in Kentucky's remote eastern mountains to strolls along the Mississippi River in its farthest western corner.

These hikes cover all regions of Kentucky and offer enough variety to satisfy people of all ages, experience, and stamina. They range in length from short loops of less than 2 miles to overnight backpacking trips, the longest of which remains the 30-mile excursion through Mammoth Cave National Park. Kentucky is full of beautiful places to hike, most of which are free and can easily be accessed from every corner of the Commonwealth.

In a backdrop of Kentucky's finest scenery, Bluegrass State hikers can immerse themselves in the region's forests, mountains, and river valleys along which travel hiking trails. Starting in Western Kentucky, you can overlook the mighty Mississippi River from the bluffs at Columbus-Belmont State Park. Or loop around Honker Lake at Land Between the Lakes National Recreation Area. Go on a family day hike at Hematite Lake, then visit nearby Center Furnace. The hike at John James Audubon State Park takes place where America's most famous naturalist identified birds during his nine-year stay in nearby Henderson. Another adventure takes you to Mantle Rock, a large sandstone arch located in a beautiful stream-crossed bottomland crossed by the Trail of Tears.

The Mammoth Cave and greater Louisville area offers a 30-mile backpack through the wilds of the aboveground parcel of Mammoth Cave National Park. Or enjoy a hike among the highlight-laden nature trails near the Mammoth Cave Visitor Center. Closer to Louisville you can view the Ohio River at Otter Creek Outdoor Recreation Area or enjoy a tour of ponds, lakes, and woods at renowned Bernheim Arboretum and Research Forest. Make a loop at revered Jefferson Memorial Forest, or seek out wildflowers at Vernon-Douglas State Nature Preserve. In northern Kentucky and the greater Lexington area, you can trek the steep slopes of General Butler State Resort Park and get rewarded with a view. Visit the salt lick, see prehistoric bones, and gaze upon buffalo at

Big Bone Lick State Park. Check out the waterfalls at Cove Spring Park near Frankfort. Soak in views, cascades, and all-around beauty at Raven Run Sanctuary. Hike lesser trod terrain to see the palisades of the Kentucky River at a special state nature preserve.

The Big South Fork and Rockcastle River Valley are chock-full of fascinating hikes featuring geological wonders and waterfalls. Grab lake vistas from outcrops at Lake Cumberland State Resort Park. Check out Gobblers Arch and Marks Branch Falls on the same hike. Soak in a view of the Big South Fork and make your way through the Cracks-in-the-Rock on the Blue Heron Loop at Big South Fork National River and Recreation Area. See an arch and giant rockhouses along with Yahoo Falls—Kentucky's highest cataract—on one hike. Be amazed at the variety of cascades while hiking to Princess Falls and Lick Creek Falls. The Eagle Falls Loop delivers aquatic beauty at Cumberland Falls State Resort Park. The hike through the Cumberland River Gorge is a feast for the eyes, and a chance to see a rare moonbow. The Scuttle Hole hike combines cataracts and views in a concentrated dose doable by hikers of all ages. Enjoy solitude en route to Bear Creek Falls and Arch Falls, where water spills through a natural bridge. Geology plays a big part when hiking at historic Bee Rock. Find Vanhook Falls, a delicate spiller deep in the wilds of the Daniel Boone National Forest.

Greater Eastern Kentucky encompasses a lot of terrain and a lot of highlight-filled hikes. Head to a plethora of overlooks at Berea Forest. Make a quaint family hike from family-friendly Turkey Foot Recreation Area, where swimming, fishing, and camping are also on the docket. Head to the outcrop where Daniel Boone himself overlooked the Bluegrass from Pilot Knob. Natural Bridge State Park is deservedly a Kentucky icon and offers a highlight reel of a hike that cannot fail to please. And then there's the Red River Gorge Scenic Area. Head to regal Courthouse Rock and unique Double Arch. Check out the historic and massive rockhouse that is D Boon Hut, as well as Grays Arch, all on one hike. The arch of Rock Bridge spans a creek that also features a waterfall, and more. Carter Caves State Park offers a nearly 8-mile loop with arches, rockhouses, creeks, bluffs, and backpacking opportunities. Head out to Lick Falls at Grayson Lake State Park, fashioning a worthy loop hike. Take a walk on Kentucky's longest rail trail—the Dawkins Line—while enjoying this newer, linear Kentucky state park.

In Southeastern Kentucky you can hike the state's highest terrain. Make an extended trek on the geologically intriguing Pine Mountain State Scenic Trail. Check out a high and mighty cataract at Bad Branch State Nature Preserve, along with a side trip to Kentucky's highest ridge. Speaking of high, take a highlight hike at Kingdom Come, Kentucky's loftiest state park. Soak in the views—and the story—from Chained Rock. What can be more Kentucky than walking through and around Cumberland Gap? Hike to the Hensley Settlement, a preserved mountaintop community. Head to the rewarding panorama at White Rocks then visit the one and only Sand Cave, spectacular in every regard.

The Bluegrass State is home to the rewarding hikes in this book. After having the privilege of researching potential hikes for this book, hiking the hikes, taking photographs, shooting video, selecting the hikes that made the grade—and the ones that didn't—exploring the parks beyond the trails, mapping the hikes, then actually writing and completing this compilation, I am excited to share these Kentucky adventures with you. The treks are an ideal mix of views, waterfalls, and geology; places where the human history of ol' Kentuck' mixes with the natural history; and where a wealth of flora and fauna makes hiking Kentucky a singular experience.

I think of the treasure trove of trails in the Bluegrass and how the hikes in this guide—a cross section of great hikes in Kentucky—create a mosaic of trail experiences reflecting the wide array of experiences to be had in this state that stretches west from the Appalachian Mountains to the Mississippi River, from the Tennessee state line north to the Ohio River. I hope the trails offered in this book will help you explore, understand, and appreciate the natural and human history of Kentucky. Enjoy!

WEATHER

Kentucky experiences all four seasons in their entirety, and sometimes all at once when you take into account the state's elevation variations, ranging from a little under 300 feet along the Mississippi River near Kentucky's border with Tennessee and Missouri to 4,145 feet atop Black Mountain, near the Virginia state line. Summer is warm to hot, and humid. Morning hikers can avoid the common afternoon thunderstorms. Electronic devices equipped with internet access allow summer hikers to monitor storms as they come up, though coverage can be spotty in places. Hikers increase in numbers when the first northerly fronts of fall sweep cool clear air across the Bluegrass State. Crisp mornings, great for vigorous treks, give way to warm afternoons, more conducive to family strolls. Autumn is a great time to hike the Bluegrass State. Winters are variable, bringing a few subfreezing days, plenty of chilling rains, and a few snows each year, more so in the east. However, there will also be plenty of fine, sunny days ideal for hiking. Make the most of them. Spring will be more variable—a mild day can be followed by a cold one. Extensive rains bring regrowth, but also keep hikers indoors. A good way to plan your hiking is to check monthly averages of high and low temperatures and average rainfall for each month in Frankfort, in the north center of the state. Frankfort averages 8 inches of snow and 47 inches of rain per year. The following climate data will give you a good idea of what to expect each month. Temperatures will be cooler and precipitation higher in the eastern highlands and warmer toward the Mississippi River.

MONTH	AVERAGE HIGH (°F)	AVERAGE LOW (°F)	PRECIPITATION (IN.)
January	43	25	3.3
February	47	28	3.4
March	57	35	4.7
April	68	45	4.5
May	76	54	5.1
June	85	63	4.3
July	87	67	4.7
August	87	65	3.1
September	81	57	3.3
October	69	45	3.6
November	57	35	3.3
December	47	29	3.7

FLORA AND FAUNA

You don't have to worry about grizzlies, mountain lions, or other four-footed predators in Kentucky. In fact, the biggest threat to hikers in Kentucky is themselves. (Hikers place themselves at risk when they are unprepared for weather changes, underestimate the trail or overestimate their hiking abilities, go off-trail, hike alone, or fail to stick to their hiking plan.) The state does have a growing population of black bears. After being eliminated in the 1800s by hunting and habitat destruction, black bears began moving in from neighboring Virginia, West Virginia, and Tennessee when regenerating oak forests matured. Sightings are most frequent in the eastern third of the state, with isolated sightings in central Kentucky. The wooded mountainous areas as well as the Big South Fork and Daniel Boone National Forest are Kentucky black bear strongholds. There has been a rise in the number of human-bear interactions. Most conflicts involve the intentional feeding of bears or access to human-related food sources. It is illegal to feed bears in Kentucky.

The large wild animal you are most likely to encounter is the elk. A program to reestablish elk in the state has proved successful; currently there are believed to be more than 15,000 elk covering sixteen counties in the southeast part of the state, the most of any state east of the Mississippi River. White-tailed deer are plentiful in the state, and a small, nonaggressive member of the cat family, the bobcat, lives in every county. Beavers, foxes, muskrats, opossums, raccoons, woodchucks, coyotes, and wild hogs are also in residence. The state bird is the Kentucky cardinal.

One of the most exciting creatures you are apt to see is the wild turkey, the largest game bird in North America; an adult male can approach 30 pounds. Kentucky's wild turkey population had been all but eliminated a few decades ago. Restoration efforts, however, have now brought the population back to well over 250,000, and it's not uncommon for one of the birds to blast out of its wooded hiding spot as you traipse by.

There are venomous snakes in Kentucky—primarily the timber rattlesnake and the copperhead, found in most parts of the state, and the water moccasin, found only in the west. Snakes strike humans only in self-defense, or when startled or afraid. The solution is to avoid scaring them. Look before you place your feet, especially in tall grass, and don't reach under or over rocks or logs without looking first. If you do encounter a snake, slowly back away and give it a chance to slither off—an opportunity it will invariably take. Don't throw rocks and sticks at the snake. If bitten, try not to panic. Running will speed up your circulation and increase the speed the venom travels through your bloodstream. Keep the bite site lower than your heart to decrease the venom spread, and seek medical attention as soon as possible.

Unlike venomous snakes, ticks are common in Kentucky—and a real pest for the hiker during the warm season. In addition to being a nuisance, ticks can cause serious health problems. Lyme disease, a flu-like sickness, the symptoms of which include nausea, fever, fatigue, and muscle and joint aches, is spread by the bite of infected deer ticks. Most ticks are not infected, and Kentucky reports few cases of the disease. However, if a red inflammation develops at the site of a tick bite, it may signal infection and should be checked by a doctor. To prevent tick bites and the possibility of disease, follow this advice from officials at Land Between the Lakes, where ticks are out in force much of the year: Wear long pants and tuck the legs into your socks or boots, or tape your pant legs closed. Spray your clothes with a tick repellent. Periodically check your clothes and body for ticks, and remove any you find with tweezers or fingers, taking care not to crush the body of an attached tick.

The flora offers as much variety as you would expect with such elevational range and sheer distance between the east and west. Extensive woodlands are found in the east, where hardwood forests of maple, tulip, birch, and beech mix with evergreens such as holly and pine, with preserved hemlock in the hollows of the Cumberland Plateau. Moving west, moisture-loving species such as sycamore and ash will be found along waterways, while great oak and hickory stands will be found in drier environments, along with cedar. Along the lowermost Ohio and Mississippi Rivers you will find bottomlands where great bald cypress trees reign, along with other swamp-loving species. It all adds up to vegetational variety of the first order that can be seen and experienced as you hike the trails of the Bluegrass State.

WILDERNESS RESTRICTIONS/REGULATIONS

The hikes in this guide primarily take place in national parks and national forests as well as state, county, and city parks. On one hike you may traverse multiple parcels of public land, going from a state park to state forest, from a national forest to a state park, and so on. Most of the time you will not know the difference; the flora and fauna of the Bluegrass State certainly don't. A couple of hikes barely edge into Virginia. Each unit will have its own backcountry camping regulations, when backpacking is allowed. For example, a backcountry permit is required for backpacking at Cumberland Gap National Historical Park, yet none is required in the Daniel Boone National Forest except for Red River Gorge, where an overnight parking permit is required.

Detailed trail and road maps are available of almost all the lands traveled in this guide. Download them; they come in handy in helping you get around.

GETTING AROUND

AREA CODES

Kentucky has five area codes. The western part uses 270 and 364, greater Louisville is 502, and greater Lexington is 859. Eastern Kentucky uses 859.

ROADS

Where feasible, hike directions originate at an interstate. The primary interstates in Kentucky are I-75, I-64, I-65, and I-24. Lesser interstates are I-155 and I-169. Kentucky also features state parkways that enhance the interstate system. If directions from an interstate aren't feasible, they are given from major federal highways and/or easily identifiable towns.

BY AIR

Kentucky has three large accessible airports: Cincinnati/Northern Kentucky International (CVG), Lexington Blue Grass Airport (LEX), and Louisville International Airport (SDF). To book reservations online, check out your favorite airline's website or search a travel site for the best price.

BY BUS

Most trailheads are not accessible via bus, but Greyhound serves some towns in Kentucky; visit greyhound.com for more information.

VISITOR INFORMATION

For general information on visiting Kentucky, check out the official tourism site for the Bluegrass State at kentuckytourism.com or call (800) 225-8747. Major cities and locales also have their own sites.

HOW TO USE THIS GUIDE

This guide contains just about everything you'll ever need to choose, plan for, enjoy, and survive a hike in Kentucky. Stuffed with Kentucky hiking–specific information, *Hiking Kentucky* features forty-five mapped and cued hikes. I grouped the hikes into six units. "Western Kentucky" covers hikes from the Mississippi River east roughly to Bowling Green. "Mammoth Cave and Greater Louisville Area" covers Mammoth Cave National Park and points north to Kentucky's largest city. "Northern Kentucky and Greater Lexington" details hikes in the Ohio River Valley toward Cincinnati as well as around Lexington. "Big South Fork and Rockcastle Valley" includes the Big South Fork National River and Recreation Area plus hikes in the southern Daniel Boone National Forest and nearby state parks. "Greater Eastern Kentucky" encompasses a big swath from east of I-75 up to northeastern Kentucky at Carter Caves plus the northern part of the Daniel Boone National Forest, including the fabled Red River Gorge. "Southeastern Kentucky" takes in Kentucky's high country, including Cumberland Gap National Historical Park.

Each hike starts with a short **summary** of the hike's highlights. These quick overviews give you a taste of the hiking adventures to follow. You'll learn about the trail terrain and what surprises each route has to offer. Following the overview, you'll find the **hike specs:** quick, nitty-gritty details of the hike. Most are self-explanatory, but here are some details on others:

Start: Tells you at exactly where to begin your hike. For example, the hike might start at a picnic area within a state park, allowing you to look for a specific trailhead rather than just the state park. The name of the trailhead often corresponds with those found on mapping apps.

Distance: The total distance of the recommended route—one-way for loop hikes, the round-trip on an out-and-back or balloon-loop hike, point-to-point for a shuttle. Options are additional.

Difficulty: Each hike has been assigned a level of difficulty. The rating system was developed from several sources and personal experience. These levels are meant to be a guideline only, and a particular hike may prove easier or harder for different people depending on ability and physical fitness.

Easy—Five miles or less total trip distance in one day with minimal elevation gain; paved or smooth-surfaced dirt trail.

Moderate—Up to 10 miles total trip distance in one day with moderate elevation gain; potentially rough terrain.

Difficult—More than 10 miles total trip distance in one day or strenuous elevation gains; rough and/or rocky terrain.

Elevation: The aggregate elevation gained and lost during a hike, whether it is a loop or an out-and-back hike. These numbers were determined using GPS data obtained during the given hike loaded onto a mapping program.

Maximum grade: The steepest portion of the hike for a sustained distance, whether you will be going up or down that grade on the specific hike. The maximum grade is calculated by dividing the elevation gained or lost by the distance covered.

Hiking time: The average time it will take to cover the route. This number is based on the total distance, elevation gain, and condition and difficulty of the trail. Your fitness level will also affect your time.

Seasons/schedule: The best time of year to hike the given hike and/or the specific hours a place is open/closed.

Fees and permits: Whether you need to carry any money with you for park entrance fees and permits.

Dog friendly: Whether dogs are allowed or not, as well as specific regulations; also if it makes sense to take your pet on the given hike.

Trail surface: General information about what to expect underfoot. Is the trail very rocky, smooth, wide, natural surface, etc.? Are parts of the path paved or concrete? This way you know what footwear to use and what conditions to expect.

Land status: Whether it is a state park, state forest, federal holding, private preserve, or other entity.

Nearest town: Helps orient you to the hike's location as well as what amenities are nearby, such as outfitters, restaurants, or an emergency clinic.

Other trail users: Equestrians, mountain bikers, in-line skaters, etc.

Maps to consult: Other maps to supplement the maps in this book. USGS maps are a good source for accurate topographical information, but the local park map may show more recent trails. Use both.

Amenities available: If restrooms, picnic areas, campgrounds, and other enhancements are at or near the trailhead.

Cell service: Whether your phone will get reception on the hike. In population-variable areas such as Kentucky, you can have reception on a ridge but not down in the valley. Also, the carrier you use can have a lot to do with whether or not you have reception.

Trail contacts: This is the location, phone number, and website URL for the local land manager(s) in charge of all the trails within the selected hike. Get trail access information before you head out, or contact the land manager after your visit if you see problems with trail erosion, damage, or misuse.

Finding the trailhead gives you dependable driving directions to where you'll want to park.

The Hike is the meat of the chapter. Detailed and honest, it's a carefully researched impression of the trail. It also often includes lots of area history, both natural and human.

Miles and Directions provides mileage cues identifying all turns and trail name changes, as well as points of interest.

HOW TO USE THE MAPS

Overview map: This map shows the location of each hike in the area by hike number.

Route map: This is your primary visual guide to each hike. It shows all the accessible roads and trails, points of interest, water, landmarks, and geographical features. The map also distinguishes trails from roads, and paved roads from unpaved roads. The selected route is highlighted, and directional arrows point the way.

TRAIL FINDER

To get our readers started on the hikes that best suit their interests and abilities, this simple trail finder categorizes each of the hikes in the book into a helpful list. Your hikes can fall under more than one category, so choose the categories that are most appropriate for your area.

HIKE #	HIKE NAME	BEST HIKES FOR WATERFALLS	BEST HIKES FOR GREAT VIEWS	BEST HIKES FOR CHILDREN	BEST HIKES FOR DOGS	BEST HIKES FOR LAKE/STREAM LOVERS	BEST HIKES FOR BACKPACKERS	BEST HIKES FOR NATURE LOVERS	BEST HIKES FOR HISTORY LOVERS
1	Columbus-Belmont State Park		•	•					•
2	Mantle Rock Loop		•	•			•		•
3	Hematite Lake Loop		•	•	•	•			•
4	Honker Lake Loop		•	•	•	•		•	
5	John James Audubon State Park			•	•			•	•
6	Mammoth Cave Backcountry Hike	•					•	•	
7	Mammoth Cave Nature Trails Circuit		•	•				•	•
8	Otter Creek		•			•		•	•
9	Vernon-Douglas State Nature Preserve							•	
10	Bernheim Forest Walk		•	•	•	•			
11	Horine Reservation Hike					•		•	•
12	General Butler State Resort Park Hike		•			•			•
13	Big Bone Lick Hike				•			•	•
14	Cove Spring Park Loop	•		•	•	•			•
15	Raven Run Sanctuary		•	•	•			•	
16	Palisades of the Kentucky River		•	•				•	

HIKE #	HIKE NAME	BEST HIKES FOR WATERFALLS	BEST HIKES FOR GREAT VIEWS	BEST HIKES FOR CHILDREN	BEST HIKES FOR DOGS	BEST HIKES FOR LAKE/STREAM LOVERS	BEST HIKES FOR BACKPACKERS	BEST HIKES FOR NATURE LOVERS	BEST HIKES FOR HISTORY LOVERS
17	Lake Cumberland State Resort Park Hike		•	•	•	•			
18	Gobblers Arch Circuit	•			•	•	•	•	
19	Big Spring Falls and Dick Gap Falls	•	•			•	•		
20	Blue Heron Loop	•	•		•	•	•		•
21	Princess Falls and Lick Creek Falls	•				•	•		
22	Yahoo Falls	•	•	•		•		•	
23	Eagle Falls Loop	•	•	•	•	•		•	
24	Cumberland River Gorge	•	•			•	•	•	•
25	The Scuttle Hole	•	•	•	•	•			
26	Arch Falls and Bear Creek Falls	•			•			•	•
27	Rockcastle Narrows and Bee Rock Loop	•	•	•	•	•		•	•
28	Vanhook Falls Loop	•		•	•	•	•		
29	Views from Berea Forest		•	•				•	
30	Turkey Foot	•		•	•	•			
31	Pilot Knob State Nature Preserve		•	•				•	•
32	Natural Bridge Highlight Hike		•	•	•			•	•
33	Courthouse Rock and Double Arch		•	•	•		•		
34	D Boon Hut and Grays Arch			•	•			•	•
35	Rock Bridge	•		•	•	•		•	
36	Carter Caves Circuit			•	•	•	•	•	
37	Lick Falls	•	•	•		•		•	
38	Dawkins Line Rail Trail			•	•				•
39	Pine Mountain State Scenic Trail		•		•		•	•	
40	Bad Branch Falls and High Rock Loop	•	•			•		•	
41	Kingdom Come Highlight Hike		•	•	•				
42	Chained Rock		•	•	•			•	•

HIKE #	HIKE NAME	BEST HIKES FOR WATERFALLS	BEST HIKES FOR GREAT VIEWS	BEST HIKES FOR CHILDREN	BEST HIKES FOR DOGS	BEST HIKES FOR LAKE/ STREAM LOVERS	BEST HIKES FOR BACKPACKERS	BEST HIKES FOR NATURE LOVERS	BEST HIKES FOR HISTORY LOVERS
43	Cumberland Gap Hike		•	•	•				•
44	Hensley Settlement						•	•	•
45	White Rocks Sand Cave Hike	•	•		•		•	•	•

Map Legend

Municipal

≡（65）≡ Interstate Highway

≡（421）≡ US Highway

≡（133）≡ State Road

≡[176]≡ Local/Forest Road

= = = = Unpaved Road

├────┼────┤ Railroad

·-··-··- State Boundary

Trails

------ Featured Trail

------ Trail

Water Features

⬭ Body of Water

Marsh

River/Creek

Intermittent Stream

Waterfall

Rapids

Spring

Symbols

≍ Bridge

▥▥▥ Boardwalk

➤ Boat Launch

≍ Bridge

▪ Building/Point of Interest

▲ Campground

∩ Cave

† Cemetery

! Gate

▭ Lodging

🅿 Parking

▲ Peak

Ⓐ Picnic Area

🏠 Ranger Station/Park Office

🚻 Restroom

◀ Scenic View/Overlook

○ Town

① Trailhead

❓ Visitor/Information Center

Land Management

National Park/Historical Park/Forest

National Recreation Area

State Park/Forest, County Park

Nature Preserve/Outdoor Recreation Area

1 COLUMBUS-BELMONT STATE PARK

Walk through big woods and along high bluffs above the Mississippi River at Kentucky's westernmost state park, also featuring Confederate earthworks from the Civil War. The short, easy adventure visits most of Columbus-Belmont State Park's facilities along the way.

Start: Near park snack bar and mini-golf
Distance: 1.7-mile loop
Difficulty: Easy
Elevation change: +/-122 feet
Maximum grade: 4% grade for 0.1 mile
Hiking time: About 1 hour
Seasons/schedule: Year-round
Fees and permits: No fees or permits required
Dog friendly: Yes
Trail surface: Forested natural surface, grass, asphalt

Land status: State park
Nearest town: Columbus
Other trail users: None
Maps to consult: Columbus-Belmont State Park
Amenities available: Snack bar, picnic shelter, campground
Cell service: Good
Trail contacts: Columbus-Belmont State Park; (270) 677-2327; parks.ky.gov/columbus/parks/historic/columbus-belmont-state-park

FINDING THE TRAILHEAD

From Bardwell, take KY 123 south for 10 miles to the town of Columbus; turn right onto Cheatham Street. (From Clinton, take KY 58 west to Columbus; turn right onto KY 123, and in 0.1 mile turn left onto Cheatham Street.) Cheatham becomes Park Road and ends in 0.8 mile at a parking lot for the picnic area. The hike starts behind and to the right of the snack bar as you face it. Trailhead GPS: 36.765787 / -89.110486

THE HIKE

This little hike takes you along a bluff high above the Mississippi River with stupendous upstream and downstream views. It is one of the most dramatic overlooks you will find anywhere in the state. Indeed, that's exactly why the little town of Columbus played a role in the Civil War.

In 1861, disregarding Kentucky's neutral status, Confederate troops fortified these bluffs to stop Union forces from using the Mississippi to penetrate the South. On November 7, 1861, under a then little-known brigadier general named Ulysses S. Grant, Union forces attacked the Confederate camp at the Missouri town of Belmont, just across the river from Columbus. The cannon fire from the Kentucky bluff helped turn back the Northern advance. Militarily the battle was inconclusive, but the aggressiveness shown by Grant's troops gave a significant boost to both Union morale and his career. The next year, after the loss of strategic forts on the Tennessee and Cumberland Rivers, the Confederates abandoned Columbus.

Gazing down on the Mississippi from a high bluff

This 156-acre state park was developed in the 1930s to commemorate the 1861 battle and preserve the extensive earthworks. Its main attribute, however, is the commanding vista of the Mississippi. The park has only a few short trails, so this hike relies on a combination of paths, paved walkways, and Park Road. Interpretive signage enhances the hike.

The hike leaves the snack bar area in vine-draped woods, soon coming alongside some large earthworks where Confederate soldiers and their guns waited for Union attack in 1861. The hike takes you to the northern tip of the park before curving south back along the bluff, where you first look down upon preserved Rebel earthworks then get those eye-popping vistas from a bluff way above the river. The views contrast with other overlooks in the mountainous districts of the state.

The hike then leaves the bluff area on an asphalt path, passing the park museum, a converted house that served as a Confederate hospital during the war. Finally you join the park's main road, returning to the parking area.

MILES AND DIRECTIONS

0.0   Start on a natural surface trail between the snack bar and mini-golf, going north into vine-draped woods rich with hackberry.

0.2   Reach an intersection. Stay with the outermost trail, now coming to preserved earthworks rising on both sides of the path. Shortly pass another trail intersection, staying right on the outside of the loop.

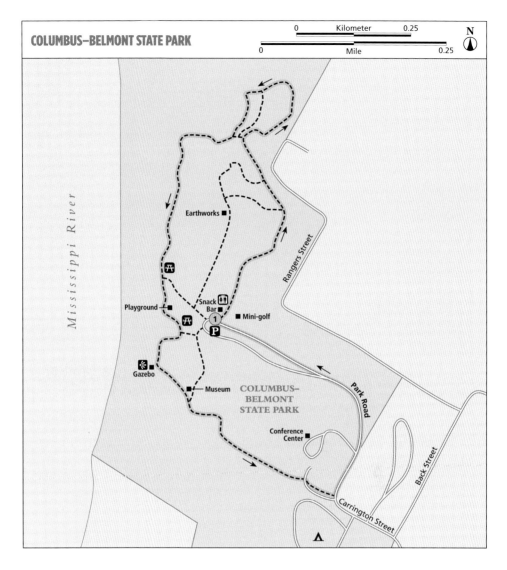

Earthworks ■

Playground ■

Snack Bar ■

■ Mini-golf

Gazebo ■

■ Museum

COLUMBUS–
BELMONT
STATE PARK

Conference
Center ■

Park Road

Rangers Street

Carrington Street

Back Street

Mississippi River

0.4 Begin curving south. Ahead, pass another intersection; stay on the outside of the loop. Partial views open of the Mississippi River. Come alongside a metal fence. Stay alongside the fence, looking down on major earthworks.

0.7 Open onto a grassy track and the picnic shelter nearest the bluff edge of the Mississippi River. Savor extensive views up- and downriver as well as across the water into Missouri and Belmont, where a Confederate encampment was located. Keep south along a wooden fence, passing the children's play area before joining an asphalt path. Follow the asphalt path uphill toward a stone gazebo.

0.9 Reach the stone gazebo and stunning panoramas of river country and beyond. Scan for barges. Follow the asphalt path away from the river, passing the historic house turned park museum.

1.2 Pass the park maintenance area. The park campground is to your right. Soon reach Park Road and turn left.

1.7 Arrive back at the parking area near the snack bar.

2 MANTLE ROCK LOOP

This Western Kentucky trek will surprise. It leads to one the longest arches in the state; goes through a pretty, stone-lined valley rife with wildflowers; then traces a historic segment of the Cherokee's Trail of Tears, when the aboriginals were forced from their Appalachian homelands to resettle in what became Oklahoma. The circuit, attractive throughout, is more than worth making the out-of-the-way trip.

Start: KY 133 trailhead
Distance: 2.5-mile loop
Difficulty: Easy
Elevation change: +/-270 feet
Maximum grade: 5% grade for 0.3 mile
Hiking time: About 1.4 hours
Seasons/schedule: Spring for wildflowers
Fees and permits: No fees or permits required
Dog friendly: No dogs allowed

Trail surface: Forested natural surface
Land status: Private preserve open to public
Nearest town: Salem
Other trail users: None
Maps to consult: At trailhead displays
Amenities available: None
Cell service: Good
Trail contacts: The Nature Conservancy; (859) 259-9655; nature.org

FINDING THE TRAILHEAD

From Marion, take US 60 west for 11.3 miles to the town of Salem; turn right onto KY 133 west. In 13 miles—2 miles beyond the community of Joy—turn left into the signed lot on your left. The hike starts at the south end of the lot. Trailhead GPS: 37.358568 / -88.421726

THE HIKE

The long arch of Mantle Rock as well as the adjacent bluffs and rockhouses of this tributary of McGilligan Creek recall cliff lines and arches of eastern Kentucky. But here they are, in wooded steep valleys draining into the Ohio River in the far west of the state. The singular features of the locale have been attracting humans for millennia, with various peoples using Mantle Rock and other rockhouses as shelters.

During the tragic winter of 1838–39, while waiting for improved weather that would allow them to cross the Ohio River, about 1,800 Cherokee—what became known as the Peter Hildebrand Detachment—took shelter under Mantle Rock and other nearby rockhouses. As a result of the Indian Removal Act of 1830, a total of 16,000 Cherokee were forcibly moved from their homeland in the Southern Appalachians, with several Cherokee groups using several different routes. It is estimated that around 1,000 Cherokee died en route to their new home in Oklahoma. Other tribes were sent west as well, many going of their own volition when they realized the futility of resisting the government.

Part of this loop hike takes you on the very road a group of Cherokee used while toiling west. A cold spell had hit, freezing the Ohio River and stopping boats from being used to carry the aboriginals across to Illinois from Barry's Ferry. The Cherokee sought refuge, huddling beneath Mantle Rock and other rockhouses you will see along the hike.

Standing under the long arch of Mantle Rock

It was a rough two weeks waiting for the ice to break, but Mantle Rock was eventually left behind.

Fast-forward 140 years. Reynolds Metal Company donated 188 acres to form the core of Mantle Rock Nature Preserve. Additional tracts were added later, enlarging the main preserve. Nearby but noncontiguous tracts were also purchased, creating a larger land mosaic and larger ecosystem for the plants and animals of this locale.

Hiking by bluffs near Mantle Rock

Not only are the bluffs and rockhouses ecologically significant, but the tract also harbors sandstone glades—dry, thin-soiled places with upthrust sandstone—where Kentucky's only known occurrence of June grass can be found. You will also see little bluestem grass, prickly pear cactus, and pinweed. The Nature Conservancy is also working to restore native prairie and these special sandstone glades using prescribed burns.

The National Park Service recognizes the Mantle Rock tract as a preserved portion of the Trail of Tears route. Enlightening interpretive information enhances the experience, taking you back to that distressing time. Today, we can not only retrace part of the Trail of Tears but also view Mantle Rock and the other geological highlights on a clockwise loop. You first descend through a meadow then reach the loop portion of the hike in woods. One direction is the original Trail of Tears route; the other leads to Mantle Rock. You soon enter an unexpected geological wonderland that includes Mantle Rock, cliff lines, and rockhouses, the same ones used by the Cherokee and a host of native peoples before them. Keep winding lower to join a bigger tributary of McGilligan Creek, then hike upstream along McGilligan Creek itself, watching for more rock formations.

You then leave the stream for the uplands, joining the old roadbed again, tracing the steps of the Cherokee. Pass sandstone glades, with their imperiled flora and an ancient oak that was around in Cherokee times before completing the fascinating circuit that proves hiking in Western Kentucky can hold its own.

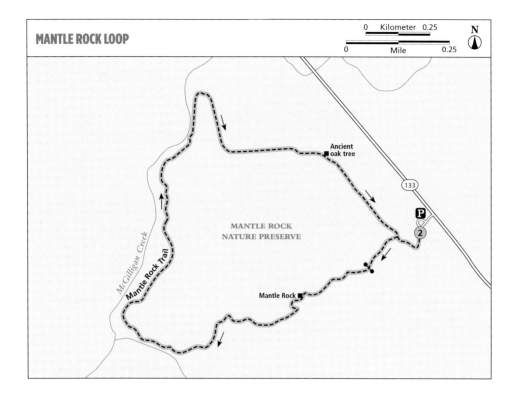

MILES AND DIRECTIONS

0.0 Start from the parking area and head southeast, descending past engaging interpretive signs. Enter woods and turn right, tracing an old roadbed, part of the Cherokee Trail of Tears.

0.1 Reach an intersection. Head left toward Mantle Rock, away from the old roadbed, running parallel to a streambed.

0.2 Pass around a gate and kiosk with more interpretive information. Cruise downhill, reaching an area of rock outcroppings.

0.4 Come to Mantle Rock, the 188-foot-long, 30-foot-high arch, running alongside a cliff, with a seasonal stream running under it. Continue beyond the arch along cliffs and beside a stream where trout lilies, Dutchman's breeches, and toothwort thrive.

0.5 Split between big boulders, keeping along a cliff line of a tributary of McGilligan Creek in boulder gardens.

1.0 Turn right, up McGilligan Creek. Seasonal tributaries cross the trail.

1.7 Turn right, tracing the original Trail of Tears route. Cross through sandstone glades.

2.1 Pass a huge ancient oak. Come near transforming prairie.

2.4 Complete the loop. Backtrack to the trailhead.

2.5 Arrive back at the trailhead.

3 HEMATITE LAKE LOOP

An ideal family day hike, this circuit at family-friendly Land Between the Lakes National Recreation Area (LBL) takes you around photo-worthy Hematite Lake. Begin at an alluring picnic area, then skirt a rolling shoreline with attractive water vistas. Reach a long boardwalk leading over wetlands on the lake's upper end, then resume along rolling wooded shoreline. Finally, cross the lake dam, soaking in more impoundment panoramas. The hike is never too steep or rugged, and it's just the right length for everyone in the group to enjoy this excursion. Other fun activities are nearby.

Start: Hematite Lake Picnic Area
Distance: 2.3-mile loop
Difficulty: Easy
Elevation change: +/-150 feet
Maximum grade: 7% grade for 0.1 mile
Hiking time: About 1.2 hours
Seasons/schedule: Year-round
Fees and permits: No fees or permits required
Dog friendly: Yes
Trail surface: Gravel, boardwalk, forested natural surface

Land status: National recreation area
Nearest town: Lake City
Other trail users: None
Maps to consult: LBL—Nature Station Trails map
Amenities available: Nature station, restrooms, picnic areas
Cell service: Decent
Trail contacts: Land Between the Lakes National Recreation Area; (800) 525-7077; landbetweenthelakes.us

FINDING THE TRAILHEAD

From exit 31 on I-24 near Lake City, take KY 453 South, entering Land Between the Lakes NRA. Continue a total of 15.4 miles. Turn left on FR 133, Silver Trail Road, and follow it for 3.2 miles to reach the Nature Station. Turn right on FR 134 and follow it downhill just a short distance. Turn right again on FR 176 and drive through Hematite Lake Picnic Area to reach the trailhead at road's end. Trailhead GPS: 36.898247 / -88.041989

THE HIKE

Hematite Lake is but one scenic corner of big and beautiful Land Between the Lakes National Recreation Area. Although shared with Tennessee, the Kentucky portion of LBL presents trails aplenty, along with other recreational pursuits, from camping to boating to fishing.

LBL offers not only conventional outdoor recreation but also historical and nature study. You can visit a living history farm from the 1850s known as The Homeplace. Check out the herd of buffalo at the Bison Range. Reach for the stars at the Golden Pond Planetarium. Drive through the Elk and Bison Prairie, where wild animals live in a restored habitat of long-ago Kentucky. The Nature Station, located very near this hike, is where kids of all ages can interact with our natural world, including close-up animal viewing.

Spring beauty brightens the woods near Hematite Lake.

Consider camping while here. Possibilities range from fully developed campsites to primitive backcountry endeavors along backwoods trails, including the North/South Trail, running more than 60 miles along the peninsula of Land Between the Lakes. More trails beckon, including the Fort Henry trails, winding among the hills and hollows of LBL's south end, allowing hikers to retrace the footsteps of Civil War soldiers, as do the nearby Fort Donelson National Battlefield Trails. Check out settler history on the Hillman Heritage trail system. The Canal Loop Trails attract both mountain bikers and hikers. Speaking of bicycling, two-wheel enthusiasts also have the Central Hardwoods Scenic Trail, excellent for casual bicyclers.

If you haven't experienced LBL, it's time to go. And the Hematite Trail is just the excuse to get you there. The hike heads west from the Hematite Lake picnic area, perfect for a pre- or post-hike meal. Come to the lake dam spillway and tread the north shore of the lake. The easy gravel track soon gives way to natural surface, and you find yourself undulating along a wooded sloping shoreline shaded by hickories and oaks, stepping over scattered rock outcrops and small stone bluffs. One bluff sports a contemplation bench and a fine vista of Hematite Lake.

From there, the Hematite Trail drops to the lake's edge, where you can get up close and personal with the water before actually traveling over it on a long boardwalk spanning the upper reaches of the impoundment—more marsh than lake—fed by the waters of Long Creek. Then you cruise the south shore, with wildflower-rich hollows divided by

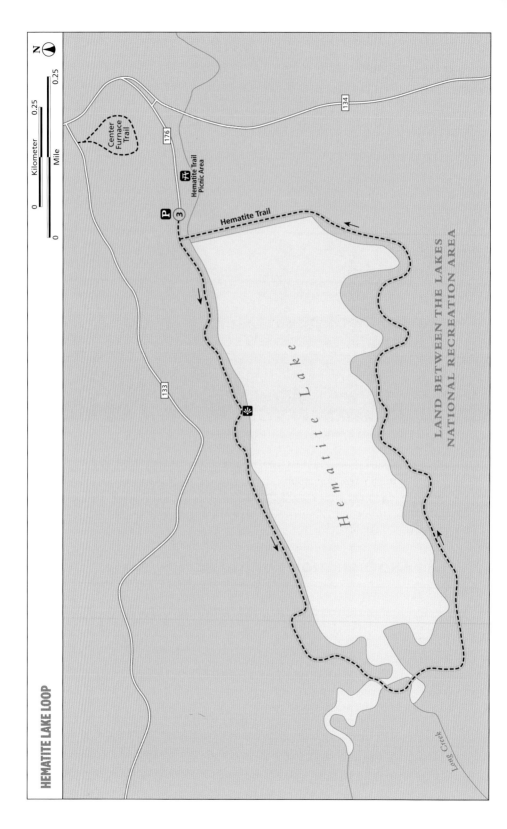

HEMATITE LAKE LOOP

Hematite Lake

Center Furnace Trail

Hematite Trail Picnic Area

Hematite Trail

LAND BETWEEN THE LAKES
NATIONAL RECREATION AREA

Long Creek

176

3

133

134

N

Kilometer
0   0.25
Mile
0   0.25

The trail leads you along the shore of Hematite Lake.

easy hills. The final section of the hike traces the lake dam north, where you can enjoy the length of the 83-acre impoundment. Finally, cross the lake spillway on concrete steps jutting above the water, a thrill for kids! (*Note:* You'll have to turn back if the spillway is flooding the concrete steps.) Now figure out all the fun activities at LBL you can add to your Hematite Lake hike.

MILES AND DIRECTIONS

0.0 Start from the picnic area and hike west on the Hematite Trail, passing around a pole gate on a gravel track. Ahead, the loop portion of the hike returns left. Reach a canoe/kayak launch, used by paddlers to explore Hematite Lake, then continue on a natural surface path in south-facing woods, rich with white oaks and maple.

0.3 A short spur goes left to a bluff and lake overlook of Hematite Lake. Continue west.

0.4 Return to the shoreline.

0.8 Begin crossing a long boardwalk over wetlands alive with amphibians in summer. Look for beaver dams in the upper lake. Bridge Long Creek.

1.1 Return to land and begin cruising the south side of Hematite Lake, rolling between low hills and gravelly drainages spanned by short hiker bridges.

2.1 Reach the lake dam. Head north along the dam, enjoying some final lake views.

2.3 Walk the concrete steps across the spillway, a thrill for kids, completing the loop. Turn right and quickly reach the trailhead/picnic area.

4 HONKER LAKE LOOP

This Land Between the Lakes (LBL) hike loops around pretty Honker Lake. Start at LBL's nature center, dropping from a wooded knob with views to cut across rich wetlands before climbing into wooded hills. Return to bottoms before joining a peninsula, then cross Honker Lake on a long dam/causeway, opening watery vistas of not only Honker Lake but also big Lake Barkley in the distance. Trek past remains of an old homesite and also relics from the days when an iron ore furnace operated nearby before closing the circuit.

Start: Land Between the Lakes Nature Station
Distance: 4.4-mile loop
Difficulty: Easy-moderate
Elevation change: +/-332 feet
Maximum grade: 5% grade for 0.3 mile
Hiking time: About 2.1 hours
Seasons/schedule: Year-round
Fees and permits: No fees or permits required
Dog friendly: Yes
Trail surface: Forested natural surface, some gravel

Land status: National recreation area
Nearest town: Lake City
Other trail users: None
Maps to consult: LBL—Nature Station Trails map
Amenities available: Nature station, restrooms, picnic areas
Cell service: Decent
Trail contacts: Land Between the Lakes National Recreation Area; (800) 525-7077; landbetweenthelakes.us

FINDING THE TRAILHEAD

From exit 31 on I-24 near Lake City, take KY 453 South, entering Land Between the Lakes NRA. Continue a total of 15.4 miles. Turn left on FR 133, Silver Trail Road, and follow it for 3.2 miles to reach the Nature Station. **Note:** The Nature Station parking lot is closed and locked at 5 p.m. If the Nature Station is closed, the immediate parking lot will be closed. If it is, park in the lot near the Nature Station entrance gate. Trailhead GPS: 36.901665 / -88.036444

THE HIKE

Land Between the Lakes National Recreation Area, shared with Tennessee, offers 170,000 acres of recreation opportunities, including hiking. LBL is situated on a peninsula between the dammed Tennessee and Cumberland Rivers, creating Kentucky Lake and Lake Barkley. A canal links Kentucky Lake and Lake Barkley, making them into one of the largest man-made bodies of water in the world. Here, anglers vie for crappie, bass, bluegill, and catfish. Fishing is big at LBL, with numerous lake access areas in addition to boat ramps at campgrounds that make getting on the water easy. Others will be getting on the water simply to boat or swim and enjoy cool water on a hot day. A few will be paddling a canoe or sea kayak, looking out on the 300 miles of undeveloped shoreline that LBL offers.

You enjoy not only these bodies of water but also lesser impounds such as Honker Lake, around which this hike leads. Honker Lake is divided from Lake Barkley only by a

This long causeway divides Honker Lake from Lake Barkley.

slim dam, over which you will walk during this hike. The trek begins at the Woodlands Nature Station, where you can engage in hands-on displays, as well as see many birds and animals up close. It's great for families. Combine a trip to Woodlands Nature Station with your Honker Lake hike.

From the hilltop trailhead, you descend to rich wooded wetlands, passing a connector with the Woodland Walk, one of the many short nature trails in the greater Nature Station sphere. A raised trail leads among sycamore, sweetgum, and other moisture-tolerant species as you cross the flats of Negrorow Branch. Wildflowers color these bottoms in

A hiker bridges a stream flowing toward Honker Lake.

spring. The scenery changes quickly as you climb into hickory/oak-dominated hills, surmounting a ridge only to drop to a second bottomland, crossing another braided stream.

The hike turns down the stream valley and crosses a spillway before opening onto Honker Dam, a long, slender causeway/dam that delivers distant water panoramas of both Honker Lake and Lake Barkley. Savor the panoramas. Angling enthusiasts may be fishing on the causeway. Then you rejoin terra firma, trekking south in rolling woods along the east shore of Honker Lake. Ahead, view old mounds left behind when ore was mined here and fed into nearby Center Furnace, built in 1852 and in operation throughout the Civil War. It is one of several historic furnace operations in this ore-rich area.

The closer you get to trail's end, the more likely you will see bluish slag remains in the path. This ore industry by-product was repurposed for graveling roads. The Honker Trail works across streams divided by hills, including big Long Creek. The final part of the hike climbs to the Nature Station, nearing an old rock quarry. The quarried stone was likely used in making nearby Center Furnace.

MILES AND DIRECTIONS

0.0 Start north from the Woodlands Nature Station on the Honker Trail, passing a covered shelter with a view. Descend a hill toward the bottoms of Negrorow Branch.

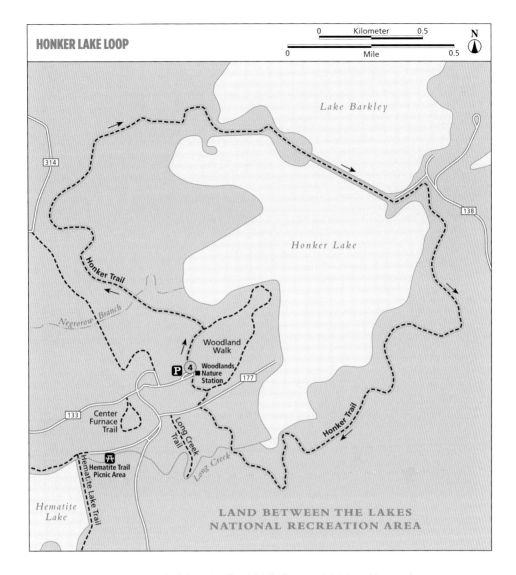

0.1 Pass the north end of the Woodland Walk. Stay straight (north), crossing open bottomland, then enter the wooded flats around Negrorow Branch, bridging several stream braids.

0.6 Top out on a wooded ridge; descend into a second bottom.

1.1 Cross a stream on a hiker bridge built in 2022, then walk under a power line.

1.6 Cross a short dam/causeway, then rise to a wooded narrow peninsula. Look for TVA survey markers.

1.9 Join the main dam/causeway. Views open to your left of Lake Barkley and to your right of Honker Lake.

2.2 Rejoin land at a canoe/kayak launch at the end of FR 138B. Head left on the forest road then shortly leave right, back on the Honker Trail.

2.8 Pass through an area of now-wooded yet unnatural earth diggings, relics of the iron ore dug to feed Center Furnace, an iron operation. Look for slag remains in the trail.

2.9 Cross a seasonal stream on a concrete bridge. Roll through hills, with the lake to your right.

3.1 Pass an old homesite marked by daffodils blooming in spring. Hike under the power line a second time.

3.6 An iron hiker bridge takes you over lake backwaters.

4.1 Bridge the Long Creek embayment. Travel through ephemeral wetlands.

4.2 Cross FR 177; climb, passing the south end of the Woodland Walk.

4.4 Arrive back at the Nature Station parking area, completing the hike.

5 JOHN JAMES AUDUBON STATE PARK

Take a walk through this unexpectedly hilly state park honoring one of early America's most renowned naturalists. Tall trees rise over flowery forest floor, and historic Civilian Conservation Corps structures make a good hiking destination even better.

Start: Park office parking area
Distance: 3.5-mile loop
Difficulty: Easy-moderate
Elevation change: +/-593 feet
Maximum grade: 10% downhill grade for 0.3 mile
Hiking time: About 1.8 hours
Seasons/schedule: Spring for wildflowers, autumn for colors
Fees and permits: No fees or permits required
Dog friendly: No dogs allowed in state nature preserve
Trail surface: A little asphalt, mostly forested natural surface

Land status: State park, state nature preserve
Nearest town: Henderson
Other trail users: None
Maps to consult: John James SP Facility map
Amenities available: Restrooms, water near trailhead
Cell service: Good
Trail contacts: John James Audubon State Park; (270) 826-2247; parks. ky.gov/henderson/parks/historic/ john-james-audubon-state-park

FINDING THE TRAILHEAD

From the junction of US 60 and US 41 on the northern side of Henderson, take US 41 north for 1.7 miles; turn right at the entrance sign for John James Audubon State Park. In 0.4 mile, turn left at the sign for the nature center and museum. Park in front of the first building, which is the park office. The hike joins gated Warbler Road. Trailhead GPS: 37.882329 / -87.557196

THE HIKE

Naturalist John James Audubon (1785–1851), famous for his realistic paintings of birds, lived in Henderson for nine years, roaming the woods and sketching wildlife. Born in what is now Haiti, the son of a French sea captain and his Creole mistress, Audubon came to Kentucky with a partner to establish a mercantile business. The enterprise proved successful, giving Audubon an opportunity to pursue his true passion, studying and painting birds.

The Ohio River community of Henderson was then—and is now—on a major flyway for migratory songbirds and waterfowl. Audubon only became famous after he left Kentucky, but the park—developed in the 1930s by the Civilian Conservation Corps (CCC) and one of the state's oldest—commemorates an important period in his development. The park museum claims to have the world's largest collection of Audubon memorabilia.

For the hiker, the park offers a pleasant ramble through mature beech and sugar maple forest to a small CCC-made lake lively with beavers, turtles, frogs, wood warblers, and waterfowl. Birds, not surprisingly, are the park's main focus, and late April through early

Dutchman's breeches rise beside the trail.

May is the prime time for visiting birders. The park is an especially good place to see rose-breasted grosbeaks, indigo buntings, scarlet tanagers, and other colorful species that, while not rare, are not your everyday robin either.

The park is now all but surrounded by Henderson sprawl, but the park's interior has been left in its natural state and has a greater away-from-it-all feel than many larger, more remote tracts. It's been at least a hundred years since the park was timbered, so many of the trees are towering. Half the park—the half you will be hiking through—is

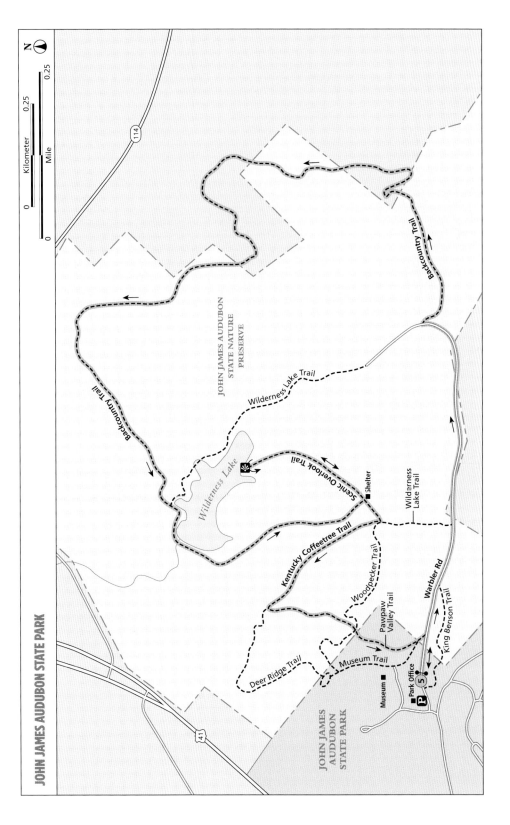

Deer are a common sight at John James Audubon State Park.

a designated state nature preserve and strictly regulated. That's why pets are prohibited. Enjoy your time here as Audubon did so many years ago. Don't sweat the plethora of trail junctions toward hike's end. All trails get you to either the park museum or the office, very near each other.

MILES AND DIRECTIONS

0.0 Start from the park office parking area and head east on gated Warbler Road. After 220 feet your return route—the Pawpaw Valley Trail—enters on the left. Keep straight along Warbler Road.

0.1 The King Benson Trail, named for a park naturalist, enters on your right. Keep walking among big hardwoods.

0.2 The Wilderness Lake Trail leaves left. Keep straight on Warbler Road, now on the park's edge, with houses in the woods to your right.

0.6 Split right on the Backcountry Trail, climbing to a ridgeline. In 0.1 mile, pass the site of an old tower. Begin a prolonged descent.

1.3 Bridge a seasonal stream on a hiker bridge. Wildflowers such as larkspur are found here in spring. Roll over a ridge, thick with hardwoods and laced with gigantic vines.

1.8 Grab a wintertime view of the Ohio River. Descend toward Wilderness Lake.

2.1 Reach an intersection at Wilderness Lake. Look for big sycamores. Stay right with the Wilderness Lake Trail. Skirt the lake's edge, then cross its dam. Climb.

2.5 Reach an intersection at a CCC-built stone storm shelter. Head left on the Scenic Overlook Trail, heading to a bench with a picturesque view of Wilderness Lake then backtrack.

3.0 Return to the CCC stone shelter. Join a new segment of the Scenic Overlook Trail, southbound and climbing.

3.1 Reach another intersection. Head right on the Kentucky Coffeetree Trail. Climb over a knob then descend.

3.2 Drop to bottoms then split left up a hollow, still on the Kentucky Coffeetree Trail.

3.4 Reach a four-way intersection. Keep straight on the Pawpaw Valley Trail as the Woodpecker Trail goes left. Shortly reach Warbler Road, turning right toward the trailhead.

3.5 Arrive back at the trailhead.

6 MAMMOTH CAVE BACKCOUNTRY HIKE

Make a big loop through the wild and beautiful backcountry of Mammoth Cave National Park, viewing many human and natural sights along the way. A recommended three-night backpack, the adventure can be easily shortened if you are pressed for time. Along the way you will view old homesites and walk former settler roads as well as tracks along bluffs and beside creeks and rivers. Observe waterfalls and stony geological wonders stretching from Raymer Hollow to the Nolin River, from Collie Ridge to the Green River. Reservable designated backcountry campsites make the overnight adventure even better.

Start: Maple Springs trailhead
Distance: 30.7-mile loop with short spurs
Difficulty: Difficult due to distance and elevation change
Elevation change: +/-4,976 feet
Maximum grade: 12% downhill grade for 0.4 mile
Hiking time: About 17.5 hours
Seasons/schedule: Best in autumn; summer could be hot
Fees and permits: Fee-based backcountry permits required
Dog friendly: Yes; can be muddy, though

Trail surface: Forested natural surface, gravel in areas
Land status: National park
Nearest town: Park City
Other trail users: Equestrians, bicycles on one small section
Maps to consult: Mammoth Cave National Park Backcountry Map
Amenities available: Restroom and picnic tables at trailhead
Cell service: Mostly good; less in some hollows
Trail contacts: Mammoth Cave National Park; (270) 758-2180; nps. gov/maca

FINDING THE TRAILHEAD

From exit 48 on I-65 at Park City, take KY 255 North for 2.4 miles. Turn left on KY 70 West for 2.5 miles then stay right with Mammoth Cave Parkway; continue for 2.3 miles to a four-way intersection. Turn left on Green River Ferry Road and drive 1.3 miles to take the Green River Ferry across the Green River. Once across the river, continue driving for 2.2 miles. Turn left onto Maple Springs Loop and follow it 0.9 mile to the trailhead, on your right. The signed Buffalo Creek Trail leaves left (west) from the trailhead. Trailhead GPS: 37.205684 / -86.139393

THE HIKE

Mammoth Cave National Park features a large backcountry area north of the Green River with more than 50 miles of trails and twelve backcountry campsites that fashion excellent backpacking opportunities—with a caveat. These trails are shared with equestrians, who tread the trails in force, creating mudholes and churned-up tread in places.

Raymer Hollow campsite

You will almost surely see equestrians while adventuring here. Therefore, if hiking on horse trails bothers you, read no further. However, I have been backpacking the Mammoth Cave backcountry for over two decades and find the good far outweighs the bad. Wildflower displays here rival Great Smoky Mountains National Park and, combined with waterfalls in spring, the colors of autumn, and geological splendor of winter, you will find it a quintessential Kentucky hiking experience. Summer is too hot here for rewarding backpacking. I recommend it as a three-night experience, but the adventure can be lengthened or shortened as desired.

A few things to know: A backcountry permit is required to overnight in the backcountry. All the campsites have a nearby water source, save for McCoy Hollow. Each site is equipped with a fire ring, tent pad, and lantern post. The trails are well marked and signed. Somewhere along the way, you will encounter mudholes created by horses.

This loop covers the full scope of the Mammoth Cave backcountry and will deliver an adventure you won't forget. Leave Maple Springs trailhead on the Buffalo Creek Trail, joining old Buffalo Road, lined with homes aplenty in pre-park days, and passing the Sal Hollow Trail. Cedar and hardwoods shade the nearly level gravel track that tacks southwesterly. At a major intersection, head right on the Dry Prong Trail, crossing a small streambed in a shallow cove. Roll through tall trees to pass a homesite to the right of the trail. Ahead, find the spur to Homestead campsite, an ideal first night's destination just a couple of miles from the trailhead. It offers a level camp with a stream just below. Ahead,

Raymer Hollow Falls

the Dry Prong Trail bridges a perennial spring branch. Note that this spring emerges from the limestone wall visible from the bridge. Continue westerly along the south rim of Dry Prong. Watch for a covered well in a trailside cedar copse to the left of the trail. You will pass views into Dry Prong hollow below. The hike drops then climbs out of normally dry Dry Prong, coming within 0.7 mile of the recommended Collie Ridge campsite.

Your ups and downs continue as you make your way to the wildflower-rich Wet Prong Buffalo Creek valley to join the McCoy Hollow Trail. This perennial stream crossing is bridgeless, and could be a ford at higher water flows. You are now on the McCoy Hollow Trail, winding your way out to bluffs overlooking the Green River after passing the pretty but waterless McCoy Hollow campsite. The hike turns in and out of hollows with waterfalls in season before coming to the highly recommended Three Springs campsite.

From there you climb to the Temple Hill trailhead then descend past rock bluffs to reach the First Creek campsites, near what once was (but is no longer) First Creek Lake. You then curve alongside the Nolin River, with more cascades dropping from the river's tributaries. The lesser used Second Creek campsite comes next, located on a high hill. Water is nearby but steeply down a hill.

The backpacking adventure then turns back east, going on and off old roads as well as along a regal bluff rich with hemlock trees, rare for these parts. The walking is easy to the First Creek trailhead and very pretty beyond as you wander back down to Wet Prong of Buffalo Creek, making a second bridgeless crossing in an alluring spot. Climb again to Collie Ridge, joining the Raymer Hollow Trail. Wind through picturesque woods and small streams to reach the fine Raymer Hollow campsite, nestled on a low bluff overlooking Dry Prong, perennially flowing at this point. The last part of the hike visits Mammoth Cave's signature cataract, Raymer Hollow Falls, then winds along the rim above Dry Prong before working back to the trailhead via Mill Branch and Maple Springs Trails.

MILES AND DIRECTIONS

0.0   Start from the Maple Springs trailhead and cross the Maple Springs Loop (a road) to join the Buffalo Creek Trail. Quickly pass the intersection with the Sal Hollow Trail and join old Buffalo Road. Head southwest. The hiking is easy.

1.1   Head right on Dry Prong Trail at major trail intersection.

1.9   A spur goes right to the recommended Homestead campsite. Camp here. Backtrack, then rejoin Dry Prong Trail, heading westbound.

4.0   Rejoin the Buffalo Creek Trail. Descend on a narrower path.

5.0   Cross normally dry Dry Prong. Begin a prolonged 300-foot climb toward Collie Ridge. Skirt along a bluff line.

6.0   Meet the Collie Ridge Trail. The recommended Collie Ridge campsite is 0.7 mile west. The loop keeps straight, joining Wet Prong Trail.

6.9   Split left on the McCoy Hollow Trail.

7.3   Come to the unbridged crossing of Wet Prong Buffalo Creek. Cross the stream then continue down the Wet Prong valley. Wind in and out of hollows with stone bluffs rising above the path.

8.9   A spur goes left 0.1 mile to the fine but waterless McCoy Hollow campsite. Ahead, come to bluffs with partial views down to the Green River, 300 feet below. Turn into and out of McCoy Hollow, then return to the Green River bluffs.

11.8   Pass a waterfall after curving around the hollow beyond McCoy Hollow.

12.5   Reach the spur trail to the recommended Three Springs campsite after passing low-flow 30-foot Kettle Falls and a shorter cascade below the trail.

13.4   Come to the Temple Hill trailhead after passing an illegal campsite. Here, head left (westerly) in the parking area then join the First Creek Trail. Cruise a ridgetop before descending along impressive bluffs.

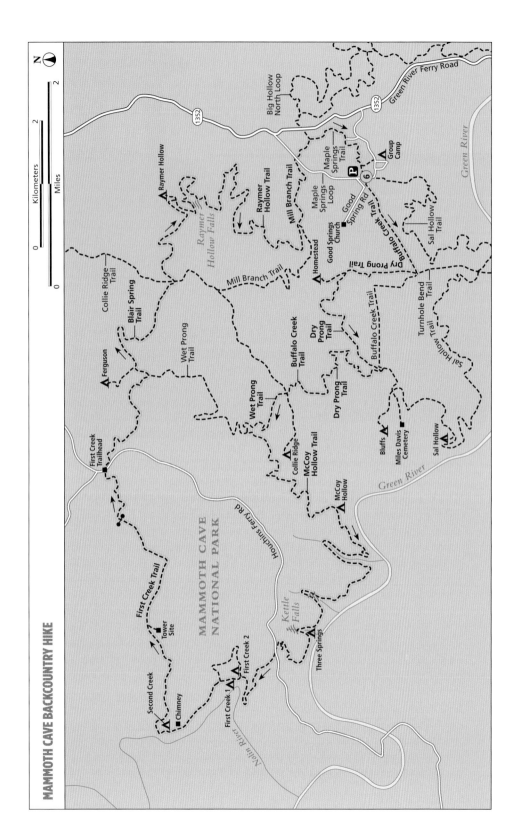

MAMMOTH CAVE BACKCOUNTRY HIKE

N

Kilometers
0   2

Miles
0   2

Green River Ferry Road

352

Big Hollow
North Loop

352

Raymer Hollow

Maple Springs
Trail

Group Camp

Maple Springs
Loop

Good
Spring Rd

6

P

Raymer
Hollow Trail

Mill Branch Trail

Good Springs
Church

Buffalo Creek Trail

Sal Hollow
Trail

Dry Prong Trail

Raymer
Hollow Falls

Homestead

Collie Ridge
Trail

Mill Branch Trail

Turnhole Bend
Trail

Sal Hollow Trail

Blair Spring
Trail

Wet Prong
Trail

Buffalo Creek
Trail

Dry
Prong
Trail

Buffalo Creek Trail

Ferguson

Dry Prong
Trail

Wet Prong
Trail

Bluffs

First Creek
Trailhead

Collie Ridge

McCoy
Hollow Trail

Miles Davis
Cemetery

Sal Hollow

First Creek Trail

MAMMOTH CAVE
NATIONAL PARK

Houchins Ferry Rd

McCoy
Hollow

Green River

Tower
Site

Second Creek

Chimney

First Creek 1

First Creek 2

Kettle
Falls

Three Springs

Nolin River

14.7 Reach an intersection. The First Creek Trail heads right and accesses First Creek 2 campsite. Stay straight on an unnamed connector and cross First Creek on a bridge near where now-drained First Creek Lake was dammed. Reach heavily used First Creek 1 campsite on your left, a good second-night destination.

15.0 Rejoin the First Creek Trail, running parallel to the Nolin River, with bottomlands below. Cross small creeks with cascades of their own.

15.6 Pass a stone block chimney to the right of the trail before curving around a bluff near the confluence of Second Creek and the Nolin River.

16.1 Pass the spur trail right to the recommended Second Creek campsite, although nearby water is far downhill. Keep east, coming along a bluff with hemlock trees.

16.7 Split right after finding a low-flow stream forming a shower-like 8-foot fall over a rock shelter.

17.1 Pass a spur leading acutely right to an old tower site. Keep straight on a wide road-like trail. The hiking is easy. Look for old homesites.

18.5 Pass a gate at the park boundary. Split right here, joining standard trail.

19.2 Reach the First Creek trailhead. Cross Houchin Ferry Road and pick up the Wet Prong Trail. Descend more than not.

20.6 Split left with the Blair Spring Trail.

20.8 Come to the unbridged crossing of Wet Prong and the spur left to the recommended Ferguson campsite. Mountain laurel abounds down here. Stay with the Blair Spring Trail, climbing along a tributary of Wet Prong, then turn toward Collie Ridge into oaks.

22.3 Meet and cross the Collie Ridge Trail, joining the well-graded Raymer Hollow Trail.

23.4 Circle an old homesite and descend.

23.7 Head left on a spur to the Raymer Hollow campsite. Enjoy the site then backtrack.

24.5 Come to 22-foot Raymer Hollow Falls after crossing Dry Prong. Observe the spring-fed cascade before climbing out of the hollow and skirting the rim of Dry Prong.

26.1 Cross a major tributary of Dry Prong. Turn back toward Dry Prong and keep winding along the rim of Dry Prong.

28.6 Meet and join the Mill Branch Trail. Keep easterly.

29.5 Cross the Good Springs Loop and stay straight.

29.7 Stay right as the Big Spring Hollow Loop heads left. Turn south.

30.7 Arrive back at the trailhead.

7 MAMMOTH CAVE NATURE TRAILS CIRCUIT

This fun little loop takes you to several highlights situated in a network of trails around the Mammoth Cave National Park Visitor Center. Leave the information-rich hub then head for the Mammoth Cave Historic Entrance. Walk a stony hillside on a level path to visit bat-rich Dixon Cave. From there trundle to the bluff edge above the picturesque Green River for a view. Next visit the old steamboat landing on Green River and River Styx Spring. Gently climb to Sunset Point and a first-rate vista. Stop by the Old Guides Cemetery en route back to the visitor center, cramming a wealth of highlights into a little more than 2 miles.

Start: Mammoth Cave Visitor Center
Distance: 2.2-mile loop with short spurs
Difficulty: Easy
Elevation change: +/-697 feet
Maximum grade: 10% grade for 0.5 mile
Hiking time: About 1.3 hours
Seasons/schedule: Year-round
Fees and permits: No fees or permits required
Dog friendly: Yes, but the area around the visitor center can be crowded.

Trail surface: Concrete, asphalt, boardwalk around visitor center; natural surface otherwise
Land status: National park
Nearest town: Park City
Other trail users: People going on cave tours
Maps to consult: Mammoth Cave National Park Visitor Center area map
Amenities available: Visitor center, dining, hotel, restrooms, cave tours at trailhead
Cell service: Good
Trail contacts: Mammoth Cave National Park; (270) 758-2180; nps.gov/maca

FINDING THE TRAILHEAD

From exit 48 on I-65 at Park City, take KY 255 North for 2.4 miles. Turn left on KY 70 West and continue for 2.5 miles. Stay right with Mammoth Cave Parkway and follow it for 2.6 miles to the Mammoth Cave National Park Visitor Center. Begin the hike from the rear of the visitor center (toward the park hotel) at the cave tour bus shelters, on the Historic Entrance Trail. Trailhead GPS: 37.205684 / -86.139393

THE HIKE

Situated on the bluffs above the Green River, Mammoth Cave National Park's visitor center area—near Mammoth Cave's Historic Entrance—contains a nearly complete recreation complex, with everything from picnic areas, cabins, hotel rooms, camp stores, historic displays, dining, and a first-rate network of interpretive trails. These interpretive trails can add much to your understanding of how Mammoth Cave was formed and the relationship between the land and water above and the cave below. Furthermore, the

A grand view of the Green River

trails tell of the interaction between humans and the Mammoth Cave through history's timeline.

Since this is an easy, short hike, consider adding one of the many other options available here to your trek. After checking out the visitor center, swing around the back of the building to pick up the Historic Entrance Trail. It starts near the bus shelter area. These buses take park visitors to cave tours that start at other caves and cave entrances besides the Historic Entrance. The Historic Entrance Trail descends a wide concrete

MAMMOTH CAVE NATURE TRAILS CIRCUIT

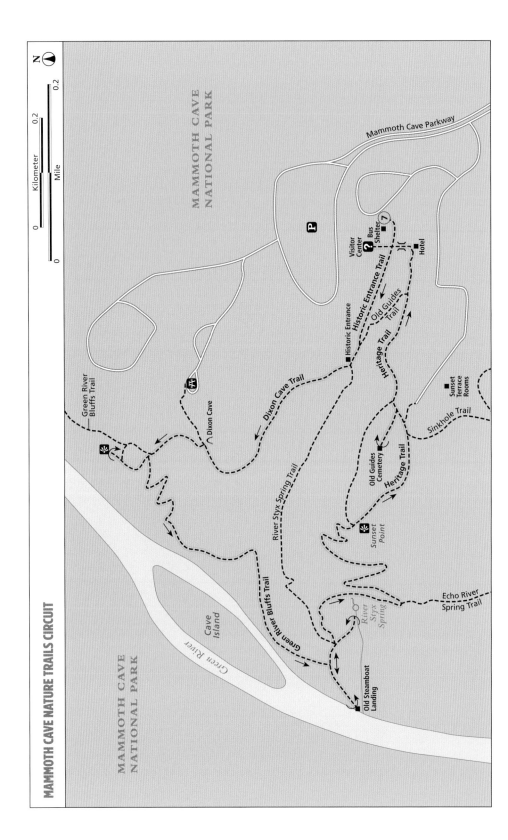

path, going under a pedestrian bridge linking the visitor center and hotel. Soon you are at the Historic Entrance, where steps lead into the world's largest known cave system. A lot of visitors have passed this way in the nearly 200 years cave tours have been undertaken. Of course, aboriginal Kentuckians explored this underground labyrinth for years untold before that. The evidence still lies inside the cave.

From here take the Dixon Cave Trail, working a hillside below a bluff line to your right. The path curves onto a dry ridgeline, where mountain laurel, dogwood, and chestnut oak thrive. A platform allows a view into Dixon Cave. This cave is fenced in to keep unauthorized explorers from disturbing the habitat of the Indiana cave bat. You'll now cross a dry rocky wash before intersecting the Green River Bluffs Trail. Head out to the overlook above the Green River. The vista delivers a long upstream look at the waterway that plays a role in the land-water relationship of the Mammoth Cave area.

From here you join the Green River Bluffs Trail. The path descends by switchbacks through cedar woods. The Green River comes into view on your right. Note Cave Island in the river. You join bottomlands where massive sycamore trees tower overhead. Ahead, a spur leads right to the old steamboat landing, where early cave tourists disembarked after traveling from afar to see this special Kentucky treasure. Interpretive signage enhances your understanding of this locale.

Next, take a boardwalk to an overlook of River Styx Spring, a large upwelling at the base of a cave-like bluff, where a pool forms then flows to the nearby Green River. This is a rich wildflower area in spring. Grab more perspectives of River Styx Spring as you climb above it then switchback uphill among cedars to Sunset Point, arguably the best overlook in the park. Here you get an unobstructed vantage downriver to the west. At this point, you are once again walking concrete pathways and are atop the bluff.

The walking remains easy while visiting the Old Guides Cemetery, an early place of interment for folks who lived in Mammoth Cave's shadow. The final part of the walk takes you by the park hotel and across the pedestrian bridge to the visitor center, with a greater understanding of the Kentucky wonderland that is Mammoth Cave National Park.

MILES AND DIRECTIONS

0.0 Start from the rear of the visitor center near the bus shelter and join the concrete Historic Entrance Trail. Head downhill under a pedestrian bridge, descending along a little creek.

0.2 Reach the Historic Entrance to Mammoth Cave after passing the short Old Guides Trail leading up to the hotel. Ahead, the River Styx Spring Trail heads downhill toward the Green River. After peering down into the Historic Entrance, split right on the Dixon Cave Trail. Ascend a hillside on natural surface path.

0.5 Climb the platform to peer into bat-heavy Dixon Cave. Here a spur leads right to the headquarters picnic area. Stay left to soon meet the Green River Bluffs Trail. Stay straight toward an overlook then backtrack to the intersection, ultimately heading southwest on the Green River Bluffs Trail, switchbacking in rocky cedar woods. Cross a stone-and-wood bridge.

0.8 Cruise bottoms of the Green River, where huge old-growth sycamores and beech rise in stately manner.

1.2   Reach an intersection. Head right to the old steamboat landing, then backtrack and take the boardwalk to River Styx Spring. Backtrack and then join the Echo River Spring Trail, circling above River Styx Spring.

1.5   Reach an intersection and head left toward Sunset Point. Switchback uphill amid hickory, cedar, and stone.

1.8   Come to Sunset Point. Soak in the westerly view and stay right, joining the concrete Heritage Trail.

2.0   Head left on the Old Guides Cemetery Trail after passing the Sinkhole Trail and a short spur to the Sunset Terrace Rooms, part of the greater hotel complex. View the Old Guides Cemetery then take the Heritage Trail toward the hotel, soon on a boardwalk. Pass the Old Guides Trail, then take the pedestrian bridge toward the visitor center.

2.2   Arrive back at the visitor center.

8 OTTER CREEK

Enjoy rolling woods at this longtime park before coming along a high bluff overlooking the mighty Ohio River. Cruise the high ridge then drop down to Morgan Cave, with its spring and cascade, before looping back to the trailhead.

Start: Former nature center parking lot
Distance: 4.0-mile loop
Difficulty: Easy-moderate
Elevation change: +/-409 feet
Maximum grade: 9% grade for 0.3 mile
Hiking time: About 2.2 hours
Seasons/schedule: Open Wed–Sun; closed Thanksgiving weekend, Christmas Eve, Christmas Day, New Year's Eve, and New Year's Day
Fees and permits: Entrance fee required
Dog friendly: Leashed dogs allowed

Trail surface: Forested natural surface
Land status: Kentucky Department of Fish and Wildlife Resources
Nearest town: Radcliff
Other trail users: Mountain bikers
Maps to consult: Otter Creek Outdoor Recreation Area
Amenities available: Campground in season
Cell service: Good
Trail contacts: Otter Creek Outdoor Recreation Area; main phone: (502) 942-9171; Trail Status Hotline: (502) 942-5052; fw.ky.gov

FINDING THE TRAILHEAD

From exit 1 on KY 841 (Gene Snyder Freeway), southwest of downtown Louisville, take US 31W south for 13.2 miles. Turn right onto Old Mill Road (KY 1638) and follow it for 2.8 miles. Turn right into the Otter Creek Outdoor Recreation Area; follow the main road for 1.2 miles and turn right into the parking area for the former nature center. Trailhead GPS: 37.940397 / -86.048860

THE HIKE

Otter Creek Outdoor Recreation Area has been through a lot of ups and downs since its conception in 1934, when the National Park Service selected 3,000 acres of gorgeous hilly land just south of the Ohio River in Meade County for residents of Louisville and other nearby communities to explore. Trails and recreational facilities were built where Otter Creek flowed into the Ohio River near Fort Knox, including YMCA Camp Piomingo. After World War II the federal government gave the park to Louisville and the park entered a golden era, with heavy use of the camps, cabins, swimming pools, restaurant/conference center, picnic grounds, nature center, and more.

Unfortunately, things went downhill. In an effort to rebound, Otter Creek Park became part of the Louisville Metro Parks system, but in 2008 the City of Louisville announced closure of the park, as it was "losing" a half million dollars per year. The state stepped in, and the park became part of the Kentucky Department of Fish and Wildlife Resources and was rechristened Otter Creek Outdoor Recreation Area.

Though the facilities aren't what they once were, the natural beauty remains. The park presents the hiker approximately 26 miles of trails along Otter Creek, the Ohio River, and the hills above the waters. Our hike travels through the heart of the park then comes

Overlooking the Ohio River from the Otter Creek Trail

along the Otter Creek valley. From there you head out to the Ohio River, where you can gaze across to Indiana from the heights above the Ohio. After that you cruise past an old rock quarry then down to Morgan Cave, named for a Civil War Confederate raider. A spring emerges from the barred cavern then forms a pretty cascade. Scoot by the park's campground before returning to the trailhead. Enjoy the deer, birds, and wildflowers and fall colors in season. Be aware that Fort Knox is nearby—any booms you hear may well be artillery, not thunder!

MILES AND DIRECTIONS

0.0 Start from the old nature center parking area and head north across a gas line clearing to enter woods and come to a trail junction. Here, the Otter Creek Trail leaves left and is our return route; for now we split right onto the Valley Overlook Trail. Travel northeast in mixed woods.

0.2 Cross Lickskillet Road in level, piney woods. Ahead, cross a road leading to some decrepit cabins. The woods roll more.

0.6 Intersect the Red Cedar Trail for the first time. Stay straight with the Valley Overlook Trail. The land to your left is part of YMCA Camp Piomingo.

1.2 Reach a trail intersection. Here, the Valley Overlook Trail splits right. Stay left, joining a connector to the Otter Creek Trail. Travel north, with Otter Creek flowing 200 feet below. Winter views into the valley and beyond extend to the east.

A spring emerges from Morgan Cave then forms a waterfall.

1.4 Reach another intersection. Here the Otter Creek Trail enters on your right. Split left (westerly), joining the Otter Creek Trail left, now on a high bluff above the Ohio River. Winter views open of the bending Ohio River and Indiana beyond. Pass a formerly cleared overlook known as the Eagles Nest. Pit Cave is on the south side of the trail. Continue in woods westbound, climbing beyond the overlook. Ahead, pass some cabins. The YMCA camp is to your left.

2.2 Cross Otter Creek Road then descend to encounter the Red Cedar Trail a second time. Continue a prolonged descent on the Otter Creek Trail.

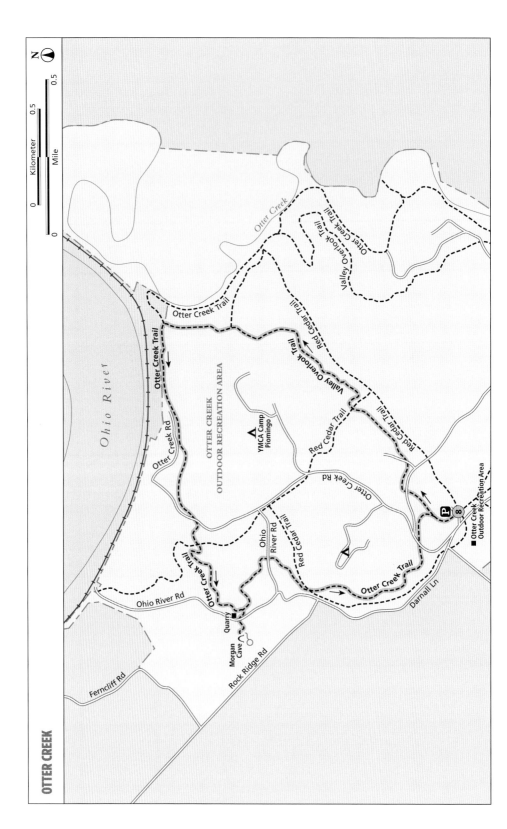

OTTER CREEK

2.6 Reach a junction after walking the lip of a rock quarry. Split right with the spur toward Morgan Cave, briefly joining Ohio River Road downhill then splitting left on a hiker trail using wood and earth steps.

2.7 Come to Morgan Cave after rock hopping a stream then climbing up to the barred cave mouth. Note the tumbling cascade flowing from the spring at the mouth of the cave. Backtrack to the Otter Creek Trail, then continue the loop.

3.1 Cross Ohio River Road a second time.

3.2 Intersect the Red Cedar Trail a third time. Stay straight on the Otter Creek Trail, circling past the park campground, visible through the trees to your left.

3.8 Cross Otter Creek Road a final time.

3.9 Complete the loop portion of the hike. Head right, backtracking to the trailhead.

4.0 Arrive back at the old nature center trailhead.

9 VERNON-DOUGLAS STATE NATURE PRESERVE

Make an undulating loop hike in this lesser visited and underutilized state nature preserve. With steep north-facing hills, the preserve, cloaked in mature hardwood forest, is rich with spring wildflowers and provides solitude for hikers who venture to this out-of-the way refuge.

Start: Audubon Trace trailhead
Distance: 3.7-mile balloon loop
Difficulty: Moderate
Elevation change: +/-708 feet
Maximum grade: 11% grade for 0.3 mile
Hiking time: About 1.6 hours
Seasons/schedule: Year-round; best in spring
Fees and permits: No fees or permits required
Dog friendly: No dogs allowed

Trail surface: Forested natural surface
Land status: Office of Kentucky State Nature Preserves
Nearest town: Elizabethtown
Other trail users: None
Maps to consult: Vernon-Douglas State Nature Preserve color brochure
Amenities available: None
Cell service: Good
Trail contacts: Office of Kentucky Nature Preserves; (502) 573-2886; eec.ky.gov/Nature-Preserves

FINDING THE TRAILHEAD

From exit 93 on I-65 just east of Elizabethtown, take the Bluegrass Parkway east for 7.1 miles to exit 8. Turn right onto Youngers Creek Road (KY 583) and follow it just a short distance. Take the next right onto Audubon Trace and follow it west 0.6 mile to the trailhead, on your left. Trailhead GPS: 37.733336 / -85.707739

THE HIKE

Central Kentucky is dotted with knobs, and this hike explores one of these large protuberances—this one covered with mature second-growth hardwoods, primarily maple, beech, tulip tree, oak, and hickory. Unlike Bernheim Forest, this 730-acre preserve is not well known. Most likely you will see no one else as you make your way through Hall Hollow then climb the ridge to the Pinnacle, the local name for a bluff overlooking the pastoral Younger Creek valley. The only intrusion on your solitude—and in some spots, it definitely is an intrusion—is the *swish-swish* of traffic on the nearby Bluegrass Parkway. Even so, the attributes of this preserve, including its many wildflowers, more than compensate for that one drawback.

The Douglas family owned the land before donating it to the National Audubon Society in 1972. The Vernons owned it before the Douglas clan bought it. They farmed Burns Hollow but planted runoff-reducing pines after allowing the fields to reforest. The land has never been commercially logged, at least not in the last century, according to the Kentucky State Nature Preserves Commission. The Audubon Society gave the property to the state in 1991.

Virginia bluebells grace this state nature preserve.

The unnamed trail—the preserve has only one—starts at the south end of the parking lot at the gate in the fence. You will head up Burns Hollow. Imagine it being denuded of forest a century ago. Heading south, you cross several wood bridges over small drainages before angling up a ridge known as Hall Hill, eventually making a gap in the ridge. This is where the loop part of the hike begins. Going counterclockwise, you will lose your hard-won elevation and descend on an old road, working into Hall Hollow, cut with a small stony creek. Look for wildflowers such as halberd-leaved violet, Virginia bluebells, and toothwort.

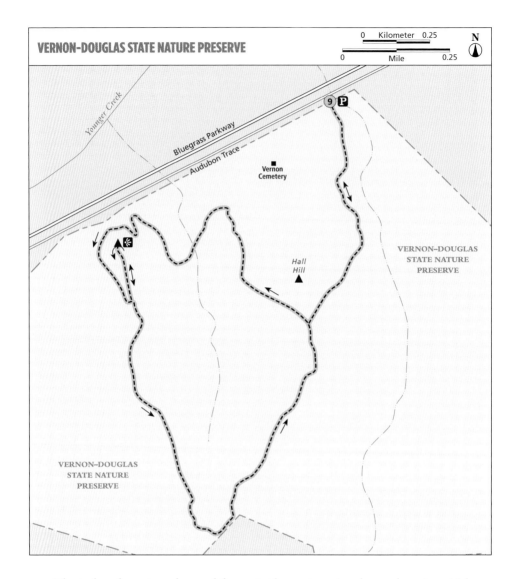

The trail works up to and around the next ridge west, passing slaty rock sections. Make the sharpest climb of the hike and you are atop this ridge and at the spur to the Pinnacle. The spur trail weaves through cedars aplenty on a stony footbed to reach the Pinnacle, a small outcrop that will likely disappoint after so grand a name. However, in winter you can gaze through lesser tree cover across the Youngers Creek Valley and to other knobs and ridges in the distance.

From the Pinnacle return to the junction and take the main trail south along the ridgetop. The large trees create a pleasing canopy. As you near a farm field, the trail curves east and then north to circle Hall Hollow. You shortly complete the loop and backtrack to the trailhead, another fine Kentucky state nature preserve checked off your list.

MILES AND DIRECTIONS

0.0 Start from the parking area and head south into woods on the only trail in the preserve, passing a trailside kiosk. Enter Burns Hollow then angle up the right side of the hollow, bridging seasonal streams among oaks, shagbark hickory, maple, and pine.

0.6 Reach a gap in the ridge you have climbed. Begin the loop portion of the hike by descending an old roadbed right and working your way into Hall Hollow.

1.1 Bridge the stream of Hall Hollow. Work your way up the next ridge west.

1.7 Reach a trail intersection in the gap of a ridge. Head left toward the Pinnacle to grab a winter view; return. Look for old barbwire fencing left over from farming days.

1.9 Continue south on the loop trail. The narrow ridge widens and the path remains level. Enjoy easy walking among tall trees. Scan for sinkholes.

2.5 The loop trail nears the preserve boundary and turns back north, running the ridge between Hall Hollow to your left and Burns Hollow to your right.

3.1 Complete the loop portion of the hike; bear right and backtrack to the trailhead.

3.7 Arrive back at the trailhead.

On this fun trail destination for everyone, explore a set of interconnected nature trails that course from the main visitor center through the planted arboretum and natural woods in the vicinity of the visitor center. This walk will likely get you itching to try the other trails winding through the large preserve.

Start: Main visitor center
Distance: 3.0-mile loop
Difficulty: Easy
Elevation change: +/-289 feet
Maximum grade: 8% grade for 0.3 mile
Hiking time: About 1.7 hours
Seasons/schedule: Year-round; summer will be hot in open areas.
Fees and permits: Entrance donation encouraged
Dog friendly: Leashed dogs allowed
Trail surface: Gravel, grass, forested natural surface

Land status: Private forest open to public
Nearest town: Louisville
Other trail users: Birders, runners
Maps to consult: Bernheim Arboretum and Research Forest
Amenities available: Restrooms, water, cafe at visitor center
Cell service: Good
Trail contacts: Bernheim Arboretum and Research Forest; (502) 955-8512; bernheim.org

FINDING THE TRAILHEAD

From exit 112 on I-65 south of Shepherdsville, take KY 245 south for 0.9 mile. Turn right into Bernheim Forest and follow the signs to the visitor center. Trailhead GPS: 37.918738 / -85.658782

THE HIKE

Bernheim Forest offers over 40 miles of trails for the Kentucky hiker. Outdoor enthusiasts from birders to runners to those desiring environmental education flock to the private research forest and arboretum, whose motto is "Connecting people with nature." And that it does. The preserve contains over 15,000 acres of native upland hardwood forest as well as a collection including 8,000 varieties of trees, shrubs, and other plants that constitute the arboretum section of the locale, creating an amalgam of both natural woodland and planned gardens.

This sizable tract came to be through the philanthropy of Isaac W. Bernheim, a German immigrant. Bernheim immigrated to the United States shortly after the Civil War. At 20 years old he wandered the Northeast, making a living as a salesman before finding his way to the Bluegrass State. Once in Kentucky, he got into the bourbon making business—and grew an empire.

The capitalist was very grateful to his adopted state of Kentucky and his adopted country, the United States. As a memorial he financially supported statues of American heroes such as Abraham Lincoln, Thomas Jefferson, and Henry Clay for public display.

In 1929 the distiller of bourbon purchased what was to become Bernheim Forest. The land was in poor condition, having been logged over and mined for iron ore.

Hiking by Lake Nevin

Nevertheless, Bernheim determined to provide a preserve where hardworking citizens could escape to enjoy nature and eye-pleasing gardens. The famed landscape architecture firm of Frederick Law Olmsted (which designed New York's Central Park, among other parks) went to work building lakes and roads and designing the gardens.

Bernheim appreciated seeing his vision come to be. Alas, he passed away in 1945, five years before the forest opened to the public in July 1950. Nevertheless, his vision of a place connecting people with nature has endured. The forest, located south of Louisville, annually attracts more than 250,000 visitors.

Our walk travels the nest of trails in the immediate visitor center area. We'll view tree collections in the preserve's arboretum, the Olmstead Ponds, a restored prairie, a small stream environment, Lake Nevin, and a ridge cloaked in naturally occurring hickory-oak woodland. A plethora of paths and intersections may confuse first-time visitors, but no matter where you go, the scenery will please the eye. The downside of a visit here is the excessive signage and its endless environmental preaching. Here at Bernheim, nature speaks for itself. Other noteworthy trails at Bernheim are the Millennium Trail, a long distance path, and the Canopy Tree Walk, where you trek an elevated boardwalk 75 feet above the ground.

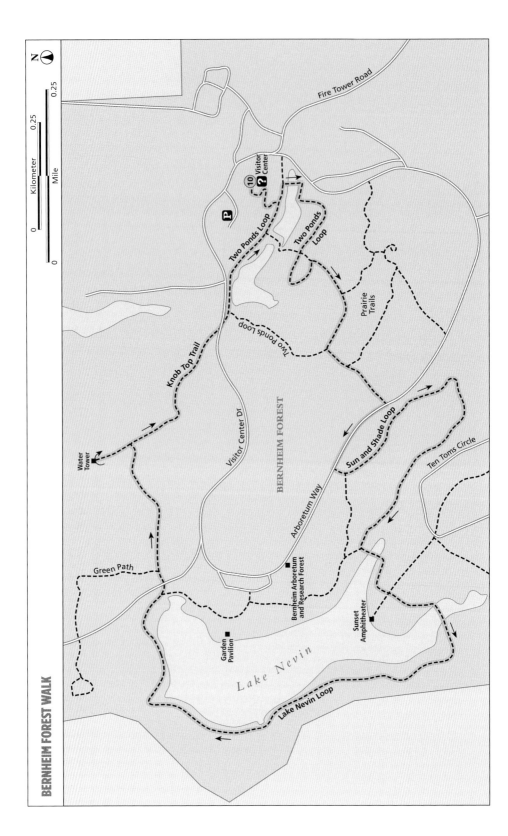

BERNHEIM FOREST WALK

N

Kilometer
0   0.25
0   0.25
Mile

Fire Tower Road

Visitor Center
10
?
P

Two Ponds Loop

Two Ponds Loop

Two Ponds Loop

Prairie Trails

Knob Top Trail

Visitor Center Dr

BERNHEIM FOREST

Water Tower

Arboretum Way

Sun and Shade Loop

Ten Toms Circle

Green Path

Bernheim Arboretum and Research Forest

Garden Pavilion

Lake Nevin

Sunset Amphitheater

Lake Nevin Loop

MILES AND DIRECTIONS

0.0 Start south from the visitor center, map in hand, and shortly reach the Olmstead Ponds, a pair of small impoundments. Once there, head left, then bridge the easterly pond on the Two Ponds Loop.

0.3 Reach an intersection. Make the mini-loop among the Kentucky Trees of Concern, then resume the Two Ponds Loop. Enter restored prairie.

0.6 Leave left from the Two Ponds Loop, heading southwest through open prairie. Shortly reach the Arboretum Way, a road. Head right on the road then split left, back in woods; split left again on the Sun and Shade Loop. Begin circling a small watershed in a mix of sun and shade.

1.4 Reach the Lake Nevin Loop. Head left, quickly bridging the marshy upper lake. Rise to an open area and the Sunset Amphitheater. Return to woods and bridge another arm of Lake Nevin. Begin circling around the west side of the lake, enjoying rewarding views.

2.0 Cross the lake outflow. Circle around the dam and cross the lake spillway.

2.3 You are near the Bernheim entrance road at the northeast corner of Lake Nevin. Cross the road left toward a grassy trail, passing the Green Path, then angle uphill, joining the Knob Top Trail as it passes a large tablet inscribed with a prayer of Isaac Bernheim.

2.6 Reach the ridge crest of the Knob Top Trail. Head left to the water tower then return right, walking the ridge.

2.9 Cross Visitor Center Drive. Rejoin the Two Ponds Loop, eastbound.

3.0 Split left to climb a small hill and arrive back at the visitor center.

11 HORINE RESERVATION HIKE

Make a loop among steep hills and hollows of an inviting tract within greater Jefferson Memorial Forest. The Red Trail is your conduit that runs along White Oak Ridge above Knob Creek. Stop and visit the Horine Cemetery before dropping to a pair of small streams. Return to the crest of the ridge and hike it back toward the park campground before completing the circuit.

Start: Horine trailhead
Distance: 4.9-mile balloon loop
Difficulty: Moderate
Elevation change: +/-599 feet
Maximum grade: 10% grade for 0.4 mile
Hiking time: About 2.6 hours
Seasons/schedule: Year-round; fall for leaf color
Fees and permits: No fees or permits required
Dog friendly: Leashed dogs allowed

Trail surface: Forested natural surface
Land status: Public park
Nearest town: Louisville
Other trail users: None
Maps to consult: Horine Reservation
Amenities available: Restrooms, seasonal water, campground
Cell service: Good
Trail contacts: Jefferson Memorial Forest; (502) 368-5404; wildernesslouisville.org

FINDING THE TRAILHEAD

From exit 121 on I-65 south of Louisville, take KY 1526 west for 2.0 miles. Turn right on Holdsclaw Hill Road and follow it 2.1 miles. Turn left into Horine Reservation and follow the main road 0.5 mile to dead-end at the hiker trailhead, just past the right turn to the conference center. Trailhead GPS: 38.076545 / 85.759361

THE HIKE

Originated in 1945 as a memorial to the brave veterans of World War II, Jefferson Memorial Forest is a Louisville outdoor icon that claims to be "the largest municipally owned forest in the United States." Over the decades the forest has expanded to more than 7,500 acres through which more than 60 miles of trails ramble. With the vastness and beauty of Jefferson Memorial Forest, it's hard to believe that these wooded ridges and hollows are anywhere near the state's biggest city.

Horine Reservation, where this hike takes place, is a later addition to Jefferson Memorial Forest. The former Boy Scout camp was deeded to the city by Dr. Emmett Horine, whose family cemetery is located on the property. Horine Reservation includes not only a fine trail system that connects to other tracts of Jefferson Memorial Forest but also a primitive tent campground (highly recommended; I've overnighted here myself) and a conference center for meetings.

Our hike tackles the Red Trail and stays with it for the entire length, though you can shorten the circuit with additional paths if desired. You'll trace the Red Trail as it runs a high wooded ridge above Knob Creek. From the ridgetops it's a full 200 feet down to the stream. The path then passes the spur to Horine Cemetery, with a mix of monuments old and new. From there, a singletrack path dives into a hollow where a feeder branch of Knob Creek flows. You'll bridge a gravelly clear stream beside which trillium, rue anemone, and other wildflowers flourish.

Another up and down and up again delivers both scenery and exercise, then you join White Oak Ridge and the hiking becomes easier and level. Pines become more common as you cruise north, passing the Shortcut before coming near the park campground. You can inspect some of the campsites from the trail and determine your favorite for future reference. All too soon the loop is complete, and then it's a short backtrack to the trailhead.

Bloodroot rises above a cluster of spring beauties.

The Horine Cemetery

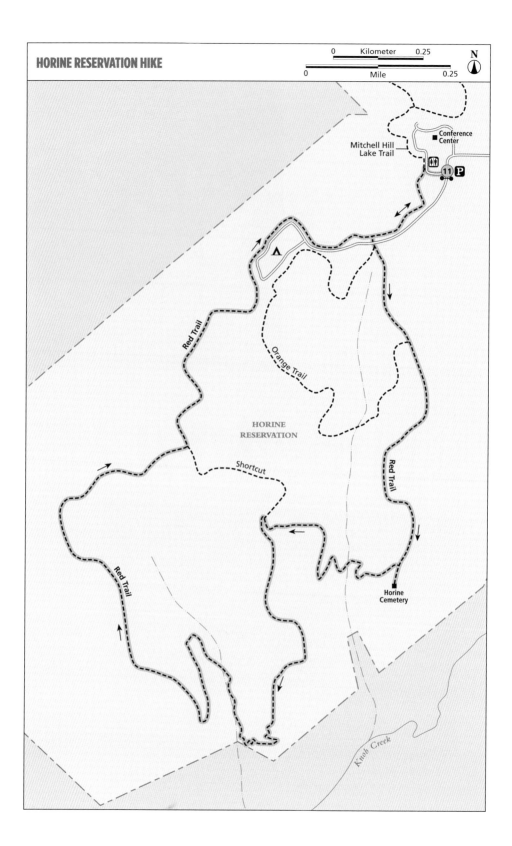

Kilometer

Mile

N

Conference Center

Mitchell Hill Lake Trail

Red Trail

Orange Trail

HORINE RESERVATION

Shortcut

Red Trail

Red Trail

Horine Cemetery

Knob Creek

MILES AND DIRECTIONS

0.0 Start from the parking area and take the road going west toward the trails (not the gated road south toward the campground). Shortly enter woods and come to an intersection. Head left toward the Red Trail on a natural surface hiker path. The ridge drops off steeply north toward the Ohio River.

0.2 Reach an intersection. Begin the loop portion of the hike by heading left on the Red Trail. Cross the campground access road then reach another intersection, where the shorter Orange Trail heads right. Stay left with the Red Trail, soon on a doubletrack, aiming for Horine Cemetery.

0.5 Meet the other end of the Orange Trail. Keep straight on the Red Trail, heading south on a high, steep wooded ridge.

1.1 A spur trail splits left to Horine Cemetery. After visiting the cemetery, resume the Red Trail, diving into and out of a hollow.

1.7 Reach an intersection. The Red Trail stays left and the Shortcut splits right. Stay left, running another ridge. Descend near the park boundary then turn north up a hollow with a gravelly, seasonal stream. Crisscross the stream then angle uphill.

3.1 Level out on White Oak Ridge. Begin working back toward the trailhead. Pines join the oaks and hickories.

3.9 Reach the other end of the Shortcut. Stay left with the Red Trail, avoiding a double-track road.

4.4 Come near the edge of the park campground. Stay on the north side of the ridge, running parallel to the camping area.

4.7 Complete the loop portion of the hike. Bear left and backtrack to the trailhead.

4.9 Arrive back at the trailhead.

12 GENERAL BUTLER STATE RESORT PARK HIKE

This loop hike follows the Fossil Trail as it winds through the steep and hilly wooded grounds above the Kentucky and Ohio Rivers on lands that were once part of the farm of the Butler clan, early movers and shakers in Kentucky history after the days of Daniel Boone. Here you will contour along towering hills offering partial views of the lands, towns, and waters beyond. Come near the park's conference center before taking a side trip to a developed overlook with a rewarding vista of the Ohio River and Carrolton, Kentucky, with the state of Indiana beyond, before looping back to the trailhead.

Start: Fossil Trail trailhead
Distance: 4.8-mile loop
Difficulty: Moderate
Elevation change: +/-963 feet
Maximum grade: 6% downhill grade for 0.3 mile
Hiking time: About 2.3 hours
Seasons/schedule: Sept through May
Fees and permits: No fees or permits required
Dog friendly: Yes
Trail surface: Natural surface foot trail

Land status: State park
Nearest town: Carrollton
Other trail users: Mountain bikers
Maps to consult: General Butler State Resort Park
Amenities available: Picnic area and views at the trailhead
Cell service: Good
Trail contacts: General Butler State Resort Park; (502) 732-4384; parks. ky.gov/carrollton/parks/historic/ general-butler-state-resort-park

FINDING THE TRAILHEAD

From exit 44 on I-71, follow KY 227 north for 2 miles to the General Butler State Park entrance and road on your left. Follow the park road 1.2 miles until you reach the turnoff for the Stone Overlook, on the right. Head for the Stone Overlook then immediately turn left into the first parking lot. The trailhead is on the southwest end of the parking lot. Trailhead GPS: 38.670351 / -85.161420

THE HIKE

General Butler State Park, one of Kentucky's first parks, is named for Gen. William O. Butler and includes a 300-acre tract of former farmland he owned. The park preserves the old Butler family home, built in 1859 and open for tours. The family cemetery and final resting place of the general are nearby. A well-known soldier and statesman, Butler served in the War of 1812 and the Mexican-American War. He was a congressman and ran unsuccessfully for governor of Kentucky and vice president of the United States.

This loop hike traverses wooded hillsides and crosses open meadows—plentiful with deer—as the hike wanders through the northwest side of the park, following the Fossil Trail its entire length. The path is named for the imprints of creatures embedded in

A fine view of Carrollton and the Ohio River

trailside rock. A short detour takes you to the Stone Overlook, built in the 1930s by the Civilian Conservation Corps. Views from the lookout stretch northward to historic Carrollton and the confluence of the Kentucky and Ohio Rivers. You will be traveling along the slopes of some of the steepest hills in the Bluegrass State—wooded bluffs rising 300 feet above the floodplain where the Kentucky River empties into the Ohio River. Stay with the blazes as the Fossil Trail goes off and on old farm roads. The path often morphs from singletrack woods path to wide grassy track to old woods road and back. Additionally, although the hike does have a gain/loss of nearly 1,000 feet of elevation, the trek has no extended climbs or descents, despite being among steep hills for the entire hike.

In addition to hiking trails, the state resort park has a fifty-three-room lodge built atop the uplands as well as cottages for overnighting. Campers have more than 100 sites from which to choose at the campground, which is open year-round. If you don't feel like cooking, the park features a restaurant for lunch and dinner. Water lovers like to explore 30-acre Butler Lake, a pretty impoundment backed against the park bluffs. No gas motors are allowed on the water, leaving it a serene experience. Bring your own canoe or kayak, or rent one from the park during the warm season. Fish for bass, bluegill, or crappie from your boat or from shore. A 1.6-mile hiking trail encircles Butler Lake, allowing you to easily access its waters. With its many amenities and activities, General Butler State Resort Park can keep you busy in addition to hiking the Fossil Trail.

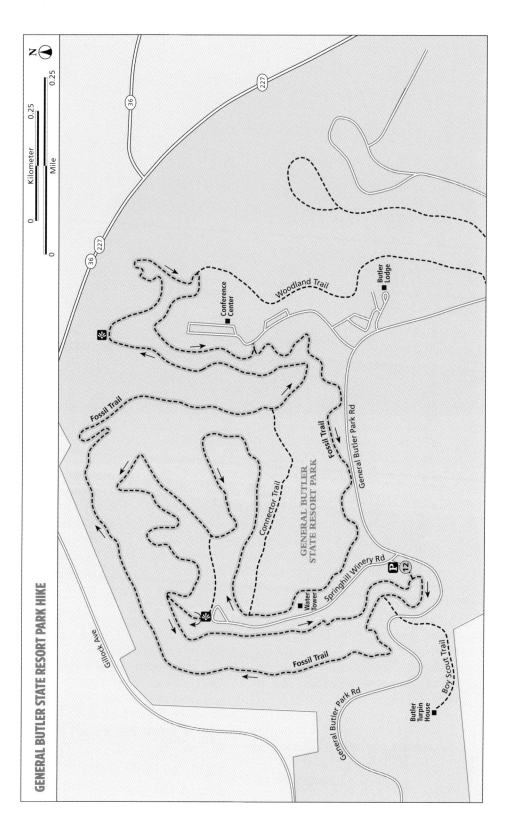

GENERAL BUTLER STATE RESORT PARK HIKE

N

0   0.25
Kilometer

0   0.25
Mile

GENERAL BUTLER
STATE RESORT PARK

Fossil Trail

Fossil Trail

Fossil Trail

Connector Trail

Woodland Trail

Boy Scout Trail

Conference Center

Butler Lodge

Water Tower

Springhill Winery Rd

General Butler Park Rd

General Butler Park Rd

Gillock Ave

Butler Turpin House

36   227

36   227

227

MILES AND DIRECTIONS

0.0 Start from the Fossil Trail parking area, enter woods, and walk a short distance to reach the loop portion of the hike. Head left, beginning a clockwise circuit of the Fossil Trail.

0.1 Reach a trail intersection. The Boy Scout Trail leads left down to the Butler-Turpin House at the base of the bluffs. Stay with the Fossil Trail, cruising down more than not on the mid-slope of the wooded bluff in rocky woods rich with oaks. The town of Carrollton, situated at the confluence of the Ohio and Kentucky Rivers, is visible through the trees.

0.6 Pass through a power line clearing offering unobstructed looks into Carrollton.

1.0 Descend by switchbacks then turn south into a hollow, away from the Ohio River. Begin gently climbing along a meadow dividing steep, wooded hills.

1.3 The Connector Trail splits right and shortcuts the loop. Stay straight with the Fossil Trail.

1.4 Turn back north and circle the other side of the hollow.

1.8 Come to a view under a power line clearing. You can clearly spot Carroll County High School and its athletic fields with the Ohio River beyond. Continue contouring along the wooded bluffs.

2.0 Pass a small stock pond on your left, now filling with sediment as the woods around it have risen and the domestic animals have long been gone.

2.1 Reach a trail intersection. The Woodland Trail goes straight toward the lodge and campground. We split right, staying with the Fossil Trail, staying in the woods while circling below the park conference center.

2.4 A spur trail goes left just a short distance to the conference center. Stay right, traveling through woods populated by the unusual Osage orange trees, with their large green but inedible fruits. The thorny tree was often planted in rows as a living fence line but now grows wild here. The Fossil Trail turns west, running parallel to a park road.

3.0 Circle by a water tower. You are at the hike's high point. Head downhill.

3.1 Stay straight as the other end of the Connector Trail enters on your right. Resume contouring along the wooded bluff.

3.6 A wide grassy track goes left to the park lookout. Stay right with the blue blazes on a grassy trail.

4.2 Reach the signed spur to the lookout while on a very steep north-facing slope, rich with wildflowers in spring. Head left (south) on the spur, rising in woods.

4.3 Reach the auto-accessible overlook and the raised rock viewing platform. Here a cleared vista opens of the Ohio River 350 feet below, clear into Indiana. Backtrack and resume the Fossil Trail, shortly turning south.

4.8 Arrive back at the trailhead after turning left when completing the loop portion of the hike.

13 BIG BONE LICK HIKE

This hike visits historic Big Bone Lick, a locale once populated by such prehistoric animals as mastodons, giant sloths, and woolly mammoths. Bogs surrounding salt licks and mineral springs, where the big bones are found, are one of Kentucky's most important archaeological sites. The State of Kentucky developed this state park as both a preserve and a recreation destination, with trails for you to explore the mineral springs that attracted prehistoric beasts, as well as the landscape, where you can observe a herd of buffalo, modern-day residents of the preserve.

Start: Park museum
Distance: 3.3-mile loop
Difficulty: Moderate
Elevation change: +/-459 feet
Maximum grade: 7% downhill grade for 0.3 mile
Hiking time: About 1.5 hours
Seasons/schedule: Year-round; summer can be hot
Fees and permits: No fees or permits required
Dog friendly: Yes
Trail surface: A little concrete, some asphalt; rest is natural surface

Land status: State park
Nearest town: Walton
Other trail users: None
Maps to consult: Big Bone Lick State Historic Site
Amenities available: Picnic tables, restrooms at trailhead
Cell service: Good
Trail contacts: Big Bone Lick State Historic Site; (859) 384-3522; parks. ky.gov/union/parks/historic/big-bone-lick-state-historic-site

FINDING THE TRAILHEAD

From exit 175 on I-75/I-71, south of downtown Cincinnati, take KY 338 North for 7.6 miles. Turn left into the state park and drive for 0.2 mile. The road splits—turn right toward the park museum and nature center. The hike heads north on a concrete sidewalk, west of the museum building. Trailhead GPS: 38.884054 / -84.752459

THE HIKE

Big Bone Lick has been noted as a significant geological location for a long time. Aboriginal Kentuckians gathered salt from the site's mineral springs. In the early 1800s, when Meriwether Lewis was en route to St. Louis to begin his memorable journey to the Pacific Ocean with William Clark, he stopped at Big Bone Lick and sent bone samples to President Thomas Jefferson. Later, on orders from Jefferson, who wanted more samples and scientific information gathered at this place, William Clark and his brother George Rogers Clark came back for a detailed exploration of Big Bone Lick. They were looking for bones of great woolly mammoths and other prehistoric animals that had been attracted to the salt licks here. This project by the Clark brothers led to Big Bone Lick being dubbed "the birthplace of American paleontology."

Since then the area has been worked over by other collectors and scientists. The mineral springs and swampy area around the salt lick held bones of the large beasts, giving the

View buffalo on this hike.

name Big Bone Lick to the area. The extraordinary concentration of animals is owed not only to the salt licks but also to the swamps around them, for the miry muck sometimes trapped the animals until they died. Human artifacts have been found here as well. This makes sense, as hunters would follow the animals to their stomping grounds. In the 1800s the mineral springs brought in visitors, and a resort hotel was located here. The locale became a Kentucky state park in 1960. It was accorded National Natural Landmark status in 2009, a prestigious moniker, since just a few more than 500 sites nationwide have been given that accolade.

Today you can walk among the springs and wetlands that were such a productive boneyard. Check out the museum for a more comprehensive understanding of Big Bone Lick. This hike first visits the mineral springs that attracted both man and beast, located along the banks of Big Bone Creek. Enjoy the interpretive information scattered along the trek. Next the hike travels along Big Bone Creek before taking the Bison Trace to visit the resident bison, North America's largest herding animals. Don't crowd too close to the fence; give them ample room, even though they are on the other side of the wire. Bring binoculars for the best looks. The buffalo are a living reminder of all the creatures that have passed this way.

The hike then loops its way through hilly terrain above Big Bone Creek. In winter you can look down on the valley below. Then the circuit makes an extended trip along the park boundary. Pastureland lies across a fence. Look for frequent deer paths crossing the fence line between the park and the pasture.

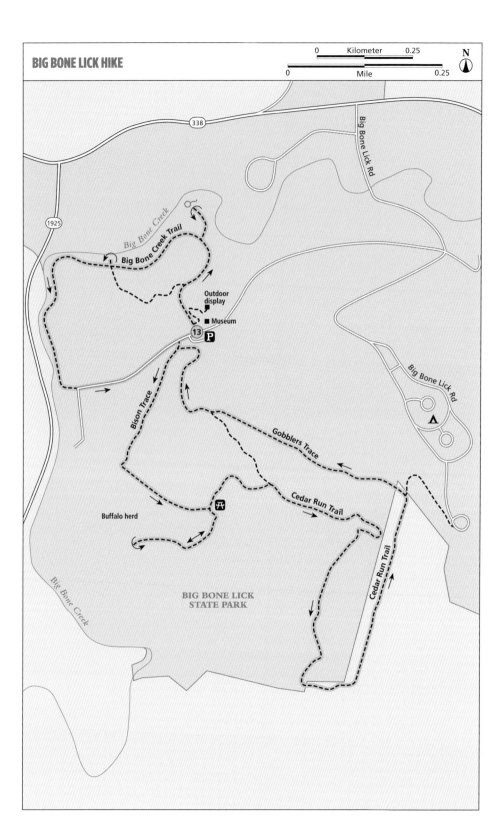

0   Kilometer   0.25

0   Mile   0.25

N

338

Big Bone Lick Rd

1925

Big Bone Creek

Big Bone Creek Trail

Outdoor
display

Museum

13   P

Big Bone Lick Rd

Bison Trace

Gobblers Trace

Cedar Run Trail

Buffalo herd

Cedar Run Trail

BIG BONE LICK
STATE PARK

Big Bone Creek

Next you take the Gobblers Trace, enjoying a glorious walk on a grassy track that drifts downhill all the way to the visitor center. Make sure to allow time to explore the displays both inside and outside the museum at this special Kentucky state historic site.

MILES AND DIRECTIONS

0.0 Start from the museum parking area and head north on the concrete walkway to the west of the museum. Pass a spur leading right to the outdoor museum display. Keep straight, joining the Big Bone Creek Trail as it starts out as an asphalt all-access track through a grassy area.

0.1 Reach a trail intersection. Stay right with the Big Bone Creek Trail toward Salt Spring as a loop trail goes left. Enjoy the interpretive signage as you walk toward Salt Spring in wooded wetlands of ash, walnut, and hackberry.

0.2 Take the spur to Salt Spring. Observe the white, chalky upwelling. Backtrack and continue on the Big Bone Creek Trail, running roughly parallel to Big Bone Creek.

0.5 Come to a four-way intersection. The paved trail goes left and a short trail leads right to Big Bone Creek. Head right for a quick overlook of Big Bone Creek, then return to the main path on a natural-surface trail running west and parallel to Big Bone Creek in bottomlands, tracing an ancient bison trail.

0.8 Turn east from Big Bone Creek on a paved trail.

1.0 Return to the parking area then split right on the gravel Bison Trace as the Gobblers Trace enters on your left.

1.2 Reach the bison herd viewing area. Enjoy watching the shaggy critters, then stay left, hiking along the fence line. Backtrack at the end of the fence line and return to the spur trail leading north (uphill) to connect with the Cedar Run Trail. Reenter woods.

1.9 Split right with the Cedar Run Trail on a rocky, singletrack path.

2.1 Bridge a little streamlet.

2.4 Curve left and climb near the park boundary. Ahead, turn left (northbound) again, running along the park boundary.

2.8 Head left on the Gobblers Trace Trail. The walking is easy among cedars and hardwoods.

3.1 Stay straight as the other end of the Cedar Run Trail comes in on your left. Continue straight toward the museum, descending off a ridge.

3.3 Arrive back at the museum parking area.

14 COVE SPRING PARK LOOP

This hike at Frankfort's Cove Spring Park combines waterfalls and Kentucky history. First, view easily accessible Hurst Falls; then make a circuit through the park, passing wet-weather cascades along tributaries flowing from the adjacent hills. Along the way you can see the stone walls of a dam that held back the waters of Cove Spring, creating the first public water supply west of the Appalachian Mountains.

Start: Trailhead at Hurst Falls
Distance: 1.3-mile loop; can be extended
Difficulty: Easy
Elevation change: +/-264 feet
Maximum grade: 10% downhill grade for 0.4 mile
Hiking time: About 1 hour
Seasons/schedule: Year-round
Fees and permits: No fees or permits required
Dog friendly: Yes

Trail surface: Natural surface foot trail, a little asphalt
Land status: City park
Nearest town: Frankfort
Other trail users: None
Maps to consult: Cove Springs Park
Amenities available: Picnic area, picnic shelter, restrooms at trailhead
Cell service: Good
Trail contacts: Cove Springs Park; (502) 875-8575; frankfortparksandrec.com

FINDING THE TRAILHEAD

From exit 58 on I-64 near Frankfort, take US 60 West/Versailles Road for 4 miles (along the way it becomes US 421, but you stay on Versailles Road), then take the ramp for US 127 North, Owenton. Get off the ramp and turn left on US 127 North, following it for less than 0.1 mile. Turn right onto Cove Spring Road, entering the park. Quickly veer left and follow the main park road to dead-end at the trailhead. Trailhead GPS: 38.218535 / -84.848124

THE HIKE

What is now Cove Spring Park—where this hike takes place—has undergone many transformations over the past 200-plus years. Located just outside the heart of Frankfort, Kentucky's capital city, the reliable waters of Cove Spring have long played a part in Bluegrass State history. Before Daniel Boone and company made their way to the Bluegrass, buffalo and aboriginal Kentuckians sought out Cove Spring for its pure and constant flow. The spring and the nearby ford of the Kentucky River were way-stops for settlers and animals traversing the heart of the Bluegrass, following the dusty and muddy trails first created by wandering buffalo.

By the 1750s, white men were pushing through what became Frankfort, battling the Shawnee who called the area home. In 1780, Stephen Frank was killed at the shallow crossing of the Kentucky River while skirmishing with the Shawnee. The spot became known as Frank's Ford. Meanwhile, wily James Wilkinson persuaded the Virginia legislature (Kentucky was part of Virginia at the time) to give him 100 acres near Frank's Ford to develop a town—an outpost of civilization and a buffer against the Native Americans.

Hurst Falls

Remember, what is now Kentucky was part of Virginia at the time. However, when Kentucky became the fifteenth state in 1792, the little town of "Frankfort" beat out Lexington to become the state's capital. The settlement at the confluence of Benson Creek and the Kentucky River grew, establishing not only the capitol building but also the state penitentiary right there in town, at the corner of High and Mero Streets. In 1800 the city sought the clean and reliable Cove Springs to supply the capital with water. A dam was built downstream of Cove Springs, using heavy limestone blocks rising nearly 30 feet from end to end across a downstream hollow. The waters of Cove Spring were soon backed up.

Richard Throckmorton figured out a way to get that good water to the fine citizens of Frankfort. He constructed a system of interconnected hollowed-out cedar logs, moving water to the town and the prison, which needed water for the inmates who worked on-site and were also leased out as convict labor for area businesses and farms.

Hurst Falls in spring

The first public supply on the west side of the Appalachians helped Frankfort grow, but the Frankfort Water Company, as it was known, was continuously fraught with problems. In the 1880s iron pipes were used to transport the water at Cove Spring. However, water pressure and supply problems continued to plague the waterworks at Cove Spring, creating an epidemic of lawsuits.

The dam remained in place until the 1980s, when it was breached. Later, Cove Spring Park was established by the city. In 2006 the City of Frankfort commenced restoring the park streams inundated by the old dam. The banks were reshaped—less channel-like and

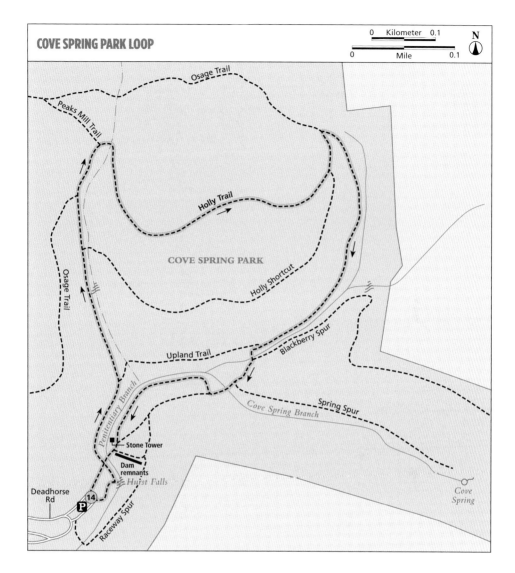

0   Kilometer   0.1

0   Mile   0.1

N

COVE SPRING PARK

Osage Trail

Peaks Mill Trail

Holly Trail

Osage Trail

Holly Shortcut

Blackberry Spur

Upland Trail

Spring Spur

Penitentiary Branch

Cove Spring Branch

Stone Tower

Dam remnants

Hurst Falls

Deadhorse Rd

14

P

Raceway Spur

Cove Spring

shallower and curved—re-creating natural flow conditions so that when floods occurred, the waters did not erode the banks and deepen the stream.

Interestingly, part of this hike takes you across what was the bottom of the water-retention pond for more than a century and a half. The pond overflow tower still stands near the old dam. As you walk through this reclaimed meadow, see how changes are taking place as the streamside once again becomes vegetated.

How about the waterfalls here? Hurst Falls is easily the park's signature cataract, and the walk to view it can be measured in feet. During dry times, only Hurst Falls will be flowing. However, during wetter times—winter through early spring and after storms—Cove Spring Park features other cascades. The preserve's trail system leads past these spillers.

Upon leaving the parking area, you immediately head for the sight and sound of Hurst Falls, a spiller dropping 20 feet from a stone wall into a shallow pond then into Cove

Spring Branch. From there you walk to and above the old waterworks dam, passing a 4-foot curtain-drop cataract on Cove Spring Branch. This artificial spiller—part of the stream restoration process—oxygenates the water to improve aquatic wildlife habitat.

You then turn into a tributary of Cove Spring Branch, joining the Holly Trail. The pathway runs parallel to the tributary, making a host of comely stairstep cascades that are quite camera-friendly when moving. Most of the singular stairstep drops are but a foot or two; however, the continuous nature of the cascades makes them quite a sight.

The hike then takes you by a concreted spring and onward to the uplands, where cedar and hickory reign among the limestone outcrops. Look for curious trailside benches made of native stone. Then you find yourself descending along another tributary featuring noisy cascades—and scads of Virginia bluebells in spring.

Next, return to Cove Spring Branch, where you can make the optional side trip to Cove Spring, tucked away in its own hollow. Finally, the hike opens onto a meadow, the restored area once underwater and covered higher than a hiker's head in silt. The transformation is impressive. Check out the naturalized shoals and pools of Cove Spring Branch and the stone tower of the water overflow structure, a rock monument to early Frankfort. Finally, return to the trailhead for a second look at Hurst Falls.

MILES AND DIRECTIONS

0.0 Start from the trailhead and walk toward Hurst Falls, visible from the parking area. A little bridge takes you across Cove Spring Branch to the 20-foot cavalcade of white, dropping in stages over a mostly vertical rock bluff. An observation deck brings you directly to the falls and the little man-made pool below it. From Hurst Falls, walk toward wooden steps climbing near the old dam site to view a 4-foot curtain fall. Climb the stairs, beginning the Upland Trail.

0.1 Head left on the Holly Trail after rising above the old dam site. Look for cascades along the tributary beside which the Holly Trail leads.

0.3 Pass a circular concrete-lined spring to the left of the trail. Keep ascending.

0.4 Keep straight beyond intersections with the Holly Shortcut and the Osage Trail to intersect the Peaks Mill Trail. Stay right here, still on the Holly Trail, stepping over the streambed of the tributary along which you have been walking. Cruise cedar woods on a hillside.

0.7 Stay on the Holly Trail as you intersect the other end of the Holly Shortcut. Just ahead, intersect the other end of the Osage Trail. Here, turn right, descending a hollow where a noisy tributary is cutting downward, still on the Holly Trail.

0.9 Reach the lower end of the hollow, where two tributaries come together. When the leaves are off the trees, you can observe a long stairstep cascade, picturesquely pouring over layers of rock.

1.0 Come to the other end of the Upland Trail. Stay left here, crossing a trail bridge and meet the Blackberry Spur and Spring Spur. Here is your chance to take the Spring Spur to visit historic Cove Spring. Ahead, cross the outflow of Cove Spring on a bridge then pass through the restored meadow on an asphalt path.

1.2 Walk by the dam remains and the standing water overflow tower.

1.3 Arrive back at the trailhead near Hurst Falls.

15 **RAVEN RUN SANCTUARY**

This loop hike takes you not only to Evans Mill Falls, a two-pronged cascade at the confluence of Raven Run and a tributary, but also to a rewarding overlook of the Kentucky River as well as other highlights—all at popular Raven Run Nature Sanctuary outside Lexington. No matter what time of year you visit, your efforts will be rewarded with scenic and historical points of interest. Waterfall lovers will find winter and spring the most rewarding times to visit the preserve.

Start: Raven Run parking area
Distance: 4.2-mile balloon loop
Difficulty: Moderate
Elevation change: +/-820 feet
Maximum grade: 9% downhill grade for 0.7 mile
Hiking time: About 2.2 hours
Seasons/schedule: Year-round; hours vary. Apr: 9 a.m.–6 p.m.; trails close at 5:30. May: 9 a.m.–7 p.m.; trails close at 6:30. June through Aug: 9 a.m. to 8 p.m.; trails close at 7:30. Sept: 9 a.m.–7 p.m.; trails close at 6:30. Oct: 9 a.m.–6 p.m.; trails close at 5:30. Nov through Mar: 9 a.m.–5 p.m.; trails close at 4:30.

Fees and permits: No fees or permits required
Dog friendly: No dogs allowed
Trail surface: Natural surface foot trail
Land status: Private preserve open to public
Nearest town: Lexington
Other trail users: None
Maps to consult: Raven Run Nature Sanctuary
Amenities available: Picnic tables and restrooms at the trailhead
Cell service: Good
Trail contacts: Raven Run Nature Sanctuary, 3885 Raven Run Way, Lexington 40515; (859) 272-6105; ravenrun.org

FINDING THE TRAILHEAD

From exit 104 on I-75 just southeast of Lexington, take KY 418 West for 2.4 miles. Turn left on US 25 (Old Richmond Road), and continue south for 3.3 miles. Turn right on KY 1975 (Jacks Creek Pike). Follow Jacks Creek Pike for 2.5 miles, then turn left, staying with Jacks Creek Pike. After 1.3 miles, stay straight with Jacks Creek Pike, joining KY 1976 as KY 1975 goes right. Continue for 1.4 more miles on Jacks Creek Pike (now KY 1976) and turn left onto Raven Run Way. Follow it 0.3 mile to dead-end at the visitor parking area for Raven Run Sanctuary. Trailhead GPS: 37.887451 / -84.397102

THE HIKE

Once an 800-acre working farm first established in 1790, what was to become Raven Run Nature Sanctuary was actively farmed until the 1930s, when the land was left fallow, growing over into the forest we see today. The land and buildings were acquired by the City of Lexington. The city, along with Friends of Raven Run, a philanthropic group, built a fine nature center (add time to check out the visitor center before your hike if possible) that is the heartbeat of the parcel, located on a tract important for both human and natural history.

The former farm site is cut by steep creeks leading down to the Kentucky River and its magnificent palisades. The site encompasses a biologically diverse array of uplands, the

Overlooking the Kentucky River in late fall

gorges cut by Chandler Creek and Raven Run, as well as the bluffs and lowlands along the Kentucky River.

Raven Run Sanctuary is a popular destination for hikers and nature lovers. From the visitor parking area you first follow a concrete sidewalk-like trail to the nature center, where you can get oriented, view the displays, and grab a trail map. Make sure to sign in before your hike.

Before your visit, check the opening and closing times for the sanctuary. The hours change seasonally, and park personnel are sticklers about the schedule. The trail system at Raven Run Sanctuary is a network of interconnected color-coded paths. Luckily, most (but not all) trail intersections are marked with a letter—for example, intersection C—allowing you to easily find your place on the preserve trail map. The Red Trail, which passes several highlights, is undoubtedly the most popular path. Our hike traces much of the Red Trail.

After leaving the visitor center, work your way through a facilities area that was part of the old farm, including the barn. You then join the Red Trail, entering full-blown woods. (Part of the sanctuary is open meadows, especially the uplands.) Working your way down to an unnamed tributary of Raven Run, roughly follow the tributary down to its confluence with Raven Run, where you find Evans Mill Falls, a layered cataract starting at the convergence of Raven Run and the unnamed tributary. Below that, discover stone remnants of the mill operation once located here. At this point, the trail and stream diverge as

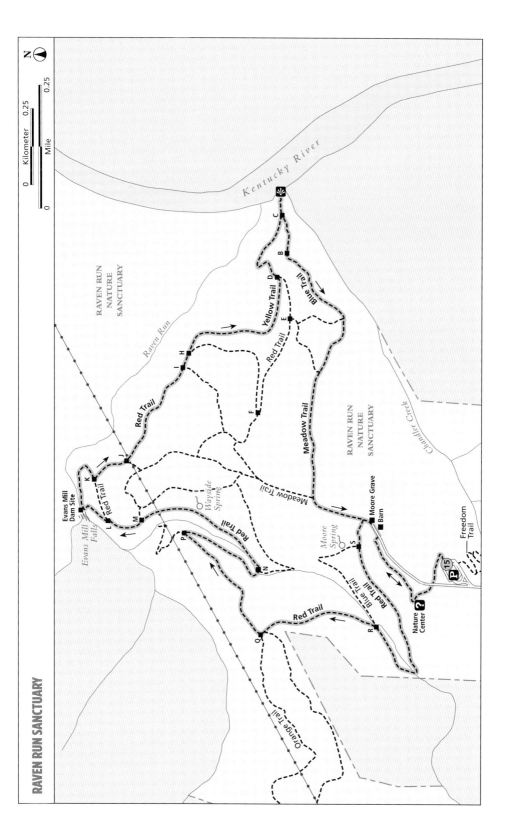

RAVEN RUN SANCTUARY

RAVEN RUN NATURE SANCTUARY

RAVEN RUN NATURE SANCTUARY

Kentucky River

Raven Run

Chandler Creek

Yellow Trail

Blue Trail

Red Trail

Meadow Trail

Meadow Trail

Red Trail

Red Trail

Blue Trail

Red Trail

Orange Trail

Freedom Trail

Evans Mill Dam Site

Evans Mill Falls

Wayside Spring

Moore Spring

Moore Grave

Barn

Nature Center

N

0   0.25 Kilometer

0   0.25 Mile

Two prongs merge to form Evans Mill Falls.

Raven Run cuts an impressive wooded gorge. The hike stays on the rim easterly all the way to an outcropping and overlook of the Kentucky River as the big waterway bends, exposing stone bluffs rising from the water's edge, a fine highlight of the hike.

You are at the hike's low point and now ascend a ridge above Chandler Creek, eventually opening onto upland meadows. From there the walking is easy, a simple cruise back to the trailhead.

MILES AND DIRECTIONS

0.0 Start from the visitor parking area and follow a winding concrete path toward the nature center.

0.1 Reach the nature center. The hike leads through the atrium of the nature center, where water and trail maps are available. Continue a wide path heading north.

0.3 Come alongside a building to your left and a barn to your right. Keep north, reaching a trail intersection. Here, head left on the Red Trail and immediately pass the Archibald Moore grave on your left.

0.4 Come to intersection S. The Blue Trail heads right toward Moore Spring. Stay straight with the Red Trail, dipping to a tributary of Raven Run among cherry, maple, and oak trees.

0.8 Reach intersection R. Stay straight with the Red Trail on a singletrack path. Ascend the slope of a hill.

1.1 Come to intersection Q. Pass both ends of the Orange Trail. Stay right with the Red Trail.

1.4 Reach intersection P. Stay right with the Red Trail as the short White Trail descends left under a power line.

1.6 Cross the tributary of Raven Run on a cool pedestrian bridge, then come to intersection N. Stay left with the Red Trail, aiming for Raven Run in a deepening hollow. Ahead, pass stone-bordered Wayside Spring.

1.9 Come to intersection M after passing under a power line. Stay with the Red Trail.

2.0 Reach intersection L. Stay left with the White Trail, descending an extremely rocky path. Raven Run and a tributary's convergence come into view. Admire the angled cascade known as Evans Mill Falls, the site of Evans Mill. Note the remaining stonework from the mill. Ahead, pass a viewing deck of the area as a sheer-walled gorge forms on the far side of the creek.

2.2 Rejoin the Red Trail left at intersection K. Head east toward the Kentucky River, roughly paralleling Raven Run as it cuts a deep gorge.

2.3 Stay straight with the Red Trail at intersection J.

2.5 Stay straight with the Red Trail at intersection I. You are 200 feet above Raven Run at this point.

2.6 Come to intersection H. Split left with the wildflower-rich Yellow Trail. Skirt a north-facing hollow and pass atop a seasonal waterfall.

2.8 Rejoin the Red Trail at intersection D. Descend.

3.0 Stay straight at intersection C, aiming for the Kentucky River overlook.

3.1 Come to an outcrop with a stellar vista of the Kentucky River and sheer bluffs rising from the water as the river curves downstream. Backtrack to intersection C.

3.2 Split left from intersection C, climbing on wooden steps. Ahead, pass intersection B, where a now-closed trail once went left, now on the Blue Trail. Climb above the valley of Chandler Creek.

3.4 Stay straight as a green-blazed trail heads right. Ahead, keep climbing past another green-blazed trail leaving right. Rise into meadows, now on doubletrack pathways, on the Meadow Trail.

3.8 Split left toward the nature center on a well-used track in meadows bordered by walnuts and cedars.

3.9 Complete the loop portion of the hike. You are near the Moore Grave. Bear left and backtrack toward the nature center and trailhead.

4.2 Arrive back at the trailhead.

16 PALISADES OF THE KENTUCKY RIVER

This hike takes place at Tom Dorman State Nature Preserve, a protected parcel in Garrard County where you can traverse attractive woods and enjoy views of regal bluffs rising from the Kentucky River. The loop portion of the hike explores points high and low along the route, from cliff lines to bottomlands and wildflower-rich hollows.

Start: US 27 trailhead
Distance: 4.2-mile balloon loop
Difficulty: Moderate
Elevation change: +/-815 feet
Maximum grade: 16% grade for 0.3 mile
Hiking time: About 2.4 hours
Seasons/schedule: Year-round
Fees and permits: No fees or permits required
Dog friendly: No dogs allowed
Trail surface: Natural surface foot trail

Land status: State nature preserve
Nearest town: Nicholasville
Other trail users: None
Maps to consult: Tom Dorman Kentucky River Palisades State Nature Preserve
Amenities available: None
Cell service: Good
Trail contacts: Office of Kentucky Nature Preserves; (502) 782-7830; eec.ky.gov/Nature-Preserves

FINDING THE TRAILHEAD

From the junction of US 27 and KY 29 on the west side of Nicholasville, follow US 27 South for 9.9 miles. Look for the trailhead parking area on your right shortly after bridging the Kentucky River. Trailhead GPS: 37.762106 / -84.617635

THE HIKE

Majestic cliffs rising 220 feet above the Kentucky River are the primary highlight of a rewarding hike at Tom Dorman Kentucky River Palisades State Nature Preserve. Located south of Nicholasville, this preserve was initially established in 1996 as Kentucky Palisades State Nature Preserve. The preserve's name was later changed, adding the name of Tom Dorman, the man responsible for saving this parcel of Kentucky River shoreline and hills. Lands continue to be added to the preserve, now coming in at almost 1,000 acres. The trail system has been expanded too, and the primary trailhead has been changed, resulting in an improved hiking experience. Elevations at the preserve vary nearly 400 feet. The forested lands are laced with sinkholes, stream hollows, and rich bottomlands, creating a diverse and rich ecosystem. The cliffs harbor rare starry cleft phlox and Eggleston's violet. We may not be able to see these plants up close, but knowing of them enhances the visit here. During spring, common wildflowers from trillium to trout lilies can be found on the preserve's north-facing slopes.

The views you get from the preserve are phenomenal. Across the river from the preserve rise steep layered cliffs that mirror the cliffs in the preserve. You will get to look out from the bluffs of the preserve and then look on the bluffs across from the preserve.

Soak in this view of bluffs rising from the Kentucky River.

The nature hike leaves the US 27 trailhead, rising along an old road, making a solid 200-foot climb before leveling off in woods of oak, maple, and cedar. Note the sinkholes in the forest. There are narrow, rock-lined, slit-like shafts as well as rounded tree-covered depressions. You will eventually come to a wet-weather stream and begin the loop portion of the hike. Here you aim for bluffs above the Kentucky River and gain your first across-the-river views. The hike continues downhill to reach bottomlands on a bend of the river, the site of an old crossing known as Knights Ferry. Here you will find evidence of old structures and, more importantly, close-up looks at the waterway in the foreground and stately layered bluffs rising from the water, curving in an arc with the bend of the Kentucky River.

What goes down must come up, and our hike weaves into and out of another hollow, rising all the while then leveling off near the old trailhead, closed back in 2020. This is the hike's high point. From here, cruise through hardwoods and evergreens, closing the circuit before backtracking to the trailhead, having gained added appreciation for Kentucky's state nature preserve program.

MILES AND DIRECTIONS

0.0   Start from the US 27 trailhead and begin walking south up an old roadway, eventually curving back north on the Upper Palisades Trail.

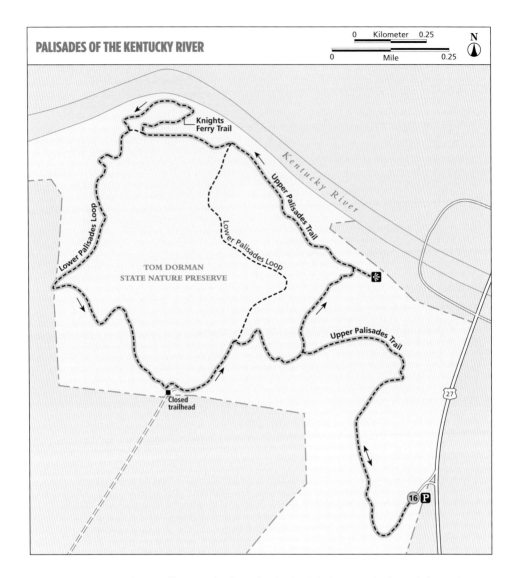

0   Kilometer   0.25

0   Mile   0.25

N

Knights
Ferry Trail

Kentucky River

Upper Palisades Trail

Lower Palisades Loop

Lower Palisades Loop

TOM DORMAN
STATE NATURE PRESERVE

Upper Palisades Trail

Closed
trailhead

27

16 **P**

0.3   Top out and level off in woods of maple, shagbark hickory, and oak. Look for trail-side sinkholes.

0.8   Reach a trail intersection just after stepping over a seasonal stream. Here, meet the Upper Palisades Trail. Your return route comes in from the left. For now, turn right with the Upper Palisades Trail, shortly passing under a power line.

1.1   Reach the bluffs of the Kentucky River. An unsigned trail splits right and goes to a view. Take the spur to the panorama then resume the main track as it heads west along the edge of the bluff, offering partial views. Descend.

1.5   Keep straight at the trail intersection, joining the Lower Palisades Loop.

1.7   Turn right on the Knights Ferry Trail, passing the stone chimney of an old structure. Hike through moist, rich-wooded bottomlands, heavy with junglesque woods of ash and sycamore. Look in the near at the river and across the water at the stony palisades rising up from the Kentucky River.

2.1 Rejoin the Lower Palisades Loop, entering a hollow, then climb sharply on wood and earth steps. Look for more sinks, as well as old fences, as you climb.

2.8 Hike under a power line. Climb a bit more.

2.9 Pass a kiosk and the old, closed trailhead, topping out. You are near the preserve's edge.

3.1 Come to a trail intersection. Split right with an arm of the Upper Palisades Trail, heading east in pines.

3.3 Complete the loop portion of the hike. Bear right and backtrack toward the US 27 trailhead.

4.2 Arrive back at the trailhead.

17 LAKE CUMBERLAND STATE RESORT PARK HIKE

This circuit explores the beauty of Lake Cumberland and protected lands of a peninsula upon which Lake Cumberland State Resort Park stands, coming near facilities that put the "resort" into this Kentucky state park. Leave from near Lure Lodge and wind along a steep shoreline opening onto a first-rate view from a stony point jutting into the water. Then make a prolonged hike along a high bluff above Lake Cumberland before turning into the hills and hollows, emerging to enjoy views of the Pumpkin Creek embayment of the lake before returning to the trailhead.

Start: Activities Center trailhead next to Lure Lodge
Distance: 4.2-mile loop with spur
Difficulty: Moderate
Elevation change: +/-1,262 feet
Maximum grade: 11% downhill grade for 0.3 mile
Hiking time: About 2.4 hours
Seasons/schedule: Year-round; summer could be noisy with boats
Fees and permits: No fees or permits required
Dog friendly: Yes
Trail surface: Natural surface foot trail

Land status: State park
Nearest town: Jamestown
Other trail users: None
Maps to consult: Lake Cumberland State Resort Park
Amenities available: Lodge and disc golf course nearby
Cell service: Good
Trail contacts: Lake Cumberland State Resort Park; (270) 343-3111; parks.ky.gov/jamestown/parks/resort/lake-cumberland-state-resort-park

FINDING THE TRAILHEAD

From exit 62 off the Cumberland Parkway at Russell Springs, take US 127 South for 13 miles. Turn left onto the state park entrance road, marked by a sign for Lure Lodge, the park's main overnight facility. Drive 5 miles and park to the right of the lodge as you face it, in front of the Activities Center. (From the south, starting at KY 90, take US 127 North for 16.5 miles; turn right onto the park road.) Trailhead GPS: 36.929785 / -85.040764

THE HIKE

This hike explores both natural and man-made offerings at Lake Cumberland State Resort Park, including something you won't find in many other parks of any kind: a huge lake. With a length of 101 miles and a shoreline totaling 1,255 miles, Lake Cumberland is one of the largest dammed bodies of water in the eastern United States. The trek takes you along an unspoiled ridge overlooking the 52,250-acre reservoir at one of the impoundment's widest points. You then meander through the park's developed area to a rock outcropping at the water's edge and end up at a commanding overlook. So grab

A sunny day on Lake Cumberland

your trekking poles and hiking shoes and enjoy all that this Kentucky state park has to offer. By the way, fall through spring is the best time to hike here. Summer can be noisy with boats on the lake—Lake Cumberland is known as the "Houseboat Capital of the World."

Lake Cumberland was created by damming the Cumberland River. Work on the project started in the early 1940s in response to devastation from the river's all-too-frequent flooding. The Wolf Creek Dam, completed by the US Army Corps of Engineers in 1951, is 240 feet high and slightly more than 1 mile long. US 127 runs on top of the dam 4 miles south of the state park road. Lake Cumberland is deep—200 feet in some spots—and, as a result, ranks as the largest man-made lake east of the Mississippi in terms of water volume, although not in surface acreage. Both Kentucky Lake and Lake Barkley in western Kentucky have more surface acreage than Lake Cumberland.

The 3,117-acre Lake Cumberland State Resort Park—heavy on developed facilities, with lodges, cabins, campground, picnic areas, and a sizable marina—was established in the early 1950s to take advantage of what was then the new reservoir. Naturally, hiking trails were included. This hike traces the Lake Bluff Nature Trail in its entirety. Along the way you will not only savor first-rate views of Lake Cumberland but also see seasonal waterfalls and beauty everywhere you look along a high bluff towering over the impoundment. Wildflowers will be seen in season as the path wanders through north-facing hollows. A plethora of informative trailside signs detailing human and

This hike features views of big Lake Cumberland.

natural aspects of the land and lake add immensely to the hike. Stop and read these educational gems while on the trail.

Finding the hike's beginning can be a challenge. The trailhead isn't obvious—it is to the right of the Activities Center as you face it. Once you get going, the highlights come fast and furious. After skirting the disc golf course, you circle around a steep-sided embayment. It isn't long before the trail leads to a commanding vista of the lake and the lands beyond it. From there, the trek runs along a bluff rising 200 feet above the water. In winter the vistas are nearly continuous. Even when the leaves are on the trees you will be rewarded with distant looks.

After leaving the lake you will be crossing park roads and nearing park facilities. These looks may lure you into staying at the cabins, lodges, or campsites. The final part of the hike takes you by the Pumpkin Creek embayment of Lake Cumberland, ending at a developed overlook. From this overlook it is but a short walk across a parking area to reach the trailhead.

MILES AND DIRECTIONS

0.0 As you face the Activities Center, take downhill steps to your right then join the signed Lake Bluff Nature Loop. Begin curving around a narrow, steep-sided lake embayment in woods of maple, beech, and oak. Bridge a gully. You can see the viewpoint the trail leads to across the embayment.

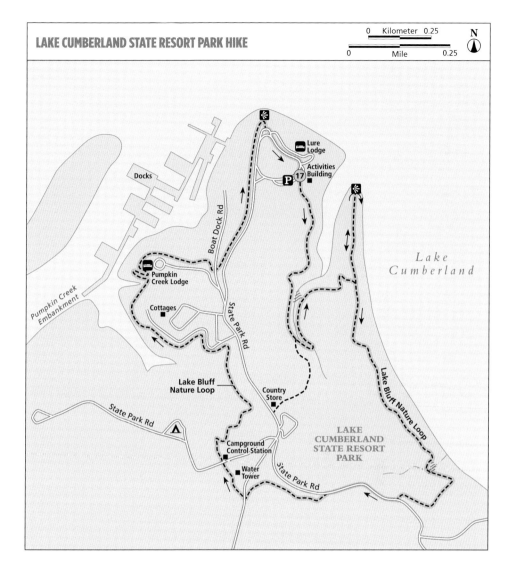

0   Kilometer 0.25

0   Mile   0.25

N

Docks

Lure Lodge

Activities Building

P 17

Boat Dock Rd

Lake Cumberland

Pumpkin Creek Lodge

Pumpkin Creek Embankment

Cottages

State Park Rd

Lake Bluff Nature Loop

Country Store

Lake Bluff Nature Loop

State Park Rd

State Park Rd

Lake Bluff Nature Loop

Campground Control Station

Water Tower

LAKE CUMBERLAND STATE RESORT PARK

0.3 Come to a seasonal waterfall that drops about 6 feet off a ledge. Step over a couple of hiker bridges spanning small seasonal feeder streams.

0.4 A signed spur goes right to the park's country store. Stay left with the Lake Bluff Nature Loop, circling the hollow.

0.8 Come to a trail intersection. Head left (north) to the primary overlook among pines and small hardwoods, walking atop rock much of the way.

1.0 Reach an outcrop and a first-rate view. Lure Lodge is across the embayment; Lake Cumberland stretches north, east, and south at a sharp bend. Backtrack.

1.8 Bridge a seasonal stream after dipping into a hollow. The stream has a seasonal waterfall with a very small watershed and thus a short time of flow. Quickly climb back out of the hollow.

1.9 Turn away from Lake Cumberland. Gently climb into oak-heavy woods.

2.0   Emerge at a park road and follow right along the road, passing some ranger residences.

2.2   Cross the park road and rejoin the woods on a footpath marked with a sign stating "Nature Trail." Shagbark hickory and white oak predominate along the trail.

2.4   Cross the main park road. Split right here after crossing the road, taking the trail uphill toward a water tower. You reach the hike's high point.

2.6   Cross the campground entrance road very near the campground control station and campsite 1. Keep north, descending in woods. Enter a wildflower-rich hollow.

2.9   Turn left (westbound), joining an old roadbed. Cottages stand uphill to your right. The waters of the Pumpkin Creek embayment come into view. Hike along a stony section of trail with water views and also looks at the massive state park docks.

3.5   A short spur trail goes right to Pumpkin Creek Lodge. Keep straight.

3.7   Cross the road leading to the boat dock. Rejoin the foot trail.

3.9   Come alongside the road leading to Lure Lodge. Keep straight toward the final overlook.

4.2   Reach the last overlook, sporting a view into the Pumpkin Creek embayment. From here, cross the parking area to arrive back at the trailhead.

18 GOBBLERS ARCH CIRCUIT

Start your hike atop Divide Ridge then drop into the geological wonderland of Marks Branch to see 80-foot Marks Branch Falls plunge into a reverberating rockhouse. Make multiple crossings of Marks Branch amid massive boulders to come near Rock Creek. The hike climbs from there, passing an unnamed 15-foot cataract before finding a high cliff line. Continue climbing to meet Gobblers Arch, a natural rock span, before completing the loop.

Start: Peters Mountain trailhead
Distance: 6.1-mile loop
Difficulty: Moderate
Elevation change: +/-1,312 feet
Maximum grade: 12% grade for 0.6 mile
Hiking time: About 3.4 hours
Seasons/schedule: Year-round; best late spring through late fall
Fees and permits: No fees or permits required
Dog friendly: Yes
Trail surface: Natural

Land status: National forest, national recreation area
Nearest town: Whitley City
Other trail users: None
Maps to consult: DBNF—Gobblers Arch Trail Map and Guide
Amenities available: Picnic tables, restrooms at trailhead; picnic area short distance away on hike
Cell service: Limited
Trail contacts: Daniel Boone National Forest, Stearns Ranger District; (606) 376-5323; fs.usda.gov/dbnf

FINDING THE TRAILHEAD

From the intersection of US 27 and KY 92 just south of Whitley City, take KY 92 West for 6.5 miles. Turn left on KY 1363, just after bridging the Big South Fork River at Yamacraw. Follow KY 1363 for 11 miles to a T intersection and the end of the blacktop. Turn left on Bell Farm Road and follow it 0.1 mile, then turn right on Peters Mountain Road (FR 139) and follow it 4.2 miles to the Peters Mountain trailhead, where parking is across the road in the Big South Fork National River and Recreation Area. Trailhead GPS: 36.623863 / -84.689823

THE HIKE

This loop hike explores a lesser-visited section of the Daniel Boone National Forest. However, after seeing Gobblers Arch and the surrounding scenery, you will wonder why it is not more visited. You get to admire not only the natural stone bridge tucked away in the national forest but also the 80-foot spiller that is Marks Branch Falls as well as another waterfall, topped off with a cliffside view. However, there is a potential price to pay—the loop requires seventeen creek crossings. During winter and early spring, you may find it difficult to do this hike dry-shod, but in summer and fall agile trail trekkers will return to the trailhead with their shoes and socks dry.

The hike starts at the Peters Mountain trailhead on Divide Road, with its picnic tables and restroom, a fine spot to begin and end your hike. Divide Road separates the Daniel Boone National Forest to the west and north from the Big South Fork National River and Recreation Area to the east and south. You will first join the Sheltowee Trace—Kentucky's master path, running more than 330 miles through the state and into Tennessee.

Marks Branch Falls dives into a stony glen.

Tread a slender footpath, working your way through plateau hardwoods and pines before dipping into the moister Marks Branch watershed.

Rhododendron cloaks Marks Branch when you come upon it after 0.5 mile. The stream is already falling in small but noisy rapids. The Sheltowee Trace is bordered in evergreens. Ahead, skirt the top of Marks Branch Falls as it plummets recklessly from a cliff line into a stone auditorium. The trail finds a route down the cliff line, leading you to a face-on encounter with the slender but superlative spiller.

Relaxing under Gobblers Arch

Here, Marks Branch pours from a cliff line, an 80-foot unimpeded free fall splashing onto a sandy landing pad framed by mineral-tinted rock. After gathering again, Marks Branch makes a serpentine flow into a riot of vegetation then courses onward toward Rock Creek to give up its waters.

Beyond Marks Branch Falls, the Sheltowee Trace courses directly down Marks Branch, crossing the stream again and again while passing huge, moss-covered boulders standing in and out of the water. Rhododendron thickens birch, tulip tree, and hemlock woods. Long, gray cliff lines lord over all. While working downstream, you will pass the intersection with the Marks Branch Trail. This path cuts the loop in half, but by taking it you will miss Gobblers Arch and the vista. The better hike stays with the longer circuit, as the vale of Marks Branch opens when nearing its mother stream, Rock Creek.

You are soon at a trail intersection near Rock Creek. A spur trail heads across Rock Creek—without benefit of bridge—to Hemlock Grove Picnic Area, with a picnic shelter. Stay with the Sheltowee Trace as it leads to the relatively faint but signed Gobblers Arch Trail. The path climbs to a cliff line and rock shelter. A gentle rise takes you past a low-flow cataract spilling 15 feet. This tributary waterfall of Marks Branch can nearly dry up in autumn.

Beyond this waterfall you are in upland oaks and pines, circling the top of cliffs falling toward Rock Creek. Ahead, an outcrop on a spur trail leads to an overlook of the Rock Creek valley below. Here, Rock Creek courses through the bottom of a mountain gorge to meet the Big South Fork, with Parker Mountain rising as a backdrop.

Past the overlook, the Gobblers Arch Trail takes you directly to and through Gobblers Arch. The stone bridge extends 18 feet wide and 8 feet high, a dry refuge with

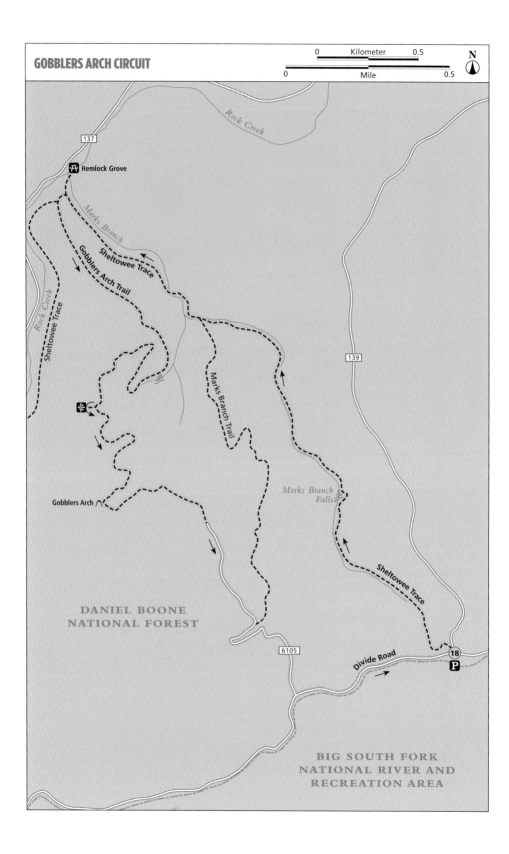

GOBBLERS ARCH CIRCUIT

0   Kilometer   0.5

0   Mile   0.5

Rock Creek

137

Hemlock Grove

Marks Branch

Sheltowee Trace

Gobblers Arch Trail

Rock Creek

Sheltowee Trace

139

Marks Branch Trail

Marks Branch Falls

Gobblers Arch

Sheltowee Trace

DANIEL BOONE
NATIONAL FOREST

6105

Divide Road

18

P

BIG SOUTH FORK
NATIONAL RIVER AND
RECREATION AREA

two openings. The hike leaves Gobblers Arch to pick up a forest road. From there the gravel track leads to Divide Road, which you follow a short distance to complete this rewarding circuit hike.

MILES AND DIRECTIONS

0.0 Start from Divide Road on the Sheltowee Trace. Join a singletrack path among oaks and hickories. Come along a cliff line before descending toward Marks Branch.

0.5 Make your first crossing of Marks Branch. Follow the stream as it cuts the beginnings of a gorge.

0.7 Cross Marks Branch then come along the cliff line above Marks Branch Falls.

0.8 Reach the base of Marks Branch Falls, dropping 80 feet into a picturesque, primeval scene. Continue down Marks Branch, sometimes in the stream, repeatedly crossing the creek amidst an implausible boulder garden.

1.2 Look for Marks Branch flowing under a house-size boulder. All the while, regal cliff lines rise above the creek.

1.6 Pass the easily missed Marks Branch Trail to the left. This intersection occurs when you are on the left bank of Marks Branch, heading downstream.

2.2 Walk around an equestrian barrier then reach a trail intersection in a growing-over field. To your right, a signed trail leads 0.25 mile to Hemlock Grove Picnic Area on FR 137. However, you must ford Rock Creek to reach the picnic area. Stay left, still on the Sheltowee Trace.

2.3 Head left on the less-used Gobblers Arch Trail. Climb.

2.7 Come to a cliff line and rockhouse.

3.0 Pass a low-flow tributary fall, pouring 15 feet into a narrow stone defile to the left of the trail.

3.7 A signed spur trail leads to an open rock slab; the Rock Creek valley opens below.

4.3 Hike through Gobblers Arch. Head left and ramble through upland hardwoods to pick up an old doubletrack trail.

4.7 Reach the dead end of FR 6105. Head south on the gravel doubletrack.

5.1 Pass the south terminus of the Marks Branch Trail, coming in from your left.

5.6 Reach Divide Road and turn left, walking the boundary between the Daniel Boone National Forest to your left and Big South Fork National River and Recreation Area to your right.

6.1 Arrive back at the trailhead.

19 BIG SPRING FALLS AND DICK GAP FALLS

Start this waterfall extravaganza at a fascinating place known as Blue Heron, where a historical outdoor mining camp museum grabs your attention. The hike leads you across the Big South Fork on a trestle bridge from the former mine site, then you ascend past bluffs to an overlook of the Big South Fork gorge. Next visit misty Dick Gap Falls and other cascades along that stream. Finally, trace an old railroad grade along the Big South Fork to view tall and slender Big Spring Falls, deep in a mountain hollow.

Start: Blue Heron parking area
Distance: 7.6 miles out and back
Difficulty: Moderate
Elevation change: +/-1,147 feet
Maximum grade: 8% downhill grade for 0.7 mile
Hiking time: About 4.3 hours
Seasons/schedule: Year-round; winter and spring for bolder waterfalls
Fees and permits: No fees or permits required
Dog friendly: Yes
Trail surface: Wood on river bridge, natural rest of the way

Land status: National recreation area
Nearest town: Whitley City
Other trail users: None
Maps to consult: National Geographic #241: Big South Fork
Amenities available: Interpretive information, restrooms
Cell service: None
Trail contacts: Big South Fork National River and Recreation Area, 4564 Leatherwood Rd., Oneida, TN 37841; (423) 286-7275; nps.gov/biso

FINDING THE TRAILHEAD

From Whitley City, take US 27 South to KY 92. Turn right and head west on KY 92 for 1.2 miles. Veer left on KY 1651 and continue 1 mile to reach KY 742. Make a sharp right here and follow KY 742 for 8.1 miles to dead-end at the Blue Heron former mining community and outdoor museum, boat ramp, and trailhead. Start the hike near the concession building on your left after driving under the trestle bridge over the Big South Fork. Trailhead GPS: 36.669317 / -84.547467

THE HIKE

This hike delivers varied highlights—big river views, mining history, gorge overlooks, and multiple waterfalls. It's a real Bluegrass State gem, all the more so knowing that almost the entire route uses the Kentucky Trail at Big South Fork National River and Recreation Area.

However, if you do this hike primarily for the waterfalls, know that the spillers are seasonal—winter and spring are the best times to catch them in full glory. And when the water is really flowing, you will find more cataracts in addition to Dick Gap and Big Spring Falls. Waterfall seekers should head elsewhere during summer and autumn.

The hike begins at the Blue Heron mining community, an interpretive site worthy of further exploration. You will be hard pressed not to look around, since the hike's

Big Spring Falls sprays down from a stone bluff.

beginning takes you near one of the old mine shafts then over a trestle bridge spanning the Big South Fork. The views from the trestle will excite—here you can gaze down on the rolling river and on the former habitation now preserved and managed by the National Park Service.

Once across the trestle, the hike joins the Kentucky Trail, tracing a railroad grade astride the Big South Fork. The track then turns into cliffy Three West Hollow. Curve around a cliff line before climbing a rock wall using steep wooden stairs flanked by rhododendron. You are now in the upper gorge, 300 feet above the Big South Fork. Emerge

This unnamed cataract drops downstream from Dick Gap Falls.

at Catawba Overlook, where big views open of Blue Heron, the bridge over the Big South Fork, the Devils Jump—a river rapid that's flipped me a few times—and at cliff lines across the gorge.

The hike bisects Dick Gap, a large once-cleared area, now reforested. Descend by an old chimney while making your way down the unnamed stream of Dick Gap Falls. A spur trail leads to the 45-foot wet-weather waterfall, cascading over a rock slab, sliding downward before free-falling into a sandy pool beneath a rock overhang, all wrapped in swaying rhododendron. The Kentucky Trail continues its pattern of going on and off old roads and paths, but the track is well marked.

When the water is up, an avid waterfall hunter will find better cataracts on the stream of Dick Gap Falls than Dick Gap Falls itself. However, to see them up close you have to scramble off the Kentucky Trail. A noteworthy 15-foot tumbler lies along the descent to a railroad grade; yet another praiseworthy waterfall is found near where the stream of Dick Gap Falls gives its waters up to the Big South Fork.

The Kentucky Trail then picks up a level railroad grade, once again cruising along the Big South Fork. Here, pass another fall after an unnamed stream emerges from a trailside culvert to tumble downslope. The hike then enters Big Spring Hollow, a deep cool cleft in the Big South Fork gorge. Take a spur leading to Big Spring Falls. The dramatic 70-foot pour-over starts its plunge as a narrow gush of white, only to splash and widen on an angled rock face then scatter outward over a rockhouse into a sea of evergreen.

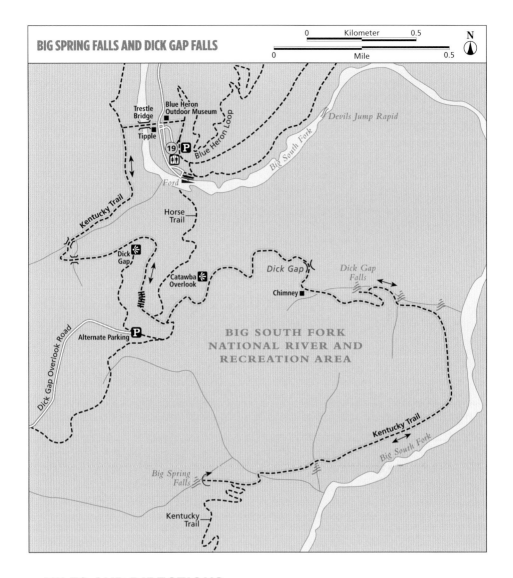

BIG SPRING FALLS AND DICK GAP FALLS

0   Kilometer   0.5

0   Mile   0.5

N

Trestle Bridge
Blue Heron Outdoor Museum
Devils Jump Rapid
Tipple
Blue Heron Loop
19 P
Big South Fork
Ford
Kentucky Trail
Horse Trail
Dick Gap
Catawba Overlook
Dick Gap
Chimney
Dick Gap Falls

BIG SOUTH FORK
NATIONAL RIVER AND
RECREATION AREA

Dick Gap Overlook Road
Alternate Parking P

Kentucky Trail
Big South Fork

Big Spring Falls

Kentucky Trail

MILES AND DIRECTIONS

0.0 Start near the concession building with the trestle bridge to your left, and join the asphalt path leading uphill to the left. Ascend.

0.1 Reach the east end of the trestle bridge. Cross the span over the Big South Fork. Enjoy views of the Blue Heron community, the river, and the gorge.

0.3 Come to a trail intersection at the end of the bridge. Head left on the Kentucky Trail, tracing a former railroad grade with the river to your left. Watch for the wheels and platform of an old mining railcar to your left. Beech and oak rise overhead. Turn into Three West Hollow. Boardwalks help you over wet sections.

0.7 Cross the stream of Three West Hollow on a hiker bridge. Shortly turn back toward the Big South Fork, crossing another hiker bridge then coming along a cliff line.

1.2 Reach and climb steep steps, surmounting a cliff line.

1.3 Come to a trail intersection. Here a horse trail descends left to a ford of the Big South Fork at Blue Heron. Stay straight and climb, immediately reaching a second intersection. A spur goes right to Dick Gap Overlook. Head left here, still on the Kentucky Trail, toward Catawba Overlook, walking through oaks and mountain laurel in uplands.

1.8 Come to the short spur leading left to Catawba Overlook. The view encompasses the Big South Fork gorge, trestle bridge, Blue Heron, and the Devils Jump. Continue on the Kentucky Trail.

2.0 Pass through Dick Gap. Descend.

2.1 Look for the remains of an old chimney to the right of the trail.

2.3 Wooden steps take you down a low cliff line.

2.4 Split left at the spur to Dick Gap Falls. Soon reach the 45-foot discharge, nestled in rhododendron. The area below the falls is very mushy. Resume the Kentucky Trail. Pass other cascades and cataracts along the stream of Dick Gap Falls.

2.7 The Kentucky Trail curves right, joining a level railroad grade. Head south with the Big South Fork to your left.

3.3 The former railroad grade passes over a stream. Below you, the bridged stream emerges from a culvert, creating a tumbling white cataract of about 20 feet. Turn into Big Spring Hollow.

3.5 Watch for a 6-foot horseshoe fall just before coming to the bridge over the stream of Big Spring Hollow. You won't miss the huge concrete building foundation to your left, just beyond the bridge. Delve deeper into the hollow.

3.6 Come to a trail intersection. Here, the Kentucky Trail splits left. We stay right on the spur to Big Spring Falls, well away from the creek below.

3.8 Come to the overlook of 70-foot Big Spring Falls. The overspill makes a slender dive from a rock precipice then splashes off a rock face, widening then splattering into a sea of rhododendron below. Retrace your steps.

7.6 Arrive back at Blue Heron and the trailhead.

20 BLUE HERON LOOP

This circuit explores the gorge of the Big South Fork. Start on the rim, trekking along bluffs to visit two fine developed overlooks, then make your way through the eerie Cracks-in-the-Rock before descending to Blue Heron Outdoor Museum, a living history replica of a coal mining town. From there, hike along the rugged Big South Fork, passing Devils Jump rapid then seasonal but scintillating Blue Heron Falls, as well as geological features. Finally, climb back to the rim of the gorge before completing the scenic loop.

Start: Blue Heron Loop trailhead
Distance: 6.5-mile loop
Difficulty: Moderate-difficult
Elevation change: +/-1,506 feet
Maximum grade: 12% downhill grade for 0.6 mile
Hiking time: About 3.4 hours
Seasons/schedule: Year-round; winter and spring for bolder falls
Fees and permits: No fees or permits required
Dog friendly: Yes
Trail surface: Mostly natural; some asphalt near overlook accesses
Land status: National recreation area

Nearest town: Whitley City
Other trail users: Equestrians on part of hike
Maps to consult: National Geographic #241: Big South Fork
Amenities available: Interpretive information, restrooms at overlook accesses
Cell service: Okay at top of gorge; none otherwise
Trail contacts: Big South Fork National River and Recreation Area, 4564 Leatherwood Rd., Oneida, TN 37841; (423) 286-7275; nps.gov/biso

FINDING THE TRAILHEAD

From Whitley City, take US 27 South to KY 92. Turn right and head west on KY 92 for 1.2 miles. Veer left on KY 1651 and continue 1 mile to reach KY 742. Make a sharp right here, and follow KY 742 for 5.3 miles. Turn left onto Gorge Overlook Road and follow it 0.4 mile to the signed Blue Heron Loop trailhead, on your left. Trailhead GPS: 36.676723 / -84.530719

THE HIKE

This very rewarding hike combines scenic views, waterfalls, and everywhere-you-look beauty with geology and mining history—all within the gorge of the Big South Fork of the Cumberland River, one of Kentucky's finest outdoor destinations. Blue Heron was a coal mining town built in 1937 on the banks of Big South Fork by the Stearns Coal and Lumber Company. Disappointed with production, Stearns closed the mining operation in 1962, and the town was abandoned. Now a major attraction of the Big South Fork National River and Recreation Area, the former coal town of Blue Heron has been re-created to inform visitors of life in the coal communities that once predominated in eastern Kentucky.

Except for the huge coal tipple, none of the original Blue Heron buildings survived. Therefore, the re-creation is dotted with new metal-frame structures representing the church, company store, school, homes, and other buildings. The recorded first-person

These steep steps lead to Cracks-in-the-Rock.

accounts of Blue Heron life by former residents are authentic and interesting, and the full-size mock-up of a mine opening is also well done.

Because the tour of Blue Heron is self-guided, how much time you spend there is entirely up to you. Distance-wise, the Blue Heron visit is only a small fraction of the total hike. Most of the walking is in the woods and along the river bottom. You also could execute this hike first and then drive to Blue Heron and tour it.

The hike begins at the dedicated Blue Heron Loop trailhead. Soon you find yourself westbound in a forest of hardwoods, evergreens, and mountain laurel. For about the

A hiker emerges from Cracks-in-the-Rock.

first mile, the trail parallels Gorge Overlook Road, which comes into and out of view then you reach the Devils Jump Overlook, with a wide overlook deck and a smaller sheltered locale. Below, admire the river and the narrow, rapid known as Devils Jump, where a boulder garden forces nearly the whole watercourse through a narrow chute. At one point the US Army Corps of Engineers wanted to build a dam at Devils Jump—a proposal that helped stimulate support for legislation to protect what became Big South Fork National River and Recreation Area.

View from the Devils Jump Overlook

The trek continues along the rim then turns away from Gorge Overlook Road and meets the spur to Blue Heron Overlook, with its circular gazebo. The climb is not difficult, but the view is similar to the one you had from the Devils Jump Overlook.

Next you begin a prolonged descent, coming to a long, steep set of wooden steps that lead down a massive boulder. Be careful here—the steps can be dangerous, especially for small children. Just beyond the bottom of the stairway, you come to Cracks-in-the-Rock—a huge rock with holes cut by nature through three of its sides. The trail goes through the rock and begins winding its way down to Blue Heron.

Once there, you can take either of the two paved walkways that go south through the exhibits. The walkway on your left takes you to the mine opening and tipple; the one on your right leads to various "ghost" structures with cutout figures and buttons that activate recorded oral histories. At one, for example, a woman's voice explains that as a girl she entertained herself by reading all the Nancy Drew books. The train station and more exhibits are located below the tipple.

Just south of the tipple, you curve to the river, heading upstream in bouldery woods. Spur trails lead to large rocks that offer nice spots for watching the water. Pass the Devils Jump then run in conjunction with the Lee Hollow Loop over an old rail line to Blue Heron Falls. Here the upper half of Blue Heron Falls spills over layered strata then dances down a vertical face onto the trail before surging onward down a concreted channel to the Big South Fork. Oddly, the concrete channel looks natural at first glance. And at second glance. A barred mine shaft stands directly to the left of the falls as you face it. Upper Blue Heron Falls spills about 60 yards upstream of the lower falls. It makes a classic Kentucky ledge dive from a rock rim then gently flows before spilling as Blue Heron Falls. You have to climb some to reach Upper Blue Heron Falls.

BLUE HERON LOOP

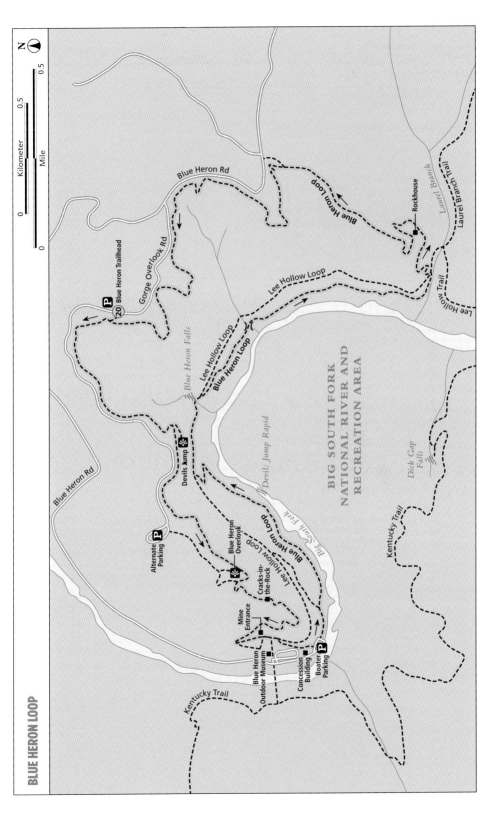

Just ahead, the Blue Heron Loop and Lee Hollow Loop separate. Descend, staying with the Blue Heron Loop and passing over several small wooden bridges returning to the riverside, with sporadic river views. You soon turn away from the river and climb east up attractive Laurel Branch. From there the ascent is via a series of steps and switchbacks. After an overall climb of about 400 feet, you are back on the gorge rim. From there, pass a spur linking the loop to the Blue Heron Campground. Begin running roughly parallel to the Blue Heron access road, returning to the hike's starting point, a fine Kentucky trail adventure under your belt.

MILES AND DIRECTIONS

0.0 Start from the parking area. Descend then split right in mountain laurel, sourwood, pines, red maple, and white oak. Come near Gorge Overlook Road.

0.6 Split left for the Devils Jump Overlook as a trail goes right to alternate parking. Follow the trail to a deck and expansive view of the gorge of the Big South Fork. Backtrack and continue along the gorge, passing a second spur to the alternate parking. Continue along the gorge rim, passing a small cozy rockhouse and cliff line.

1.4 A spur leads right (uphill) to the Blue Heron Overlook. Begin a steady decline.

1.6 Descend steep steps down a boulder then split left, cutting through Cracks-in-the-Rock—a combination rockhouse, cliff line, and cool cave. Resume the downgrade.

1.9 Reach the first spur down to the Blue Heron Outdoor Museum. Explore at will. The loop continues, passing a second spur right to Blue Heron. Next, reach the pedestrian bridge over the Big South Fork and a worthwhile river view. Split right just beyond the bridge, dropping toward the boater parking, passing the concession building along the way.

2.2 Hike east from the boater parking with the Big South Fork to your right. Soon, a spur leads left to the Lee Hollow Loop. Keep straight on the hiker-only Blue Heron Loop as it narrows to a singletrack path under sycamores.

2.7 A sign alerts you to Devils Jump, roaring to your right. High bluffs rise across the river. Ahead, bridge a seasonal stream and enter a reclamation area where mine tailings were piled. Ahead, climb steep steps.

3.0 Meet and run in conjunction with the Lee Hollow Loop. Head right on an old railbed in pines. Look down on the river, bluffs, and reclamation area. Pass a barred mine shaft to the left of the trail, as well as coal seams.

3.2 Come to Blue Heron Falls as it spills above the trail. Note the barred mine shaft next to the falls. The slide cascade shoots below the trail, while Upper Blue Heron Falls makes its drop over a ledge well above the path. Just ahead, split right with the Blue Heron Loop. Descend on irregular trail.

3.5 Bridge a stream. Descend to bottoms amid big trees and big boulders.

4.1 Reach an intersection, crossing the Lee Hollow Loop. Climb from the gorge on steps and switchbacks, passing a low, long rockhouse. Ahead, gain the nose of a ridge, now trekking in pines and xeric hardwoods, as well as over rock slabs.

5.1 Pass the spur right to Blue Heron Campground. Now, run alongside Blue Heron Road then Gorge Overlook Road, curving away on rib ridges. The walking is easy.

6.5 Arrive back at the trailhead.

21 PRINCESS FALLS AND LICK CREEK FALLS

This hike leads down the gorgeous Lick Creek Valley to several water-falls within its confines. Yet it's not all about falling water, as you will tackle metal ladders, majestic rockhouses, and bridgeless creek crossings amid everywhere-you-look beauty. Allow plenty of time to enjoy the sights.

Start: Lick Creek trailhead near Whitley City
Distance: 7.4 miles out and back with spur
Difficulty: Moderate-difficult
Elevation change: +/-1,020 feet
Maximum grade: 9% grade for 0.7 mile
Hiking time: About 4.2 hours
Seasons/schedule: Year-round; spring best for waterfalls
Fees and permits: No fees or permits required
Dog friendly: Yes

Trail surface: Natural; does have creek crossings
Land status: National forest
Nearest town: Whitley City
Other trail users: None
Maps to consult: DBNF—Lick Creek Falls Map and Guide
Amenities available: None
Cell service: Good at first; less so toward Princess Falls
Trail contacts: Daniel Boone National Forest, Stearns Ranger District; (606) 376-5323; fs.usda.gov/dbnf

FINDING THE TRAILHEAD

From traffic light #4 on US 27 at the intersection with KY 478 in Whitley City, head west on KY 478 for 0.1 mile. Turn left on KY 1651 South and follow it for 1 mile to turn right onto Ranger Road. Follow Ranger Road just a short distance to a gravel parking area on your right, between two houses. Trailhead GPS: 36.714975 / -84.480969

THE HIKE

This hike explores one of the prettiest valleys in the Daniel Boone National Forest. Along the way the trek visits a pair of major waterfalls—Lick Creek Falls and Princess Falls—along with another lesser-visited cataract amid a wild gorge with geological features you expect in this part of the Bluegrass State. Here the three distinctly dissimilar cataracts feed the blue-green stream as it courses among massive boulders, where the trail uses ladders to descend cliff lines and then uses stone steps to curve under a massive rockhouse you won't forget.

The waterfalls themselves hold their own and more in the beauty department. Lower Lick Creek Falls is an unusual cataract. It makes an angled stairstep descent—nothing unusual about that. It is the massive boulder perched atop the pour-over that makes this spiller stand out. Lick Creek Falls is a slender free-faller parachuting 40 feet from a cut in an overhanging stone lip enveloped in a sandstone rockhouse. Princess Falls is altogether different from the other two cascades. Located on Lick Creek itself (the other two are located on a tributary of Lick Creek), Princess Falls is situated on a bend in the stream.

Princess Falls is long and wide.

Here, Lick Creek flows over an extended rock slab then makes an abrupt right turn, spilling 18 feet over a 45-foot-wide ledge into a sizable pool, creating a broad curtain fall.

The wildness of the hike is belied by its beginning, starting on the edge of Whitley City. Hike through ridgetop pines and oaks. It isn't long before you leave civilization behind to enter the gorge of Lick Creek, using the aforementioned metal ladders to descend cliff lines. And the excitement continues when you curve under a stone-littered rockhouse of impressive proportions. The whole scene is ethereal. Furthermore, when the rains have been falling, the rockhouse has a slender spiller of its own.

Then you reach Lick Creek itself, working downstream in classic Eastern Kentucky landscape of big boulders, cliff lines, and rich woods. It isn't long before you are turning up another tributary of Lick Creek to visit Lower Lick Creek Falls and Lick Creek Falls. These two spillers are perhaps misnamed, since they are not on Lick Creek itself. Names aside, the two falls are worth the side trip and offer exciting waterfall photography opportunities.

A trip along a dripping cliff line ends in the grotto from which Lick Creek Falls makes its 40-foot dive. The cliff walls are stained with iron and, along with other colored rock, add a splash of tint to the splashing waterfall.

Now, on to Princess Falls. A short backtrack followed by a trail split and rock hop gets you heading down Lick Creek past big pools and scads of rhododendron. A few manageable creek crossings lie ahead, then you come to a campsite near a tributary of Lick Creek before reaching a stream curve and Princess Falls.

Lick Creek Falls

If you stay with the trail beyond 18-foot Princess Falls, you can drop below the falls from the bottom. If the water is high, expect to get your feet wet when looking upstream at Princess Falls. Nonetheless, the cataract can be viewed from 360 degrees, allowing you to fully appreciate the wider-than-long cataract that flows into a large plunge pool bordered by a campsite.

From here you can simply take the Lick Creek Trail directly back to the trailhead, avoiding the spur to Lower Lick Creek Falls and Lick Creek Falls. However, it will be rewarding to experience a second time the ethereal rockhouse and ladders climbing the cliff lines on your way back.

MILES AND DIRECTIONS

0.0 Start from the trailhead and look left for the trail sign and pole gate. Pass the pole gate and walk along the wood's edge near a private house to your left. Pick up Lick Creek Trail, at this point a doubletrack path running along the Daniel Boone National Forest boundary.

0.1 Stay right with the Lick Creek Trail, descending.

0.3 Pass under a power line.

0.9 Begin descending from the uplands.

1.2 Descend the first of two metal ladders, whereby hikers can safely scale a pair of sheer cliff lines. Dip to come along an unnamed tributary of Lick Creek.

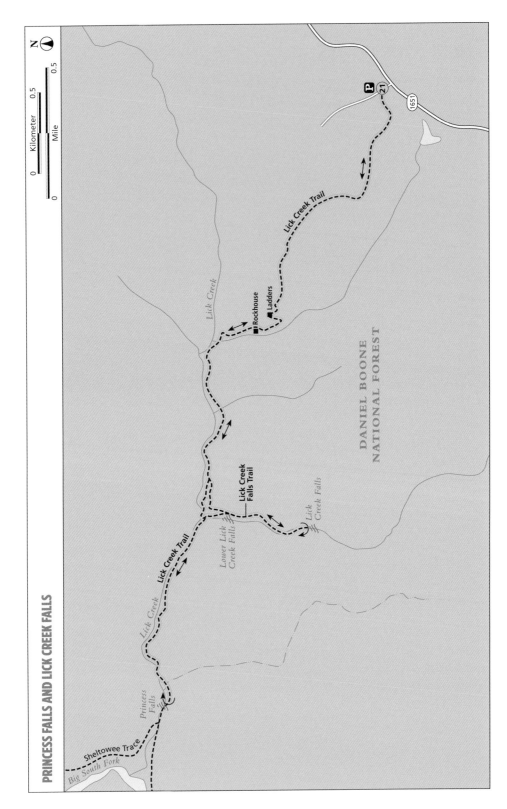

PRINCESS FALLS AND LICK CREEK FALLS

N

Kilometer
0   0.5

Mile
0   0.5

Lick Creek Trail

P
21

1651

Lick Creek

Rockhouse

Ladders

DANIEL BOONE
NATIONAL FOREST

Lick Creek
Falls Trail

Lower Lick
Creek Falls

Lick
Creek Falls

Lick Creek Trail

Lick Creek

Princess
Falls

Sheltowee Trace

Big South Fork

A water-level view of Princess Falls

1.4 The trail curves under a gigantic rockhouse scattered with fallen boulders with a very low-flow fall. Take the stone steps between boulders and beneath the overhang of nothing but rock.

1.6 Reach Lick Creek and turn downstream. The creek flows to your right among mid-stream boulders shaded by tall trees.

2.3 Head left on the Lick Creek Falls Trail. Turn up an unnamed feeder stream of Lick Creek. Join a slope well above the creek.

2.5 Come to another signed trail intersection. Stay left toward Lick Creek Falls. Listen for Lower Lick Creek Falls, a 16-foot cataract complemented by a hanging boulder. There is no easy way to reach the falls. To reach it, scramble steeply downhill to your right. Approach the falls from the lower end, then head upstream. Here you will face the falls, with the imposing boulder standing atop the angled, widening white cataract descending in increments before gathering in a shallow, sandy pool.

2.8 Reach 40-foot Lick Creek Falls, pouring into a stone amphitheater. Backtrack.

3.1 Head left at the signed junction where you were earlier. Descend toward Lick Creek.

3.3 Return to the Lick Creek Trail after crossing Lick Creek just upstream of a huge boulder. When the water is up, this crossing may be a ford. Once on the Lick Creek Trail, head left (westerly), downstream.

3.7 Make a more difficult crossing of Lick Creek. Keep down the left-hand bank of the stream.

4.0 Come to a pair of creek crossings. (**Option:** A user-created trail sneaks along on the left-hand bank and avoids the two creek crossings.) If you do make these crossings, note the illegal ATV trail coming in from the north bank.

4.1 Reach Princess Falls after passing through a campsite near a tributary stream entering from the left. Backtrack.

4.9 Keep straight beyond the trail intersection with a path leading right for Lick Creek Falls.

5.1 Pass the second intersection leading right to Lick Creek Falls. Keep straight on the Lick Creek Trail.

5.8 Turn right, away from Lick Creek.

6.2 Pass under the otherworldly rockhouse, then come to the metal ladders ascending cliff lines. Continue backtracking

7.4 Arrive back at the trailhead.

This hike amid a nest of nature trails takes you to Kentucky's highest waterfall—Yahoo Falls—plus a few other highlights, including Roaring Rocks Cataract and Yahoo Arch. First, walk to the base of the 113-foot-high spiller that is Yahoo Falls, tumbling into a world-class rockhouse, then circle past veiled Roaring Rocks Cataract. From there, take the side trip to Yahoo Arch, located in the adjacent Daniel Boone National Forest. See this geological curiosity then return to Yahoo Falls, walking along the rim of the cliff line over which Yahoo Falls spills, gaining top-down views of the falls before returning to the trailhead.

Start: Yahoo Falls parking area
Distance: 2.7-mile loop, including out-and-back to Yahoo Falls
Difficulty: Easy
Elevation change: +/-659 feet
Maximum grade: 12% grade for 0.2 mile
Hiking time: About 1.5 hours
Seasons/schedule: Year-round
Fees and permits: No fees or permits required
Dog friendly: Yes, but Yahoo Falls area can be busy.

Trail surface: Natural surface
Land status: National park, national forest
Nearest town: Whitley City
Other trail users: None
Maps to consult: National Geographic #241: Big South Fork
Amenities available: Picnic tables, restrooms at parking area
Cell service: Iffy at best
Trail contacts: Big South Fork National River and Recreation Area; (423) 286-7275; nps.gov/biso

FINDING THE TRAILHEAD

From the intersection of KY 700 and US 27 just north of Whitley City, take KY 700 West for 3.9 miles. Turn right onto Yahoo Falls Road and follow it for 1.5 miles to reach a restroom and parking area for Yahoo Falls at the lower end of the parking area loop road. The trail starts on your right. Trailhead GPS: 36.773629 / -84.524114

THE HIKE

Yahoo Falls is the centerpiece of a nest of nature trails at Yahoo Falls Scenic Area, part of the Big South Fork National River and Recreation Area, a unit of the National Park Service. This is a scenic designation–worthy parcel of the Bluegrass State, some of the best of the best, where nature's splendor is concentrated in one spot.

There's only one little problem—the mazelike network of trails can be confusing. But even if you get lost—rather, briefly discombobulated—you will still stumble onto the highlights of this locale: the overlook of the Big South Fork, metal stairs descending a cliff, an immense rockhouse once occupied by aboriginal Kentuckians, a garden of massive boulders topped off by Kentucky's highest cataract. A side trip will take you to Yahoo Arch, a stone span located on a spur trail linking to the Yahoo Falls Scenic Area.

Your best bet to stay on track is to study then photograph the map in this guide and take a picture of the map at the trailhead with your phone. Even if you don't follow this

Yahoo Falls is Kentucky's highest cataract.

hike exactly, you will find the waterfalls quite rewarding—after all, Yahoo Falls is Kentucky's tallest waterfall.

The hike first leaves the trailhead on the signed path toward Yahoo Falls. Ahead, take the short spur left to an overlook of the Big South Fork of the Cumberland River, the waterway that created a magnificent gorge. Here the river bends left near its confluence with Yahoo Creek, flowing quietly bordered by glorious forests. Savor this perspective; you'll then begin your loop to enter the Yahoo Falls trail maze. A GPS unit, Magic 8

Yahoo Falls tumbles 113 feet.

Ball, lucky rabbit's foot, divining rod, and a deck of tarot cards may help you get through. Okay, that's a little exaggeration.

Take a cool, steep metal stairwell down a steep bluff. After reaching dry ground, you will cruise along the base of a cliff line toward Yahoo Falls. The waterfall is echoing in the distance, reverberating throughout the immense semicircular rockhouse ahead, below which grows junglesque flora. Even pre-Columbian Kentuckians used this considerable rockhouse.

Work past some tempting spur trails and aim for the resounding waterfall. Ahead, Yahoo Falls makes its long dive from an overhanging ledge, a slender curtain of white landing on rocks before gathering in a shallow pool. The 113-foot falls and enormous shelter fashion an outstanding waterfall picture. Waterfall photographers have multiple angles from which to capture the spiller backed by an immense rockhouse.

The official trail leads beneath the rockhouse and behind Yahoo Falls then works behind a dark boulder jumble. Keep your phone handy. One shot after another opens up. Work your way to Yahoo Creek, where a garden of gargantuan boulders seem to block the trail. Here the path keeps upstream on Yahoo Creek, squeezing among the boulders.

The walking becomes easy again as you cruise up along Yahoo Creek then come to Roaring Rocks Cataract. The 30-foot faucet-like waterfall dashes through another boulder garden. Mostly obscured by thickets of rhododendron, the falls are very difficult to photograph, yet still a praiseworthy sight.

Ahead, climb away from Yahoo Creek then reach the side trail to Yahoo Arch. Here, head left on the much less used singletrack path running parallel to Yahoo Creek. Enter the Daniel Boone National Forest, though you won't know the difference. Switchbacks uphill bring you to an impressive cliff line, with three highlights concentrated in one area ahead. First, come to a deep rockhouse certainly long used as a shelter. Then comes Yahoo Arch, 17 feet high and 70 feet long. The Yahoo Arch Trail leads you under the span. Adjust your eye to the dim light, then look around for a 4-foot-high window arch, on the right side of Yahoo Arch.

After backtracking to the scenic area, carefully walk along the cliff line above Yahoo Falls. Three designated overlooks give you a chance to safely look down into the chasm below, where Yahoo Falls sings its watery song, echoing off the chasm walls below. A bridge leads over the stream forming Yahoo Falls. One last top-of-the-rim overlook of Yahoo Falls awaits. Beyond there, the loop concludes. Make the short backtrack to the trailhead.

The Yahoo Falls area offers additional trails, such as the Sheltowee Trace, as well as scattered picnic sites with tables. After the hike you will understand why this is dubbed Yahoo Falls Scenic Area.

MILES AND DIRECTIONS

0.0 Start from the trailhead parking area toward Yahoo Falls. Shortly reach a spur trail leading left to an overlook of the Big South Fork, at this point usually backed up as uppermost Lake Cumberland.

0.2 Come to a trail junction and the loop portion of the hike. Turn left here, aiming for the base of Yahoo Falls. Ahead, a long set of metal stairs leads you below a sheer bluff.

0.3 A spur trail heads left to the Sheltowee Trace. Our hike keeps straight, running along the base of the cliff line from which Yahoo Falls drops.

0.4 Come to 113-foot Yahoo Falls, the centerpiece of an enormous rockhouse that has to be seen to be comprehended. Steps lead to the splashy shallow pool of the long, narrow cataract. Circle behind Yahoo Falls and around the rockhouse to next turn left at an intersection, descending away from the cliff line. A short switchback leads you to still another trail junction. The trail leading left bridges the creek of Yahoo Falls. However, this hike turns right up Yahoo Creek.

YAHOO FALLS

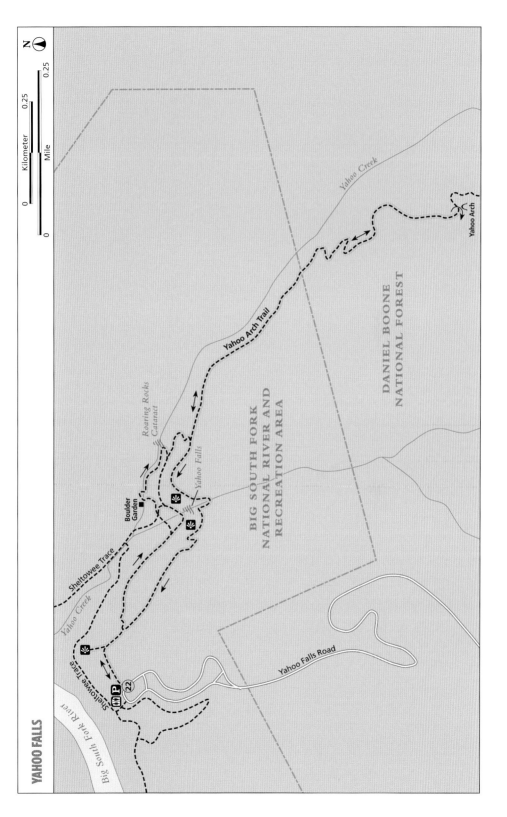

N

Kilometer
0   0.25   0.25

Mile
0   0.25

Big South Fork River

Sheltowee Trace

Yahoo Creek

Boulder Garden

Roaring Rocks Cataract

Yahoo Falls

Yahoo Arch Trail

Sheltowee Trace

Yahoo Creek

Yahoo Arch

BIG SOUTH FORK NATIONAL RIVER AND RECREATION AREA

DANIEL BOONE NATIONAL FOREST

Yahoo Falls Road

22

0.5   Seemingly dead-end at big boulders on Yahoo Creek. Work your way upstream of the boulder field, crisscrossing Yahoo Creek.

0.6   Come to Roaring Rocks Cataract. The 30-foot faucet spiller dances through boulders and rhododendron. Cross Yahoo Creek beyond the falls and come to a cliff line and trail intersection. Turn left here and climb.

0.7   Reach yet another intersection. Here, take the Yahoo Arch Trail left toward Yahoo Arch.

1.4   Find a deep rockhouse after walking along a cliff line. Just ahead you will walk under Yahoo Arch. Backtrack.

2.1   Return to the main loop and stay left, hiking the cliff line above Yahoo Falls, passing two overlooks.

2.3   Cross the creek of Yahoo Falls and pass one last overlook of Yahoo Falls below. Continue back toward the trailhead.

2.5   Complete the loop portion of the hike and begin backtracking toward the trailhead.

2.7   Arrive back at the trailhead.

23 EAGLE FALLS LOOP

This triple-waterfall hike visits thunderous 67-foot Cumberland Falls, noble 40-foot Eagle Falls, and under-visited 10-foot Eagle Creek Cascade. The trek also affords vistas of the Cumberland River and its gorge. First, admire Cumberland Falls, a river-wide horseshoe-shaped cataract of muscle, mist, and magnificence. Trace cliff lines above the Cumberland River to reach river bottom, where Eagle Falls dives into a boulder-bordered pool. Walk up the rugged Eagle Creek watershed to find Eagle Creek Cascade and wooded hills. The balance of the hike loops you back to the trail, with a side trip to a historic overlook.

Start: Kentucky 90 trailhead
Distance: 2.2-mile balloon loop with spurs
Difficulty: Moderate
Elevation change: +/-708 feet
Maximum grade: 12% grade for 0.4 mile
Hiking time: About 1.4 hours
Seasons/schedule: Year-round; best waterfalls in winter and spring
Fees and permits: No fees or permits required
Dog friendly: Leased dogs allowed

Trail surface: Forested natural surface
Land status: State park
Nearest town: Corbin
Other trail users: None
Maps to consult: Cumberland Falls State Resort Park facilities map
Amenities available: Restrooms, gift shop across river
Cell service: Good
Trail contacts: Cumberland Falls State Resort Park; (606) 528-4121; parks.ky.gov/parks/resortparks/cumberland-falls

FINDING THE TRAILHEAD

From Exit 25 on I-75 near Corbin, take US 25W south for 7.5 miles to KY 90. Turn right and take KY 90 West for 8.4 miles, bridging the Cumberland River just above Cumberland Falls. From the bridge, continue on KY 90 for 0.3 mile farther to reach the Eagle Falls trailhead, on your right. Trailhead GPS: 36.836592 / -84.345119

THE HIKE

For a short hike of only 2.2 miles, you will find this trek challenging. The short distance, however, gives it a moderate rating. You will climb and descend hills, use staircases, walk steps, and pick your way along sandy shores and through boulder gardens. Do not be dissuaded—anyone can execute this hike with adequate time. Allow yet additional time to take pictures and videos of this trio of first-rate cataracts.

From the trailhead, the hike quickly sidles alongside the Cumberland River, just a short distance upstream of Cumberland Falls. The track squeezes past cliffs then climbs. Cumberland Falls is below, obscured by trees. Climb past an overlook then join another cliff line where incredible upriver views of Cumberland Falls are among the finest vistas in the entire state. Here, Cumberland Falls brews up a hurtling 67-foot-high, 125-foot-wide vertical plunge, collapsing in spiraling spray. One look and you will see why Cumberland Falls is known as the "Niagara of the South."

Eagle Falls spills into a rock garden.

Beyond here you begin the loop portion of the hike amid rugged terrain inside the gorge of the Cumberland, finally dipping to reach the Cumberland River, aided by steps and stairwells. The river bottom is uneven but picturesque. The path courses through boulders, sandbars, and brush before reaching 40-foot Eagle Falls. View Eagle Creek free-falling from a rock lip into a boulder-bordered basin. These rocks allow for multiple photography vantages of the spiller. Below the waterfall plunge pool, Eagle Creek gurgles through boulders then makes one last 6-foot drop before giving its waters up to the Cumberland River.

Hiker profile provides a height comparison to 40 foot Eagle Falls.

Explore Eagle Falls and the adjacent beach on the Cumberland River before back-tracking to the loop portion of the hike, where Eagle Creek dashes among rocks below rhododendron, evergreens, and ferns. Ahead, find Eagle Creek Cascade, a 10-foot angled slide fall, pouring over a slab of stone before ending in a final, vertical descent on a bend in Eagle Creek.

The loop part of the hike shortly leaves Eagle Creek, climbing past a rock overhang en route to a hilltop. From here the trail dips along a hollow to finish out the circuit. At this point, take the spur to the historic overlook with its Civilian Conservation Corps (CCC) gazebo. The CCC was a government works organization employing young men during the Great Depression of the 1930s. The CCC developed many of the trails and facilities at Cumberland Falls State Resort Park. The overlook and gazebo are a fitting tribute to those men of yesteryear.

MILES AND DIRECTIONS

0.0   Start on the Eagle Falls Trail, leaving KY 90 and working downstream. Pass warning signs about being swept over Cumberland Falls, which is already audible.

0.1   The trail comes fast against a dripping cliff line. Climb well above Cumberland Falls.

0.2   Squeeze under a rock overhang then reach a view of the Cumberland River gorge, downriver of the falls.

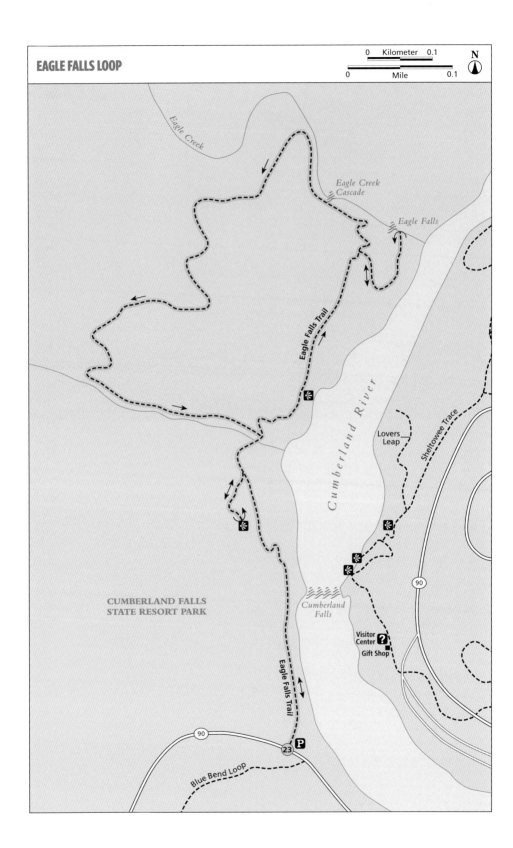

0   Kilometer   0.1

0   Mile   0.1

N

Eagle Creek

Eagle Creek
Cascade

Eagle Falls

Eagle Falls Trail

Cumberland River

Lovers
Leap

Sheltowee Trace

CUMBERLAND FALLS
STATE RESORT PARK

Cumberland
Falls

Visitor
Center
Gift Shop

90

Eagle Falls Trail

90

23

P

Blue Bend Loop

Looking upstream at crashing Cumberland Falls

0.3 Reach a spur trail to a historic overlook of the Cumberland River gorge, complete with a gazebo constructed by the Civilian Conservation Corps in the 1930s. For now, keep straight with the Eagle Falls Trail, soon passing an incredible overlook of Cumberland Falls.

0.4 Step over a stream and come to the loop portion of the Eagle Falls Trail. Stay right here, continuing downstream along the Cumberland River. Ahead, stop by a second Cumberland Falls overlook.

0.6 Reach another trail intersection. Head right here on the spur to Eagle Falls. Metal, stone, and wood steps lead down to the river bottom.

0.7 Come to 40-foot Eagle Falls. Here the cataract pours curtain-style into a plunge pool bordered by boulders. Backtrack to the loop portion of the hike.

0.8 Resume the loop, now heading up Eagle Creek.

0.9 Reach Eagle Creek Cascade, a 10-foot slide fall located on a bend in Eagle Creek.

1.1 Pass a rock shelter littered with stone debris.

1.3 Top out on a hill. Walk among pines and oaks before descending into a moist hollow.

1.5 Come alongside a Cumberland River tributary.

1.7 Finish the loop portion of the hike. Backtrack.

1.8 Head right up wooden steps aplenty to reach an overlook and a wooden gazebo built by the Civilian Conservation Corps. Bear right and backtrack toward the trailhead.

2.2 Arrive back at the trailhead.

This hike explores the wild and beautiful Cumberland River through an incredible gorge where it holds designation as a Kentucky Wild River. The trek, starting at Kentucky wonder Cumberland Falls State Resort Park, first leads to big, brawling Cumberland Falls, a popular area featuring several designated overlooks of the 67-foot "Niagara of the South." Continue down the Cumberland River gorge, where several lesser known waterfalls set in a geological paradise await. Finally, find Dog Slaughter Falls tucked away in a rugged vale, making its curtain spill into a stone bordered pool.

Start: Cumberland Falls State Resort Park
Distance: 7.0 miles out and back
Difficulty: Moderate-difficult due to terrain
Elevation change: +/-1,136 feet
Maximum grade: 7% downhill grade for 0.2 mile
Hiking time: About 3.8 hours
Seasons/schedule: Year-round; falls better winter through spring
Fees and permits: None
Dog friendly: Yes, but the first 0.5 mile can be busy with people.
Trail surface: Concrete on first 0.5 mile; natural rest of way

Land status: State park, national forest
Nearest town: Corbin
Other trail users: None
Maps to consult: Cumberland Falls State Resort Park, DBNF Sheltowee Trace Section 27: Moonbow
Amenities available: Gift shop, office, picnic area, restrooms at trailhead
Cell service: Good
Trail contacts: Cumberland Falls State Resort Park; (606) 528-4121; parks.ky.gov/parks/resortparks/cumberland-falls

FINDING THE TRAILHEAD

From exit 25 on I-75 near Corbin, take US 25W south for 7.5 miles to KY 90. Turn right and take KY 90 West for 8.3 miles, turning right into the large Cumberland Falls parking area before the bridge over the Cumberland River. Trailhead GPS: 36.837905 / -84.343513

THE HIKE

Cumberland Falls State Resort Park is not only one of Kentucky's most beautiful places—where the melding of forest, rock, and water fashion your trailside landscape—but also where you can view the famed "moonbow" created by the spray rising from Cumberland Falls. Purportedly one of only two moonbows in the world, this phenomenon occurs when a full moon shines on the waterfall's mist—in much the same way as the sun creates a rainbow during daytime at Cumberland Falls, a regular occurrence in and of itself. You can check the Cumberland Falls State Resort Park website for specific dates and times of the moonbows (cloud cover notwithstanding).

This hike takes the park's Moonbow Trail (with which the Sheltowee Trace runs in conjunction) from the visitor center area on KY 90 to view the Bluegrass State's most powerful cataract bellowing from a horseshoe-shaped sandstone rim. The trail then

Hiking through the Cumberland River Gorge

explores the portion of the Cumberland that is a state-designated Kentucky Wild River, and, boy, does it live up to that name. A plentitude of waterfalls spill near the trail, culminating in the visual highlight that is Dog Slaughter Falls, officially on the list of top-ten all-time Kentucky waterfall names.

The beginning of the hike is busy and developed. Scores of people regularly stop at Cumberland Falls, as demonstrated by the large parking area. Wander past the visitor center, gift shop, and other amenities to shortly reach Cumberland Falls. Here the entire flow of the Cumberland River drops 67 feet in a 125-foot-wide horseshoe-shaped curtain. The spray and mist, noise and vigor make Cumberland Falls one of America's natural wonders.

Multiple overlooks deliver different vantages of the cataract—from above, beside, and below. A concrete trail takes you downriver to Lovers Leap, a sometimes crowded spot that delivers the best view of the falls. The area is centered by a memorial to Kentucky native T. Coleman DuPont. DuPont purchased Cumberland Falls and the adjoining tracts then donated the land to the Commonwealth of Kentucky, creating the state park. The big river, big falls, big bluffs, and big gorge combine to create a big-time panorama.

Beyond this overlook, the hike leaves the crowds behind. You are now cruising the bottoms alongside the designated Kentucky Wild River, where enormous boulders line the now-narrower watercourse, creating sporadic rapids. The rocky terrain makes for slow travel as cliff lines rise overhead. Rock House Falls adds to the trailside beauty with its low-flow 30-foot drop. In places, the bluffs recede and the Moonbow Trail/Sheltowee

Dog Slaughter Falls

Trace cuts through bottomland, where sand beaches gather along the Cumberland and river birch trees spread their limbs. The next cataract is Anvil Falls, a 20-foot slide cascade that disappears into a boulder field. The low-flow tributary falls can devolve to mere drips in late summer and autumn.

Continue in geological wonderment of cliffs, rockhouses—even a rockfall arch. Pass Veil Cascade ahead. The delicate 10-foot curtain-type fall drops directly beside the trail. Beyond here, the hike scenery mixes beaches and bouldery fields as it follows the curve of the Cumberland River. You can't miss Catfish Creek Cascades, as it is located uphill from where the Moonbow Trail/Sheltowee Trace crosses Catfish Creek on a wooden hiker bridge. Look up Catfish Creek for the cataract spilling 12 feet over a rock face then caroming amid mossy boulders before flowing under the bridge upon which you stand. It takes a little work to photograph the spiller. This bridge roughly marks your entrance into the Daniel Boone National Forest, leaving the state park behind.

The scenery stays first-rate as you enter the valley of Dog Slaughter Creek. Wind among immense boulders and under rockhouses to reach Dog Slaughter Falls, making a wide, curtain-type 20-foot dive into an alluringly big plunge pool. Boulders and other rock perches make for multiple photography vantage points. It's a cool place to hang out. Allow plenty of time to backtrack. I guarantee you will see additional beautiful sights on your return trip, executing one of Kentucky's best all-around hikes, deserving of a return trip.

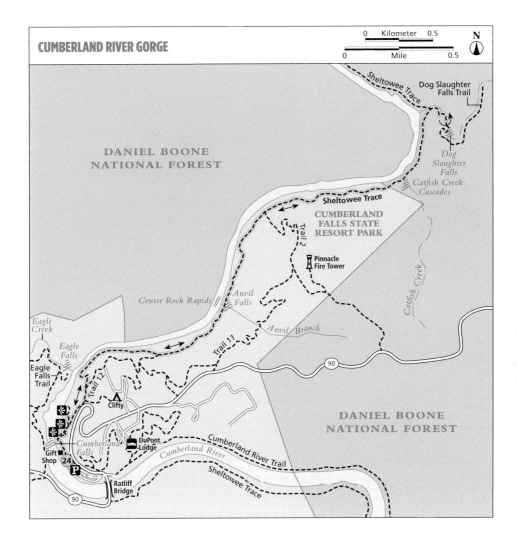

0   Kilometer   0.5

0   Mile   0.5

N

DANIEL BOONE
NATIONAL FOREST

Sheltowee Trace

Dog Slaughter
Falls Trail

Dog
Slaughter
Falls

Catfish Creek
Cascades

Sheltowee Trace

CUMBERLAND
FALLS STATE
RESORT PARK

Trail 2

Pinnacle
Fire Tower

Catfish Creek

Center Rock Rapids

Anvil
Falls

Anvil Branch

Eagle
Creek

Eagle
Falls

Trail 11

90

Eagle
Falls
Trail

Trail 12

Clifty

DANIEL BOONE
NATIONAL FOREST

DuPont
Lodge

Cumberland River Trail

Cumberland
Falls

Cumberland River

Gift
Shop   24

Sheltowee Trace

P

Ratliff
Bridge

90

MILES AND DIRECTIONS

0.0 Start from the large parking area on KY 90 and walk past the visitor center to quickly reach the first overlook of Cumberland Falls. From there, walk downstream to curve under a cliff line to a lower view of the falls. This viewpoint is close enough to the falls to get misted on. Resume downstream toward the Lovers Leap view.

0.3 Reach the Lovers Leap view. Enjoy the large-scale waterfall scene, then backtrack a little to pick up the Moonbow Trail/Sheltowee Trace. Pass a couple of quick intersections with Trail #12. Stay with the Moonbow Trail/Sheltowee Trace.

0.7 A series of switchbacks and a staircase take you back to the Cumberland River bottoms. The crowds have been left behind. Ahead, look across the river for Eagle Falls. Course down the incredible Cumberland River gorge.

1.1 The trail splits right. Here the old abandoned part of the Sheltowee Trace once kept directly along the river. However, the current route goes underneath low-flow Rock House Falls, spilling 30 feet from the stone above. This is the first of the low-flow seasonal falls between reliable Cumberland Falls and Dog Slaughter Falls. Ahead, climb beyond a trail leading uphill into the park trail network before the Moonbow Trail/Sheltowee Trace returns to the river, cruising bottoms and along bluffs.

1.6 Reach Anvil Falls, a 20-foot slide cascade slipping down a ledge to disappear into a boulder field then flow as a creek under the trail. Just ahead, walk to a riverside boulder to see Center Rock Rapids, where the Cumberland loudly crashes white through a watery boulder jumble.

1.8 Walk under an immense rockhouse with a massive overhang.

1.9 Pass beneath a rockfall arch after dancing through boulders and along a cliff line.

2.2 Reach a trail intersection. Trail #2 leaves right. Keep on the Moonbow Trail/Sheltowee Trace.

2.5 Reach Veil Cascade, a delicate 10-foot curtain-type fall.

2.9 Cross a wooden bridge over Catfish Creek and view Catfish Creek Cascades from the span. Ahead, enter the Daniel Boone National Forest, leaving the state park and staying closer to the Cumberland River.

3.3 Turn right onto the Dog Slaughter Trail. Dance among big boulders to enter the valley of Dog Slaughter Creek.

3.5 Reach 20-foot Dog Slaughter Falls as it discharges over a stone rim into a boulder-bordered pool. Retrace your steps.

7.0 Arrive back at the trailhead.

25 THE SCUTTLE HOLE

This highlight-filled hike features not only 60-foot Dutch Branch Falls but also three eye-opening overlooks of the Rockcastle River arm of Lake Cumberland. Relish additional geological highlights, from majestic cliff lines to a stone channel through which Dutch Branch flows before diving off a ledge to form the centerpiece cataract of this engaging Daniel Boone National Forest trek.

Start: KY 3497
Distance: 2.7-mile balloon loop with spur
Difficulty: Moderate
Elevation change: +/-634 feet
Maximum grade: 20% grade for 0.2 mile
Hiking time: About 1.6 hours
Seasons/schedule: Year-round; Feb through Mar for best falls
Fees and permits: No fees or permits required
Dog friendly: Yes

Trail surface: Natural
Land status: National forest
Nearest town: London
Other trail users: None
Maps to consult: DBNF—Scuttle Hole Trail Guide and Map
Amenities available: Campground and boat ramp a little beyond the trailhead
Cell service: None
Trail contacts: Daniel Boone National Forest, London Ranger District; (606) 864-4163; fs.usda.gov/dbnf

FINDING THE TRAILHEAD

From exit 38 on I-75 near London, head west on KY 192 for 14 miles to KY 1193. Turn left on KY 1193 and follow it 1 mile to KY 3497. Turn right on KY 3497 and continue 5.1 miles to the Scuttle Hole trailhead, on your right. Trailhead GPS: 36.958689 / -84.345871

THE HIKE

Dutch Branch Falls gives reason enough and more to visit this neck of the woods. However, other highlights await, namely the views of Lake Cumberland, where the stilled waters of the Cumberland and Rockcastle Rivers merge. Management of the Daniel Boone National Forest recognized this special area and laid out a nature trail system that will leave you a happy hiker.

The trailhead, located on a turn in KY 3497, gives no indication of what lies below in the valley of Dutch Branch. You join the Scuttle Hole Trail as it dips to quickly meet Dutch Branch in thick hemlock, mountain laurel, and rhododendron woods. The stream slides down a smooth rock channel backed by a parallel low cliff line. Then you are cruising directly down the stream channel with cliff lines rising on both sides of the trail and creek, complemented by a little slide cascade!

Next thing you know, the trail is taking you along the high cliff line over which Dutch Branch Falls plummets 60 feet into a semicircular rock amphitheater. You cannot see the falls from here, but you can hear them. Hang on—you will get the opportunity to admire Dutch Branch Falls in its fullness. Ahead, views of Dutch Branch valley open from the gorge rim.

Dutch Branch Falls

You then reach the junction to cut through the Scuttle Hole to Dutch Branch Falls, but for now stay right, heading out to the panoramas. It isn't long before you reach the first developed overlook, marked with stonework and a fence. Gaze to the west, with Dutch Branch valley to your left and the Rockcastle River arm of Lake Cumberland in the distance. Two more overlooks lie ahead, the last of which allows a most-expansive view across the Rockcastle River embayment to sheer stone cliffs.

Gazing into the Rockcastle River valley

After backtracking, you drop through the Scuttle Hole, where stone steps lead through a break in the cliff line. Admire the geology while scuttling down toward Dutch Branch, where smaller cascades preview Dutch Branch Falls.

Then turn uphill, bordered by boulders on one side and Dutch Branch on the other, gurgling unseen amid its own boulders and thickets of rhododendron. Ahead, a side trail leads to 60-foot Dutch Branch Falls, pirouetting from the high cliff circling the defile below. Dutch Branch Falls flows best winter through mid-spring, reducing to a trickle in autumn.

Continue exploring the Dutch Branch valley, heading along a glorious cliff line rising mightily overhead. The trail then switchbacks down to the now closed Rockcastle Campground access road. From here, climb the Dutch Branch Trail then back through the Scuttle Hole and back to the trailhead, delighting in Kentucky hiking at its best.

MILES AND DIRECTIONS

0.0   Start at the Scuttle Hole trailhead on KY 3497. Join a singletrack path descending gently to Dutch Branch, swaddled in evergreens. Cross Dutch Branch and turn downstream as Dutch Branch flows along a low channel-like cliff line.

0.3   Come to the top of a high cliff line, the precipice from which Dutch Branch tumbles 60 feet into an overhanging, echoing amphitheater of rock. You can't see anything

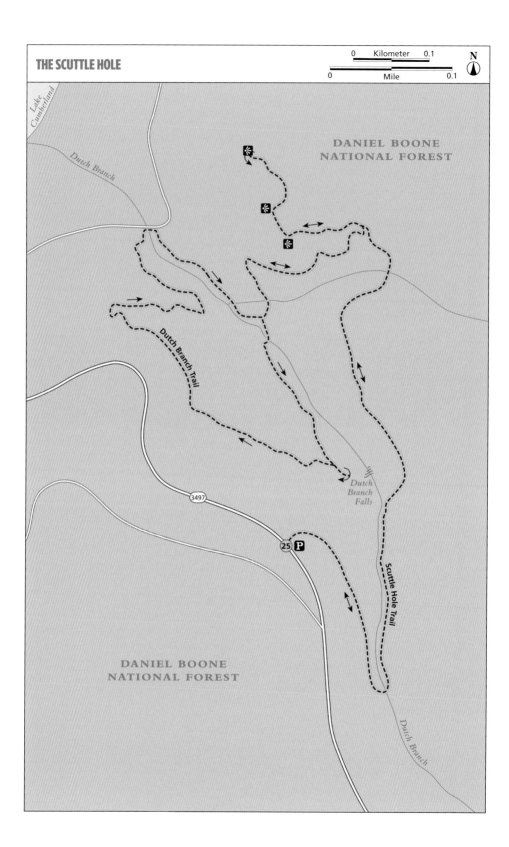

THE SCUTTLE HOLE

0   Kilometer   0.1

0   Mile   0.1

N

DANIEL BOONE
NATIONAL FOREST

Dutch Branch

Lake
Cumberland

Dutch Branch Trail

Dutch
Branch
Falls

3497

25 P

Scuttle Hole Trail

DANIEL BOONE
NATIONAL FOREST

Dutch Branch

but the top of the falls from here. Keep hiking along the rim of the Dutch Branch gorge. Views open of the widening Dutch Branch valley.

0.6 Reach a trail intersection. For now, stay right toward the overlooks before returning to this intersection and visiting the waterfalls. Soon pass the first two developed overlooks.

0.8 Reach the final overlook. The Rockcastle River arm of Lake Cumberland opens before you, including cliffs above the embayment of Pole Bridge Branch. Savor the scenery then backtrack.

1.0 Descend through the Scuttle Hole on stone steps. Pass an inspiring rockhouse to the right of the trail.

1.1 Intersect the Dutch Branch Trail, which has come up from Rockcastle Campground. Turn left, climbing along Dutch Branch. Just ahead, span Dutch Branch near a small cascade. Climb.

1.2 Reach a trail intersection and head left on a spur trail. Ahead you will meet the amphitheater of stone where Dutch Branch nosedives into a rock heap. Backtrack.

1.3 Resume the Dutch Branch Trail. Hike in the shadows of a monumental cliff line. During leafless times, scan across the Dutch Branch valley to find the developed overlooks.

1.6 Descend from the cliff line on switchbacks.

1.8 Come to the old Rockcastle Campground access road. Walk just a few feet on the campground road to bridge Dutch Branch via culvert. Turn right and join the Dutch Branch Trail. Climb the narrow path in a steep vale.

1.9 Come to a trail intersection. You were here before. From here, work your way up through the Scuttle Hole, now backtracking.

2.7 Arrive back at the trailhead.

26 ARCH FALLS AND BEAR CREEK FALLS

This hike features not only waterfalls but also an arch and magnificent cliff lines. Take the Nathan McClure Trail into the valley of the Rockcastle River, first viewing 18-foot Chimney Cascade. Next comes Arch Falls, a truly unique cataract that starts its 50-foot dive by passing through a stone arch. Ahead, lesser, ephemeral waterfalls spill off ledges. Your end destination is 20-foot Bear Creek Falls, a big, wide perennial cataract that plunges from a ledge into Lake Cumberland.

Start: FR 122
Distance: 7.4 miles out and back
Difficulty: Moderate, but trail can be muddy.
Elevation change: +/-935 feet
Maximum grade: 11% grade for 0.3 mile
Hiking time: About 4.1 hours
Seasons/schedule: Feb through Apr for boldest falls
Fees and permits: No fees or permits required
Dog friendly: Yes, but trail is shared with equestrians.

Trail surface: Forested natural surface
Land status: National forest
Nearest town: Somerset
Other trail users: Equestrians
Maps to consult: Daniel Boone National Forest—Nathan McClure Trail #530
Amenities available: None
Cell service: Iffy at best
Trail contacts: Daniel Boone National Forest; (606) 864-4163; fs.usda.gov/dbnf

FINDING THE TRAILHEAD

From exit 38 on I-75 near London, head west on KY 192 for 18 miles to the bridge over the Rockcastle River. Continue on KY 192 for 3.5 more miles, then turn left on Old Whitney Road. Follow it for 1.1 miles; the road becomes gravel FR 122. Continue on FR 122 for 2.7 miles, then veer left onto FR 122A. Follow FR 122A for 2.6 miles to reach the Nathan McClure Trail where it leaves acutely left and uphill from FR 122A. There is no official parking area; park on the road shoulder. Trailhead GPS: 36.975082 / -84.361701

THE HIKE

This is a spectacular hike, full of continuous beauty as well as high-level highlights. If you come after rains, you will be rewarded with more waterfalls in addition to the three major cataracts on this hike—Chimney Cascade, Arch Falls, and Bear Creek Falls. For here in the valley of the Rockcastle River, many a seasonal tributary tumbles from rock rims, creating cataracts that delight the hiker in winter and spring before the spillers empty into Lake Cumberland, a highlight unto itself. Majestic bluffs, spring wildflowers, and rock formations will vie for your attention. The downside of this hike? When the waterfalls are flowing, the trail can be muddy in places. Also, you share the path with equestrians, which can be troublesome.

Bear Creek Falls is located at hike's end and is accessible not only by foot but also by boaters motoring up Lake Cumberland. The scenery around Bear Creek Falls is alluring—the

Arch Falls spills through a natural span.

nexus of mountain stream and mountain lake, where a semicircular rock bluff provides an elevated perch for viewing Bear Creek Falls, framed in wooded wonderment.

The hike uses the Nathan McClure Trail, named for an eighteenth-century Native American fighter. In 1788 Lieutenant McClure was escorting Kentucky settlers west from the Cumberland Gap. Native Americans stole the settler's livestock and horses, and McClure and his patrol went after them. McClure was subsequently killed then buried hereabouts.

Bear Creek Falls makes a 20-foot dive into Lake Cumberland.

The hike's beginning belies its forthcoming beauty as the trail surmounts a nondescript brushy hill before descending into the luxuriantly vegetated valley of Pole Bridge Branch. You will bridge the creek then traverse a narrow swath of the vale to soon find a lone chimney located beside the path, overlooking Chimney Cascade. The difficult-to-reach cataract pours through a narrow boulder jumble then widens and slides down a convex-angled rock slab, dropping a total of 18 feet.

The Nathan McClure Trail leads out to the Rockcastle River arm of Lake Cumberland, across the water from Rockcastle Campground. The trail turns north up the lake arm, undulating along a rugged tree-covered hillside, ultimately rising to Arch Falls. Here, a seasonal stream pours through an 8-foot-long arch known as Nathan McClure Arch #2 then bounces down a few short ledges before free-falling to splatter at the base of a long rockhouse. It is a rare sight indeed to have a waterfall flowing through an arch. You can circle behind the waterfall and also climb up to viewpoints of the water flowing through the arch.

It is important to pay attention to the trail ahead, as the path goes on and off an old roadbed. Beyond Arch Falls, the trail leads past several cascades, including Morning Falls, so named because the morning light shines upon its flowing waters, and Lake Falls, which makes a drop just above Lake Cumberland.

Eventually you turn into the Bear Creek embayment of Lake Cumberland. Then comes the star of the show—20-foot Bear Creek Falls. This brawny wall of white is well known, since it can be accessed not only by trail but also, more commonly, by boat. During the spring and summer, when the lake is at full pool, boaters regularly work their way

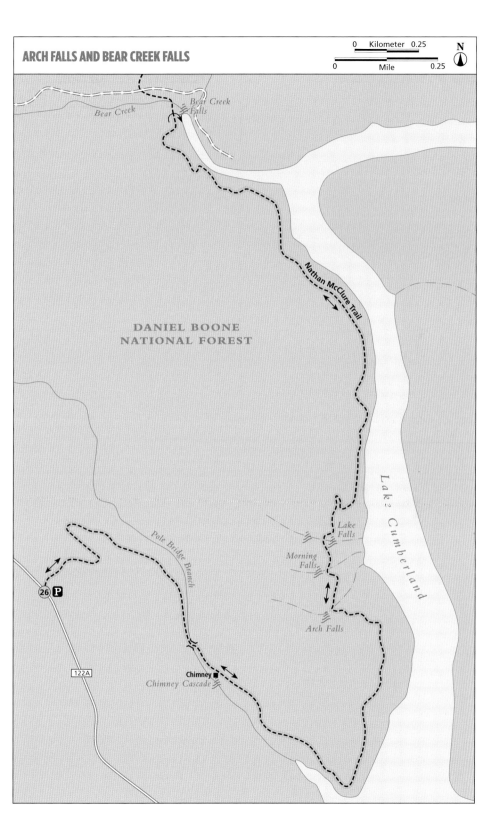

ARCH FALLS AND BEAR CREEK FALLS

0 Kilometer 0.25

0 Mile 0.25

N

Bear Creek

Bear Creek Falls

Nathan McClure Trail

DANIEL BOONE
NATIONAL FOREST

Lake Cumberland

Pole Bridge Branch

Lake Falls

Morning Falls

Arch Falls

26 P

122A

Chimney

Chimney Cascade

to the base of this wide, curtain-like cataract. For hikers, the waterfall can be viewed from a cleared cliff. At higher flows, Bear Creek Falls will be accompanied by a tributary falls spilling into the water across the embayment from the overlook. You can safely walk to the top of Bear Creek Falls. However, viewing the falls from lake level—unless you are in a boat or the lake pool is drawn down—is a challenge. Nonetheless, the cataract makes for a fine exclamation point to a rewarding waterfall hike.

MILES AND DIRECTIONS

0.0   Start where the Nathan McClure Trail leaves northeast from FR 122A. Join the doubletrack Nathan McClure Trail (Trail #530) and climb into pines, soon topping out in piney, brushy woods.

0.2   Curve left (westerly) then descend toward Pole Bridge Branch, curving right into evergreens.

0.6   Span Pole Bridge Branch on a trail bridge. Continue down the left bank of the creek, squeezing through a defile. The creek then falls away sharply.

0.9   Come along a lone chimney beside the trail on the right. From here, walk toward the cliff line and peer down on Chimney Cascade, making its convex slide. The steep terrain makes the spiller challenging to reach up close.

1.3   Leave the embayment of Pole Bridge Branch and turn north up the Rockcastle River arm of Lake Cumberland. Soon cross the first of several tributaries flowing from cliff-laden Gulf Ridge above.

1.9   Come to 50-foot Arch Falls after climbing. Here a low-flow stream pours through a cliff-top arch then dances over layers of rock before diving past a vertical rock face. A big rockhouse stands to the right of the falls.

2.0   Pass a low-flow waterfall well upstream of the trail, dropping from a cliff line. This will be one of the first ephemeral falls to dry up.

2.1   Come to Morning Falls. This spiller lies just below the trail, diving 12 feet from a stone lip. An upper falls can be viewed on this same stream, plunging from a high cliff.

2.2   Pay close attention here. At this point an old roadbed, used as a social trail, keeps straight then curves left to climb Gulf Ridge. This is the wrong way. Instead, look for the acute right turn descending toward Lake Cumberland. This correct route is blazed and gets closer to the water then turns back north.

2.5   Come to Lake Falls. Here a stream makes a narrow 12-foot drop below the trail, while Upper Lake Falls executes a wider 10-foot drop from an undercut rock lip. Neither is easy to reach. In winter you will see imposing cliff lines across the Rockcastle River. Dip into other drainages ahead.

3.1   Turn left into the Bear Creek embayment.

3.7   Reach the cliff-top overlook of Bear Creek Falls, a wide rumbler crashing 20 feet from a rock lip directly into Lake Cumberland. Look for the companion waterfall dropping into the lake very near Bear Creek Falls. Scramble to the fall's base if the lake is down. Retrace your steps.

7.4   Arrive back at FR 122A.

27 ROCKCASTLE NARROWS AND BEE ROCK LOOP

Execute a fine loop starting at a fine national forest recreation area centered on the Rockcastle River. Cross a historic bridge over the river then climb past a deep rockhouse to reach Bee Rock with its rewarding views. After topping a ridge, you pass a wildflower-rich hillside then cruise along the Rockcastle, a designated Kentucky Wild River. Soak in the eye-pleasing land- and waterscapes before cruising through the Bee Rock Campground, which will entice you to overnight at this parcel of the Daniel Boone National Forest.

Start: Bee Rock Campground, south side
Distance: 5.0-mile balloon loop
Difficulty: Moderate
Elevation change: +/-1,390 feet
Maximum grade: 16% downhill grade for 0.4 mile
Hiking time: About 2.8 hours
Seasons/schedule: Year-round
Fees and permits: No fees or permits required
Dog friendly: Yes
Trail surface: Natural, some rock sections

Land status: National forest
Nearest town: Corbin
Other trail users: None
Maps to consult: Daniel Boone National Forest, Bee Rock Area Trails
Amenities available: Campground, picnic area, boat ramp, water during warm season
Cell service: Bad
Trail contacts: Daniel Boone National Forest, London Ranger District; (606) 864-4163; fs.usda.gov/dbnf

FINDING THE TRAILHEAD

From exit 38 on I-75 near London, head west on KY 192 for 18 miles to the bridge over the Rockcastle River. Turn right into Bee Rock Campground on FR 624, the south side of the Rockcastle River, before crossing the river bridge. Follow FR 624 for 0.4 mile to the Sublimity Bridge, on the left. Trailhead GPS: 37.027940 / -84.321521

THE HIKE

This hike takes place at the Daniel Boone National Forest's Bee Rock Recreation Area, deep in the gorge where the Rockcastle River, an officially designated Kentucky Wild River, flows into Lake Cumberland. The trek stays along the Rockcastle River and Lake Cumberland for most of its distance. It also offers a little history, a fine vista, and even some falling water in season.

And don't forget fine Bee Rock Campground. I've spent many a night there and highly recommend it. The camp, divided into two sections by the Rockcastle River, offers walk-in and drive-up campsites, restrooms, and water spigots in season. The destination, geared toward tent, truck, and pop-up campers, offers a wide array of spacious sites, each with tent pad, fire ring, and lantern post, situated amid big boulders and rich forest. Part of the campground is open year-round. The campground got a full rehabilitation in 2022 after being damaged by flooding.

The view from atop Bee Rock

This is a good year-round hike. (Caveat: Start early on summer mornings.) The hike begins on the south side of Sublimity Bridge, constructed by the Civilian Conservation Corps in the 1930s. For many a year it led autos across the Rockcastle River before the current KY 192 bridge replaced it. Nowadays the span is open only to hikers and bicyclists. Look up and down the water as you cross. In summer, Lake Cumberland will likely be at full pool. During winter, when the lake is drawn down, the Rockcastle River may be flowing free hereabouts. While you are at it, gaze directly up from the bridge. The

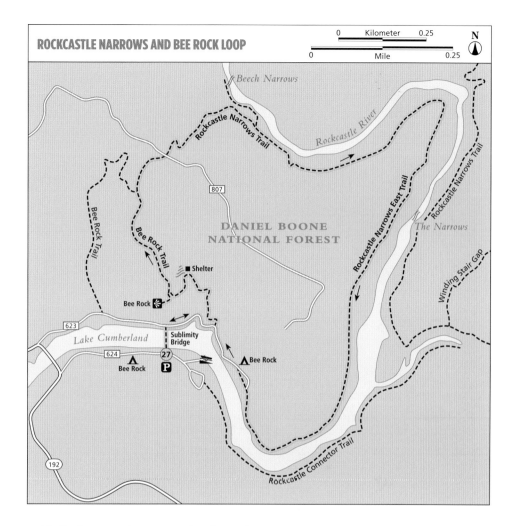

bluff of Bee Rock rises 300 feet from where you are, standing proud above the forest, capped by a lid of woods.

After crossing the river, you walk the campground then pick up the Bee Rock Trail, weaving upward through moss-backed boulders standing in repose amid thick woods. Since you are in a gorge, it isn't long before you are up against a cliff line.

Ascend a singletrack path, turning into a bouldery hollow. Work along a ragged cliff line then come to a big ol' rockhouse, incised deep into the cliff line. The trail travels into this dim, damp refuge, the front of which is partly blocked with boulders, technically a rockfall arch. Utah excepted, Kentucky has more natural arches than any other state. A 20-foot faucet fall splashes by the rockhouse.

You are now trekking along the base of the cliff line forming Bee Rock. Not for long, however, as the path leads to the top of Bee Rock via a break in the cliff line. The hike leads through scraggly pines before reaching Bee Rock. The view, fronted by a low stone wall, extends south directly down to Sublimity Bridge then southwest down the Rockcastle gorge, where seemingly tiny KY 192 bridge spans Lake Cumberland, bordered in

Sublimity Bridge stands in front of Bee Rock.

deep woods broken by tan cliff lines. As you may guess, Bee Rock once was home to a massive hive. Area beekeepers who had troubles with these wild bees mixing with their hives blasted part of the cliff, destroying the hive and letting loose a stream of honey that purportedly flowed 300 feet into the Rockcastle River below. To flow that far, it had to "bee" a whole lot of honey.

The Bee Rock Trail stays in upland woods, passing the left turn to complete the 2.4-mile Bee Rock loop, where a couple of waterfalls tumble in winter and spring before drying up in summer. Our hike joins the Rockcastle Narrows Trail, where you reach and cross remote Bee Rock Road (CR 807), then switchbacks downhill 350 feet to the Rockcastle River. This north-facing slope is rich with wildflowers during spring. The path can be hard to follow in places. Come within sight and sound of the Rockcastle River. A spur trail leads left (upstream) along the cobbled waterway to the Beech Narrows, a boulder-strewn rapid that gets whitewater boaters' pulse up.

Now you run parallel to the river through deep forests of tulip trees and evergreens rising from ferny woods. You will mimic a hairpin river bend then climb, passing vehicle barrier boulders. Look down on The Narrows, where the boulders may or may not be inundated, depending on the season. Sooner or later the river transitions to lake and you suddenly reach the far end of FR 623 and Bee Rock Campground. Now you can cruise the campground on the forest road, analyzing the sites and picking your favorite camp, plotting and planning a future camping trip.

Consider enhancing your hike with not only camping but also fishing, paddling, or boating. After all, visitors have been coming to Bee Rock for a natural respite since the early 1800s, when Sublimity Spring Resort Hotel was erected at this very spot. The resort was built as a place to escape the summertime illnesses that plagued the Deep South, such as malaria and yellow fever. The informative kiosk near the trailhead details the sales pitch of founder Christopher Columbus Graham: "an Eden for children, a sanitarium for invalids, a paradise for lovers, and a haven of rest for the tired." May you find Bee Rock as relaxing as they did back in the 1800s.

MILES AND DIRECTIONS

0.0   Start north on the Sublimity Bridge from the south side of Bee Rock Campground.

0.1   Turn right onto FR 623, the north side road of Bee Rock Campground. Keep east, hiking past campsites 1–4.

0.3   Split left from FR 623 and join the singletrack Bee Rock Trail, officially Trail #529.

0.4   Bridge a small tributary of the Rockcastle River.

0.6   Circle under a big rockhouse, fronted by broken boulders. A small stream creates a low-flow cataract. Ahead, climb a break in the cliff line.

0.8   Reach a trail intersection in low pines and mountain laurel. Here, stay left to find the official Bee Rock Overlook and gain excellent vistas of the Rockcastle Valley below, including the Sublimity Bridge. Hopefully, you can still see your vehicle parked down there. Backtrack to the last intersection and stay left (northbound).

1.2   Meet and join the Rockcastle Narrows Trail as the Bee Rock Loop heads left.

1.9   A signed spur trail leads 0.25 mile up the Rockcastle to the Beech Narrows, a boulder-strewn rapid.

2.1   Rock hop a brook with a backcountry campsite nearby. Keep hiking parallel to the river.

2.7   Turn sharply south, then climb.

3.2   Look down on The Narrows. Continue downstream, heading south.

4.2   The trail curves northwest with the waterway.

4.4   Reach the east end of the campground. Join the forest road, passing campsites.

4.9   Turn left at the Sublimity Bridge.

5.0   Arrive back at the trailhead.

28 VANHOOK FALLS LOOP

This loop hike not only takes you by two named waterfalls but also four unnamed lesser cascades set in the Rockcastle River valley within a remote, lesser-visited section of the Daniel Boone National Forest. The Rockcastle Narrows East Trail and the Sheltowee Trace first lead you to Vanhook Cascade, a 10-foot angled slide cascade. Next comes one of Daniel Boone National Forest's signature spillers—35-foot Vanhook Falls. The hike turns down Cane Creek then up the Rockcastle River, passing the legendary rapid known as The Narrows. Make the only sustained climb of the trek, passing a low-flow cataract before returning to the trailhead.

Start: FR 119 gate
Distance: 6.6-mile balloon loop
Difficulty: Moderate; does have significant elevation change
Elevation change: +/-1,697 feet
Maximum grade: 15% grade for 0.6 mile
Hiking time: About 3.3 hours
Seasons/schedule: Year-round
Fees and permits: No fees or permits required
Dog friendly: Yes

Trail surface: Natural
Land status: National forest
Nearest town: Corbin
Other trail users: None
Maps to consult: Daniel Boone National Forest, Rockcastle Narrows East #401
Amenities available: None
Cell service: Bad
Trail contacts: Daniel Boone National Forest, London Ranger District; (606) 864-4163; fs.usda.gov/dbnf

FINDING THE TRAILHEAD

From exit 38 on I-75 near London, head west on KY 192 for 5.7 miles and turn right onto paved Line Creek Road. Follow Line Creek Road for 2.7 miles then veer left onto gravel FR 56. After 1.8 miles, veer left onto FR 119 (away from New Hope Baptist Church). After 3.2 miles, stay left with FR 119 as FR 457 goes right and uphill. Continue for 2.1 more miles on FR 119, parking at the intersection of FR 119 and FR 1198. Park in the gravel to the right of the road, just after FR 1198 goes right. Trailhead GPS: 37.049606 / -84.291748

THE HIKE

Want to please a skeptical hiker who wants a truly rewarding hike? Take them on this circuit, complete with waterfalls, watercourses big and small, and a healthy dose of everywhere-you-look beauty. Set in a remote section of the Daniel Boone National Forest in the craggy and stunning Rockcastle River Valley, the circuit follows four distinct waterways, each adding aquatic grandeur to the trek.

As far as waterfalls are concerned, Vanhook Falls (often misspelled as Van Hook) is the star of the show. It makes a 35-foot dive from a rock rim into a stone-bordered cathedral of overhanging rock, lording over scads of rhododendron. Vanhook Cascade slides into a dark grotto and is often quickly passed by, since it is found 0.25 mile before Vanhook Falls. Stop and appreciate this cataract.

Vanhook Falls rains down in a curtain of white.

Also welcome the other less-heralded spillers on the way. The first unnamed fall you will encounter is a 5-foot ledge drop on Yuel Branch, just before this stream merges with Vanhook Branch. The next pour-over is on Vanhook Branch. It makes a distinctive horseshoe-shaped 7-foot drop into a stone-walled mini-gorge. The two named falls then come next. Beyond them, the trail goes directly by a low-flow fall making a 6-foot slide then dropping an additional 16 feet from a rim into a maw of darkness enveloped by rhododendron. The path cuts back across the creek at a small ledge. The final cataract is near hike's end, where a low-flow seasonal creek drops 30-plus feet from a cliff line, but it can run dry by autumn.

You will get plenty of waterfall action on this hike, especially in spring. And the hike segment along the Rockcastle River displays powerful, hard-edged beauty that cannot be denied. However, even if the falls and the Rockcastle River aren't rocking, the nonaquatic scenery will more than suffice. Additionally, it is a lesser-done hike, offering suitable opportunities for solitude. The trek starts out easy enough, following gated FR 119 south for 0.25 mile then joining the Rockcastle Narrows East Trail, a singletrack path heading into the valley of Yuel Branch. The woodland is lush here as you slowly drift deeper toward the water, crossing Yuel Branch twice before it gives up its waters to Vanhook Branch. This is also where you join the Sheltowee Trace and encounter your first bonus ledge drop.

The Sheltowee Trace and Vanhook Branch separate for a while, but when they come back together you will find the 7-foot horseshoe-shaped fall. Just a little downtrail come

A close-up view of Vanhook Falls

to 10-foot Vanhook Cascade, located where the Sheltowee Trace crosses Vanhook Branch. Here, just below where you cross Vanhook Branch, the brook bounces over layered strata then makes a final slide into a dark pool bordered by low but sheer rock walls. This stream crossing and falls are slippery, so exercise caution.

Vanhook Falls lies just a short piece down the Sheltowee Trace. Here discover a wooden observation deck with a bench and an excellent view of Vanhook Falls. However, you can walk closer to the falls and even behind the cascade as the stream collapses from the overhanging brow of stone. The whole scene is enrapturing and worth a lengthy stop.

Next the circuit leaves the Sheltowee Trace and heads down the Cane Creek valley, curving into evergreen hollows and onto ridges of pine well above Cane Creek. Ahead, pass a tributary fall that is difficult to access, but you will certainly hear it. This spiller slides to a straight drop, seemingly into a black hole.

Then you open onto the perceptibly wider valley of the Rockcastle River, though these lowermost regions of the river are often stilled as part of Lake Cumberland. When lake levels are down in fall and winter, however, the Rockcastle will flow free in this area. The trail winds among big boulders and thick woods in the almost junglesque valley, shortly reaching "The Nars," aka "The Narrows," a tapered part of the Rockcastle River caroming through a boulder garden that challenges whitewater boaters. While hiking this area you will understand why this part of the Rockcastle is a designated Kentucky Wild River.

The Rockcastle Narrows East Trail steeply climbs away from the river to pass the final waterfall of the loop—a low-flow dropper dripping from a cliff line, sometimes known as Stairway to Heaven Falls. Your 400-foot ascent ends upon picking up a grassy roadbed to soon reach closed FR 119. From there it is an easy, simple backtrack to the parking area.

MILES AND DIRECTIONS

0.0 Pass around the pole gate on FR 119, and start heading southbound on the doubletrack.

0.2 Come to a trail intersection. Head left onto the singletrack Rockcastle Narrows East Trail, leaving the forest road behind. Dip into thick woods.

0.9 Rock hop evergreen-shaded Yuel Branch. You are now on the left-hand bank, heading downstream.

1.1 Intersect the Sheltowee Trace. Head right here (southbound) on Kentucky's master path. Quickly cross Yuel Branch a second time. Note the 5-foot ledge waterfall just below this second crossing.

1.9 Listen for a 7-foot horseshoe-shaped waterfall on Vanhook Branch spilling into an eroded, rhododendron-cloaked stone fissure. The trail and creek are near each other at this point.

2.2 Reach a trail junction. You will return here later. Head left toward Vanhook Falls on the Sheltowee Trace. Descend to reach Vanhook Branch. Carefully cross the stream just above Vanhook Cascade, a 10-foot angled slide fall. Continue toward Vanhook Falls.

2.4 Circle above the rim of Vanhook Falls then turn onto a stairway and wooden deck at Vanhook Falls. The 35-foot pour-over makes its curtain free-fall into a rock hollow echo chamber, reverberating the spill. Backtrack to the last trail intersection.

2.6 Reach the trail intersection just after again crossing above Vanhook Cascade. Here, head west on the continuation of the Rockcastle Narrows East Trail, down the Cane Creek valley. Watch for a spur leading right (uphill) to the terminus of FR 119.

3.3 Walk near a low-flow falls sliding 6 feet then diving 16 additional feet off a rock rim. Listen for this falls, then work your way toward it.

4.2 Intersect the faint Winding Stair Gap Trail after coming along Cane Creek amid pines. The Rockcastle Connector Trail—with no bridge crossing Cane Creek—is across Cane Creek and leads you to Bee Rock Campground. Stay straight here, curving north along the Rockcastle River.

4.8 Reach the Rockcastle River Narrows. Continue upriver.

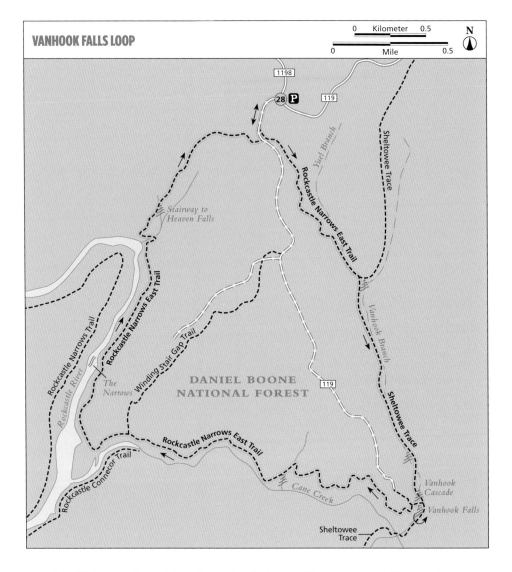

5.4 Work around a muddy hollow as the Rockcastle River curves west. Beware of user-created trails working around this messy area. After crossing the stream of the hollow, stay west along the Rockcastle River.

5.5 Turn right along the easily missed blazed path rising right, away from the water. Don't be deceived by a user-created trail continuing along the Rockcastle river bottom. Climb.

5.7 Come alongside a low-flow cataract, Stairway to Heaven Falls, spilling from a cliff line. Keep climbing via switchbacks.

6.1 Level off at a closed forest road, accessing a wildlife clearing. The walking is easy from here on out.

6.4 Turn left (northbound) onto FR 119.

6.6 Arrive back at the trailhead.

29 VIEWS FROM BEREA FOREST

Easily one of the better hikes in the Bluegrass State, this loop with several spurs leads you to numerous rock outcrops atop Indian Fort Mountain, delivering a series of gratifying views to please even the most jaded hiker. In addition to the panoramas, the hike is also enhanced with visits to other geological wonders, such as the Devils Kitchen rockhouse, regal bluffs, and slender stone passages, all preserved by Berea College.

Start: Main trailhead near forestry visitor center
Distance: 7.3-mile loop with spurs
Difficulty: Moderate-difficult
Elevation change: +/-2,102 feet
Maximum grade: 13% grade for 0.4 mile
Hiking time: About 4 hours
Seasons/schedule: Year-round; clear days for best views
Fees and permits: No fees or permits required
Dog friendly: Yes
Trail surface: Forest natural surface; some naked rock

Land status: College forest open to public
Nearest town: Berea
Other trail users: None
Maps to consult: Indian Fort Mountain Trails at the Pinnacles
Amenities available: Information, restrooms at Forestry Outreach Center
Cell service: Good
Trail contacts: Berea Forest; (859) 756-3315; forestryoutreach.berea.edu/trails/

FINDING THE TRAILHEAD

From exit 76 on I-75 south of Richmond, take KY 21 East through the town of Berea and Berea College for 4.5 miles to the large Berea Forest parking area, on your left. Trailhead GPS: 37.554377 / -84.240809

THE HIKE

Located in the town of the same name, Berea College is a highly rated liberal arts school that gives a tuition-free education to promising youths from Appalachia and beyond. In fact, inability to pay is a requirement for admission; students work instead. In addition to the pleasant campus, the college manages some 8,000 acres of fine Kentucky forestland, much of it donated in the early 1900s to provide the college with timber income and forestry demonstration sites. Included in these holdings is Indian Fort Mountain, a deservedly popular hiking area full of cliffs and overlooks. The area is open to the public, but camping is not allowed. This hike takes you to an impressive array of observation points.

Indian Fort Mountain is crisscrossed by many trails that are well cared for by Berea forestry staff. The trail network is such that if you want to shorten your hike and just

Fog hangs in the valley below East Pinnacle.

visit one or two overlooks, you can. I recommend the whole enchilada as you appreciate the import of Indian Lookout Mountain, one of Kentucky's singularly intriguing
peaks.

The trailhead's large parking area attests to the trail system's popularity. However, the
plurality of destinations spread hikers all over Indian Fort Mountain. The Indian Fort
Trail leaves the trailhead and connects you to the balance of pathways atop Indian Fort
Mountain. Your first marker is Indian Fort Theater, an amphitheater, on your right.

As you climb gradually, note that the forest is dominated by oak and hickory, with
some pines and yellow poplars. Much of this land was farmed at one time, and the hardwoods are tall but thin. After climbing to an intersection, you will start the main loop,
with East Pinnacle as destination number one. After climbing to a protruding ridgeline
cloaked in rock and pines, pass numerous well-worn side trails to lookouts on both sides.
Keep going to trail's end and the stone viewing platform that is East Pinnacle, affording
sweeping views to the east of the Red Lick Creek watershed below as well as Pilot Knob
and a host of mountains stretching as far east as the sky allows.

Your hike next climbs to the main ridge of Indian Fort Mountain, where the walking
is easy and mostly level. You will head out on spur trails to two more overlooks—Buzzards Roost Vista and Eagles Nest View. Eagles Nest features boulders from which you
can take in the views.

Eagles Nest View presents a spectacular overlook.

Your next major highlight is the Devils Kitchen. Here a spur runs atop a cliff line then curves under it to find intriguing rock formations and a rockhouse with a clearly form-ing arch and a hole atop (metal bars keep hikers from falling into the rock house) as the trail to Indian Fort Lookout runs just above the Devils Kitchen. Indian Fort Lookout,

Yet another overlook at Berea Forest

your next highlight, is a wide-open rock slab where you can take in views that sweep across the farmland below to Berea and Richmond beyond.

From here the trail follows the edge of the cliff line toward West Pinnacle. You soon come to another overlook, this one with fine views looking south. Here it's easy to get stumped, because the trail to West Pinnacle—your next destination—is hard to find. The only path immediately visible goes northeast, back toward Indian Fort Lookout, which you don't want. But if you closely examine the boulders on the west edge of the over-look, you will find a steep dirt path—almost a chute—cutting down through the rocks on the west side of the cliff. Take this route downhill. You will need both hands, but it's not dangerous.

Your next highlight is the mushroom-shaped tower of rock called West Pinnacle. There is a way to get on top, although at first you may not think so. Midway up the west side of the huge rock, there's a ledge. Put your feet on the ledge and, holding the top of the rock with your hands, inch your way to the middle of the west side. There you will find a large hole running down the rock that looks as if it were made by a giant corkscrew. Bracing your body against the inside of the hole, you can push yourself up and come out on the flat top of West Pinnacle. You will feel like a true climber. Children should not try it on their own, however; a fall could cause serious injury. The view is worth the small rock scramble, and the top of the rock is wide and flat. This is an excellent vantage point that on a clear day affords views of Lexington, 36 miles to the northwest. After this final highlight, it is a simple woods walk back to the trailhead.

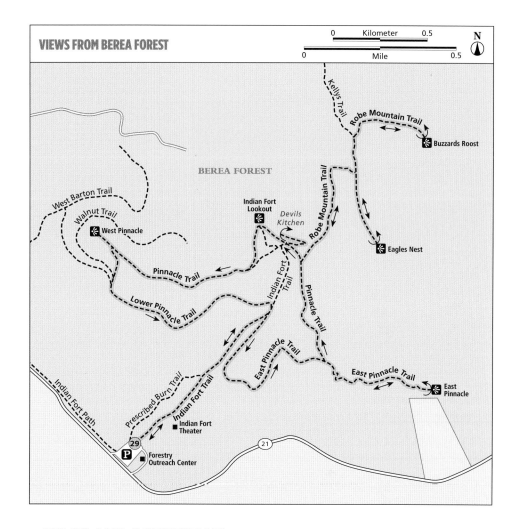

VIEWS FROM BEREA FOREST

MILES AND DIRECTIONS

0.0 Start north from the parking area on the asphalt Indian Fort Trail under a stately oak hall.

0.2 Come to the Indian Fort Theater, an outdoor amphitheater. Keep straight, now on natural surface path, climbing.

0.3 The Prescribed Burn Trail leaves left. It offers interpretive information about fire in forests. Continue climbing in thick woods.

0.6 Reach a major signed intersection and the loop portion of your hike. Head right on the East Pinnacle Trail, contouring on the side slope of a mountain. Watch for old closed trails. Pass through oak-dominated woods broken by rocks.

1.3 Come to an intersection in young woods. Stay right toward East Pinnacle, trekking a ridgeline of rock from which pines rise.

1.7 Come to East Pinnacle and a first-rate panorama from a rock perch with plenty of posing and relaxing spots. Backtrack.

2.1 Continue west on the Pinnacle Trail, climbing in oak/cedar/dogwood woods, shortly leveling out on the main ridge of Indian Fort Mountain.

2.6 Come to another intersection. Head right on the Robe Mountain Trail toward Buzzards Roost.

2.9 The Eagles Nest Trail splits right; stay left for the moment and soon reach another intersection. Here, Kellys Trail splits left toward Robe Mountain; we stay right here, descending.

3.3 Come to Buzzards Roost Vista, where an outcrop pocked with pines offers some views. Backtrack, passing Kellys Trail again.

3.8 Take the spur to Eagles Nest View, heading south, dropping to a spectacular overlook down Baker Hollow across to Owsley Fork Reservoir, as well as forested mountains and fields. Backtrack to Robe Mountain Trail, then head left, south, still backtracking.

4.7 Split right toward Indian Fort Lookout, entering an area with a potentially confusing nest of trails. Ahead, you'll come to a cliff line and intersection. Split right and walk east along the top of a cliff line, shortly descending below the cliff line toward the Devils Kitchen.

4.9 Reach the rockhouse of the Devils Kitchen. Note the hole in the rockhouse overhead and the clear beginnings of an arch. Backtrack.

5.1 Return to where you were before, now heading west along the cliff line. Note the hole down into the Devils Kitchen. Watch out for user-created trails in this area.

5.2 Open onto the stone terrace of Indian Fort Lookout. Stunning panoramas open to the west. After soaking in the vista, leave south atop the clifftop of the mountain.

5.3 Come to an intersection and a fine stone overlook of forested hills. Here, head right (west) down into a rocky crevice with steep enough sections to require the use of hands and feet. Drop to a gap and climb over a knob, still heading westerly.

5.8 Reach another intersection after passing a limited view and descending past strange layered rock and small rock knobs. Keep west toward West Pinnacle, climbing among rocks and trees.

5.9 Reach West Pinnacle. The best view from here requires a little scrambling then pushing through a hole to reach the top. Descend back to the last intersection, then follow the Lower Pinnacle Trail past the Walnut Trail and the West Barton Trail. Cruise easterly in tall woods along a mountain slope. The walking is easy.

6.7 Complete the loop portion of the hike. Here, head right on the Indian Fort Trail, backtracking toward the parking area.

7.3 Arrive back at the parking area.

Enjoy this fine hike at a desirable yet unsung recreation area in Daniel Boone National Forest. The hike first follows War Fork downstream then turns up a hollow to traverse wooded slopes before dropping to Hughes Fork, another of the many area streams. Complete the loop by passing a handsome seasonal waterfall. After your return, consider swimming, fishing, or camping at this pretty parcel of the Bluegrass State.

Start: Turkey Foot Recreation Area
Distance: 4.1-mile loop
Difficulty: Moderate
Elevation change: +/-756 feet
Maximum grade: 10% downhill grade for 0.5 mile
Hiking time: About 1.9 hours
Seasons/schedule: Spring best for water flow and wildflowers
Fees and permits: No fees or permits required
Dog friendly: Yes

Trail surface: Natural
Land status: National forest
Nearest town: McKee
Other trail users: None
Maps to consult: DBNF—Turkey Foot Trail #303
Amenities available: Campground, swimming/picnicking area
Cell service: Limited
Trail contacts: Daniel Boone National Forest, London Ranger District; (606) 864-4163; fs.usda.gov/dbnf

FINDING THE TRAILHEAD

From exit 76 on I-75 near Berea, drive east on US 421 for 18 miles to McKee. Once in McKee, turn left on KY 89 North, passing through the town square. Stay with KY 89 North for 3 miles to a sharp, signed right turn onto paved FR 17 (Macedonia Road). Follow Macedonia Road for 0.5 mile, turning left onto a paved road that becomes FR 4 (Turkey Foot Road) after 1 mile. Continue forward on gravel FR 4 for 2 more miles to FR 345. Turn right onto FR 345 and follow it 0.2 mile to the right turn into Turkey Foot Campground, crossing a low-water bridge. Stay left on the recreation area road toward the picnic area (the other way goes through Turkey Foot Campground) and park at the far end of the picnic area, near a small field. Trailhead GPS: 37.470648 / -83.914688

THE HIKE

When rambling through Eastern Kentucky, I often make my way to Turkey Foot Recreation Area, situated in lovely Jackson County. Formerly the location of a Girl Scout camp, this Daniel Boone National Forest parcel offers not only a fine loop hike but also a shady, picturesque picnic area, a fishing hole, and a primitive but desirable campground at which I have overnighted in all seasons. The camp is cut into a hill rising from the valley stream known as War Fork. Each campsite offers a fire ring, picnic table, lantern post, and tent pad. Vault toilets complete the picture. Bring your own drinking water. There is no charge to overnight at this open-year-round campground.

Located where Elsam Fork, War Fork, and Hughes Fork converge (the meeting of the stream valleys creates a "turkey foot," giving the locale its name), Turkey Foot Recreation

Turkey Foot Cascade

Area also offers fishing for stocked trout in late winter and spring, while bass and bream inhabit the waters year-round. Even if you don't fish, bring a pre- or post-hike meal to savor beside the translucent aquamarine waters at the recreation area.

For us hikers, the actual trail trek is what gets our mojo on. Savor the Turkey Foot Loop as it travels along War Fork then through an area of sinks, rich with spring wildflowers. These sinkholes are part of the greater above- and belowground hydrology in

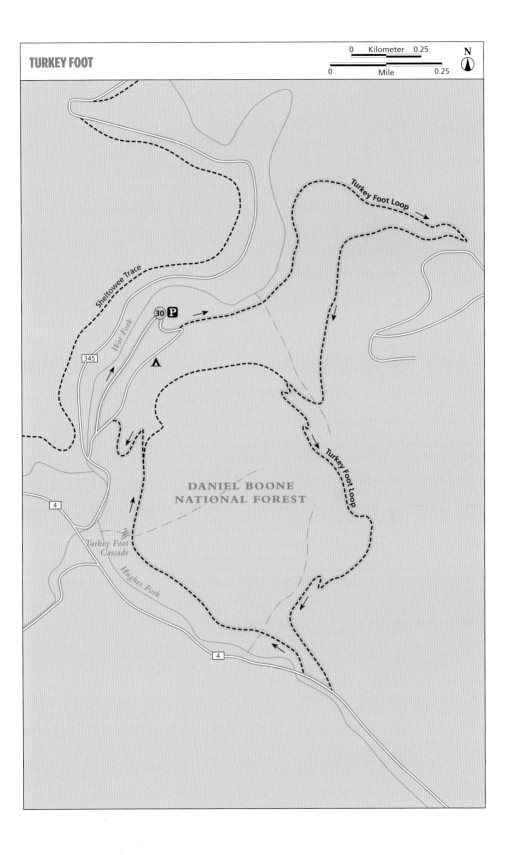

TURKEY FOOT

N

0   Kilometer   0.25

0   Mile   0.25

Turkey Foot Loop

Sheltowee Trace

War Fork

30 P

345

DANIEL BOONE
NATIONAL FOREST

Turkey Foot Loop

4

Turkey Foot
Cascade

Hughes Fork

4

the War Fork Valley, a place where the main stream runs underground in places, springs emerge from cliffs, and sinks like this drain the woodlands.

The hike rises to the national forest boundary and turns south. Ahead, you reach a trail intersection, enabling hikers to opt for a 2.0-mile loop instead of the 4.1-mile trek. The longer loop then surmounts a hill on the sharpest climb of the hike (which doesn't last long) then dips into the Hughes Fork watershed.

After briefly walking FR 4, the trail reenters woods then rejoins the old logging grade. Look for remains of old rail ties, evenly spaced along the trail bed. You briefly split from the grade to visit Turkey Foot Cascade, a 12-foot two-stage cataract. Its flow ranges wildly, but it's best midwinter through mid-spring. Ahead you will reach the loop short-cut. From here the main circuit descends to the recreation area campground. Inspect a site or two. Beyond the campground it's a simple walk through the picnic area back to the trailhead.

MILES AND DIRECTIONS

0.0 Start from the trailhead parking near the small field at the picnic area's north end. Follow the recreation area loop road right and uphill, going counterclockwise on the loop road. Avoid the trailhead field and any trails emanating from it. Ascend 300 feet along the loop road then split left onto signed singletrack Turkey Foot Loop, in a hemlock copse. Head northeast along a bluff above War Fork as seeping springs trickle toward War Fork.

0.5 Enter a sinkhole garden. Watch just ahead for the trail turning right (eastbound), heading up a wildflower-filled hollow to surmount a low cliff line.

1.0 Come close to the national forest boundary. Avoid the private road leading to a small farm. Stay with the Turkey Foot Loop as it cuts acutely right, picking up an old doubletrack in woods. The path levels out. Curve around a ridge presenting partial views across War Fork.

1.2 Meet an obvious cut in the slope, location of a long-ago logging rail line. The forest has since regrown wonderfully. Straight-trunked tulip trees rise from the forest floor.

1.7 Come to a signed trail junction. If you want to shortcut the hike, stay straight. Our longer loop cuts sharply left, climbing as a singletrack path.

2.2 Reach the hike's high point, then dip south into the Hughes Fork watershed for a 0.5-mile unabated descent.

2.7 Pop out onto FR 4. Turn right on the gravel forest road, bridging Hughes Fork then splitting right, back into the forest. Join the old railroad grade.

3.3 Split left from the railroad grade. Ahead, walk directly above Turkey Foot Cascade.

3.5 Reach the other end of the loop shortcut after rejoining the railroad grade. Stay left at the intersection, then begin switchbacking downhill.

3.8 Come to Turkey Foot Campground near campsite 1. Split left then join the main road right through the picnic area.

4.1 Arrive back at the parking area beside the small field.

31 PILOT KNOB STATE NATURE PRESERVE

This gratifying hike leads you to a fantastic panorama atop Pilot Knob, where you can soak in vistas of mountains to the east and Bluegrass to the west. Set in a state nature preserve, the trek leads through rich forest on a well-graded track rising to bluffs that you first circle around then rise atop. The view, known as Boone's Overlook, is thought to be the spot where ol' Dan'l first laid eyes on the Bluegrass. The ramble is well worth it in any season, as long as the skies are clear.

Start: Brush Creek Road trailhead
Distance: 2.4 miles out and back
Difficulty: Easy-moderate
Elevation change: +/-661 feet
Maximum grade: 12% grade for 1.0 mile
Hiking time: About 1.2 hours
Seasons/schedule: Year-round
Fees and permits: No fees or permits required
Dog friendly: Dogs not allowed

Trail surface: Natural surface foot trail
Land status: State nature preserve
Nearest town: Stanton
Other trail users: None
Maps to consult: Pilot Knob State Nature Preserve
Amenities available: None
Cell service: Good
Trail contacts: Office of Kentucky Nature Preserves; (502) 573-2886; eec.ky.gov/Nature-Preserves

FINDING THE TRAILHEAD

From exit 16 off the Bert T. Combs Mountain Parkway near Clay City, take KY 15 North. In 3 miles turn right onto Brush Creek Road. Brush Creek Road immediately crosses over the parkway; in 1.5 miles the pavement ends. Park in the gravel area on your right. **Note:** This parking lot is also a turnaround for school buses, so be sure to allow sufficient turnaround space if visiting during the school week. Trailhead GPS: 37.912086 / -83.945069

THE HIKE

Pilot Knob affords visitors a vista made famous in history books as the point where famed Kentucky explorer Daniel Boone is said to have gotten his first view, in 1769, of the rolling, fertile hills of Kentucky's Bluegrass region from the aptly named "Boone's Overlook," on the southeastern end of a tall sandstone outcropping. While there is no definitive evidence that Boone did in fact stand at that exact spot on the most obvious promontory along the line of knobs marking the western entrance to the more rugged hills of eastern Kentucky, historians believe it is highly likely.

What is certain is that this 1,350-foot-elevation lookout provides a good lesson in Kentucky geography. To the east and south rise the forested ridges and high country of the Cumberland Plateau. To the west and north begins the relatively flat farmland of central Kentucky, the Bluegrass.

Daniel Boone purportedly spied the Bluegrass from Pilot Knob.

Even though the nature preserve has been expanded to a total of 1,257 acres from its original 385 acres when opened in 1985, the trail system has been reconfigured—and downsized—to leave intact more of this special swath of the Bluegrass State. The top of Pilot Knob is only 1.2 miles from the parking area, but you can add the Millstone Quarry Loop for an additional 1.0 mile of trail trekking. The quarry was in operation in the early 1800s, quarrying stones used in grinding corn and other agricultural products.

So what exactly is a Kentucky state nature preserve? According to the Energy & Environment Cabinet of Kentucky—an umbrella of several land-and water-related

The view from Pilot Knob

government arms—a state nature preserve "is a legally dedicated area that has been recognized for its natural significance and protected by law for scientific and educational purposes. Dedicated state nature preserves are established solely to protect and preserve rare species, the natural environment, or exceptional natural scenery or environmental education opportunities." Kentucky currently has sixty-three state nature preserves, as well as a host of other protected parcels in the form of state natural areas, heritage lands, and wild river corridors. State nature preserves effect the highest form of preservation among these protected parcels.

Pilot Knob State Nature Preserve encompasses several forest types, from oak–maple woodlands down low to the stunted Virginia pines atop Pilot Knob. The headwaters of Brush Creek, which you will cross at the hike's beginning, are located in the preserve and add a riparian element to the ecosystem here.

You use the Oscar Geralds Jr. Trail to reach Pilot Knob. The path has been rerouted to make it less erosive and more maintainable. It first crosses Brush Creek—without benefit of bridge, which could mean a wet ford in spring—then methodically works its way along a ridgeline toward Pilot Knob. The path then skirts the south side of the upthrust, passing a tiny spring before finally attaining the crest of the knob then working over the high point to make a short descent to an outcrop, where a royal vista spreads before you—a spot where you can stand and gaze admiringly from the same spot Daniel Boone did when he first beheld the Bluegrass and the mountains whence he came. On your return trip, consider taking the Millstone Quarry Loop to enhance your hike.

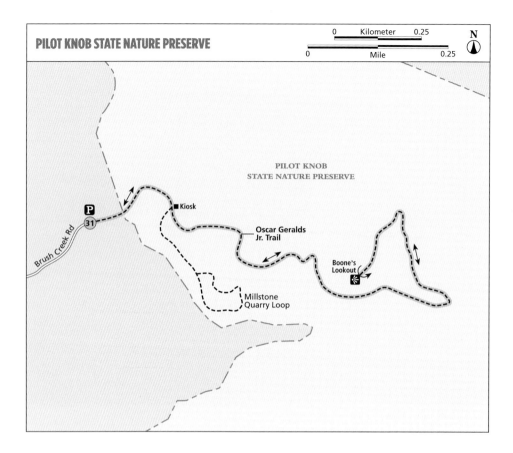

MILES AND DIRECTIONS

0.0 Start from the gravel parking area/bus turnaround on a wide doubletrack, quickly coming to Brush Creek. Walk upstream along the creek. Come to a crossing point, which may be a ford during wet times, then cross the creek, squeezing past an ATV buffer.

0.2 Reach a trail intersection and informative kiosk. Here, the Millstone Quarry Loop leads right; we stay straight on the Oscar Geralds Jr. Trail, aiming for Pilot Knob. Climb in white oaks, beech, and maples.

0.5 Briefly level off, then begin working around the south side of Pilot Knob, now among sassafras, hickory, and redbud. You are traveling directly below the lookout.

0.7 Cross a small spring branch on a boardwalk as the water dribbles over slickrock.

0.8 Make the crest of the knob, then cut northwesterly.

1.0 Turn south and roll over the wooded crest of Pilot Knob.

1.2 Reach Boone's Lookout and a vivid panorama of the melding of Kentucky's mountains and Bluegrass country as far as the eye can see. The outcrop offers multiple vantages. Retrace your steps.

2.4 Arrive back at the trailhead.

32 NATURAL BRIDGE HIGHLIGHT HIKE

Natural Bridge State Park is full of special attributes clustered in one preserve, and this hike visits lots of them, the main highlight being massive Natural Bridge. Along the way you will see Balanced Rock then the Natural Bridge, admiring it from above and below, walking atop the arch then making your way through Fat Man's Squeeze. The Needle's Eye Stairway then leads you to a fine view from Lover's Leap. Next, gain a vista into the Middle Fork Red River Valley from another outcrop. Pass the arch skylift access then cut under Natural Bridge a final time, dropping back to the trailhead on the Original Trail.

Start: Near swinging bridge and gift shop

Distance: 3.0-mile figure eight loop with spur

Difficulty: Moderate; does have significant elevation change

Elevation change: +/-1,404 feet

Maximum grade: 20% grade for first 0.6 mile

Hiking time: About 1.8 hours

Seasons/schedule: Year-round; could be rough in snow

Fees and permits: No fees or permits required

Dog friendly: Dogs not allowed on state park trails

Trail surface: Natural surface, lots of open stone

Land status: State park

Nearest town: Slade

Other trail users: None

Maps to consult: Natural Bridge State Park

Amenities available: Picnic area, shelter, restrooms near parking area

Cell service: Good

Trail contacts: Natural Bridge State Resort Park; (606) 663-2214; parks.ky.gov/slade/parks/resort/natural-bridge-state-resort-park

FINDING THE TRAILHEAD

From exit 33 on the Mountain Parkway near Slade, head south on KY 11 for 2.5 miles. Turn right onto the road indicating "Activities Center and Trails." Cross Middle Fork Kentucky River then take an immediate right into a teardrop-shaped parking area. The hike starts near the swinging bridge over the river. Trailhead GPS: 37.775455 / -83.677623

THE HIKE

You will earn your rewards on this highlight-laden hike, as it involves 1,400 feet of climbing and descending by the time you have made your tour de force of Natural Bridge State Park. Be forewarned: The trails can be busy, especially around Natural Bridge, where visitors are brought up by skylift. Solitude seekers will want to make their treks during weekdays and colder times if possible.

Some visitors take the skylift to the top of Natural Bridge.

You will start on the Original Trail, built in the 1890s by the Lexington and Eastern Railroad for passengers to tour the famed Natural Bridge. Other trails at the state park are also historical, many constructed by the Civilian Conservation Corps back in the 1930s. After a short stint on the Original Trail (you will come back to it later), the hike climbs on the Balanced Rock Trail, noted for its 600 stone stairs. You'll get a good workout—passing Rockhouse Cave along a cliff line—en route to Balanced Rock, an upturned stone edifice that is actually a single rock appearing to be two. The pillar's inverted middle will eventually give way and break into two stones, losing its balance.

Resume your climb, rising to a piney ridge affording scattered southerly vistas before Kentucky's long-distance master path, the Sheltowee Trace, splits left. Our hike goes right toward the Natural Bridge, passing the wooden gazebo built nearly a century ago. Then you walk out onto the Natural Bridge—a classic curved natural arch on bottom with a flat top. Its symmetry is what makes Natural Bridge so appealing. It looks like what people imagine an arch to be. And the arch's size never fails to impress: 78 feet long, 65 feet high, and 20 feet wide—big enough for lots of people to cross with ease.

After exploring the arch, a stairwell leads to the base of the span and Fat Man's Squeeze, an intriguing slender passage between massive boulders that becomes a human traffic jam—only one hiker can pass through at a time, while hikers are going both ways. After getting through Fat Man's Squeeze, you then pick up the Battleship Rock Trail. As its

Standing beneath the Natural Bridge

name implies, you will be traveling along the base of a massive bluff with rising walls of stone, imposing cliffs, and rock houses.

The geological features continue when you pick up the Needle's Eye Stairway, a series of carved stone steps built in 1934 by the CCC, working your way to the top of the cliff line above. Places like this are what make hiking in Kentucky so memorable. (You'll remember the steepness of the Needle's Eye Stairway.) You will further recall the view from Lover's Leap as it opens to the Red River Gorge beyond and the stone pillar just in front of you. After backtracking on the Laurel Ridge Trail, you can enjoy yet another vista. The view from this open sandstone rock along Laurel Ridge Trail delivers an additional perspective of the Natural Bridge. Hikers will be visible on the deck of the arch. Gaze down at the park lake, Hemlock Lodge, and Hoedown Island.

You are still heading for an encore trip to Natural Bridge when you pass the park skylift. The cleared woods allow views of Middle Fork Kentucky River and the land beyond, as well as the chairs bringing other visitors to the top of the arch. After cruising atop the wide bridge, the hike works under the arch a final time then picks up the Original Trail, winding along a small brook that ends in a cave. Pass rain shelters before returning to the trailhead. Consider enjoying other park offerings, from overnighting in the lodge, a cabin, or the campground; to hiking other trails; to paddling or fishing the park lake.

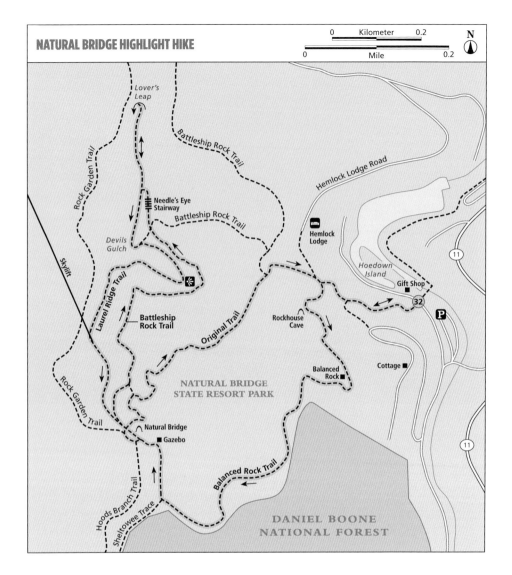

0   Kilometer   0.2

0   Mile   0.2

N

Lover's Leap

Battleship Rock Trail

Rock Garden Trail

Hemlock Lodge Road

Needle's Eye Stairway

Battleship Rock Trail

Devils Gulch

Hemlock Lodge

Skylift

Laurel Ridge Trail

Hoedown Island

Gift Shop

Battleship Rock Trail

Original Trail

Rockhouse Cave

32

P

Rock Garden Trail

NATURAL BRIDGE STATE RESORT PARK

Balanced Rock

Cottage

11

Natural Bridge

Gazebo

Balanced Rock Trail

Hoods Branch Trail

Sheltowee Trace

DANIEL BOONE NATIONAL FOREST

11

MILES AND DIRECTIONS

0.0   Start on the Original Trail, heading uphill from the park activities center trailhead, next to the gift shop and swinging bridge.

0.2   Pass a spur to the park cabins then reach a major trail intersection, signboard, and benches. Ahead is your return route, the Original Trail. Head left here on the Balanced Rock Trail.

0.4   Come to Balanced Rock after passing barred Rockhouse Cave.

0.6   Reach a level resting rock, likely winded from the 400-foot climb thus far. Continue westerly along the ridgeline.

0.8   Reach an intersection. The long-distance Sheltowee Trace and the Sand Gap Trail split left. We stay right, dropping to a saddle then climbing over open rock.

0.9 Walk onto the deck of Natural Bridge. Enjoy the views then backtrack to take the stairway to the arch base, working through Fat Man's Squeeze, a narrow passageway between the Natural Bridge and an adjacent boulder. Once under the bridge, join the Battleship Rock Trail, passing a short connector to the Original Trail.

1.4 Reach a trail intersection. The Battleship Rock Trail splits right; we stay straight, ascending the Needle's Eye Stairway.

1.5 Turn right onto the level, pine-bordered Laurel Ridge Trail, aiming for Lover's Leap.

1.6 Come to Lover's Leap and savor the vista to the north, then backtrack, staying on the Laurel Ridge Trail past the Needle's Eye Stairway and the Devil's Gulch Trail.

1.9 Come to a fine view on the Laurel Ridge Trail from an expansive stone slab. Find Natural Bridge from the overlook. Continue toward Natural Bridge.

2.1 The park skylift enters on your right. Enjoy the view northwest. The trail can become crowded from here to the Natural Bridge, but the path is level.

2.2 Open onto the Natural Bridge. Look back where you were 0.6 mile back. That sandstone outcrop is clearly visible. Cross the Natural Bridge then take the stairway to the base of the arch, making your way through Fat Man's Squeeze a second time then joining the Original Trail. Begin a prolonged descent, passing a spur to the Battleship Rock Trail as well as shelters built by the CCC.

2.7 A spur goes left to the Battleship Rock Trail. Stay right with the Original Trail, still descending.

2.8 Reach a four-way intersection. You have been here before. Here a spur goes left to Hemlock Lodge and the Balanced Rock Trail heads right. We stay straight on the Original Trail.

3.0 Arrive back at the trailhead.

33 COURTHOUSE ROCK AND DOUBLE ARCH

One of the finest hikes in the Red River Gorge, this circuit shows off three major highlights—Courthouse Rock, Double Arch, and Haystack Rock—as well as lesser places where you can gain additional open vistas. Start on the Auxier Ridge Trail as it travels atop an open sandstone ridge replete with views. From there, dip to deeply wooded Auxier Branch, working your way to the base of a cliff line. Trace thick woods then find Double Arch—a two-layered span with a 300-degree view atop the arch. Complete the circuit after another panorama, tracing a gated forest road open only to forest personnel.

Start: Auxier Ridge parking area
Distance: 6.1-mile loop with spur
Difficulty: Moderate-difficult
Elevation change: +/-1,320 feet
Maximum grade: 13% downhill grade for 0.7 mile
Hiking time: About 3.8 hours
Seasons/schedule: Year-round; summer can be hot
Fees and permits: Permit required if camping in the Red River Gorge between 10 p.m. and 6 a.m.
Dog friendly: Yes

Trail surface: Natural, open road, gravel/dirt roadbed
Land status: National forest
Nearest town: Slade
Other trail users: None
Maps to consult: USFS Red River Gorge Brochure, Auxier Area Trails
Amenities available: Vault toilets
Cell service: Better on ridges
Trail contacts: Daniel Boone National Forest, Cumberland Ranger District; (606) 776-5456; fs.usda.gov/dbnf

FINDING THE TRAILHEAD

From exit 33 on the Mountain Parkway near Slade, take KY 15 South for 3.3 miles. Turn left on Tunnel Ridge Road and continue 3.7 miles to dead-end at the Auxier trailhead. Trailhead GPS: 37.820091 / -83.681078

THE HIKE

This fine hike will take you by the best trail-accessible highlights of the Auxier Ridge area. Here, proud sandstone ridges rise from rich forest offering views, arches, rockhouses, and other scintillating geological topographies. Have the batteries charged on your phone to record the experience. The Auxier area trails can be very busy, so consider starting your hike early in the morning or during other less-popular periods. Departing from the Auxier trailhead, you will head north on the outcrop-rich Auxier Ridge Trail, allowing looks into beyond. Yet other parts are richly forested, adding contrast to the sandstone. You will be able to identify the major landmarks—Courthouse Rock, Double Arch, and Haystack Rock—in relation to one another as you progress the circuit, since

Courthouse Rock

each highlight offers a vista into the outlands of the Red River Gorge and, at places, from one overlook to another.

The hike first works north along Auxier Ridge in black gum, sourwood, and pines, contrasting with the whitish-tan of the open sandstone spots over which you hike. In places, steps have been chiseled into naked rock. You won't be able to miss a trailside geological wonder in the form of a mushroom-shaped rock directly on the track. It is sights like this that account for the official name of this parcel of national forest: Red River Gorge Geological Area. The Red River Gorge is truly a diamond in the crown of Bluegrass State natural features.

Keep north, with the vales of Auxier Branch and Fish Trap Branch falling away from both sides of Auxier Ridge. The open sandstone along the path and limited tree cover afford vistas aplenty—and little shade. What pines and hardwoods do grow here are subject to periodic, low-intensity forest fires. Look for blackened trunks. You'll pass the Courthouse Rock Trail wandering the western edge of Auxier Ridge. It offers the opportunity for a shorter 5.1-mile balloon loop hike.

Undulate on the crest, passing through some sections of wider, more forested ridgeline before reaching the Haystack Rock vista point. Just below the wide overlook, Haystack Rock rises from the woods. Scan across Auxier Branch to the visible span of Double Arch, where you will be before long. Look for the lowest valley that marks the course of the Red River, 400 feet lower than where you stand.

Looking on Double Arch

More rambling leads to the view of Courthouse Rock. You might see rock climbers tackling the monolith. If you don't know what you are doing, Courthouse Rock is a great place to get hurt. Appreciate Courthouse Rock from afar, then join incredible steps and stairs leading downhill from the stone ridgeline. Standard footpath takes you onward past the other end of the Courthouse Rock Trail down to thickly wooded, clear, and cool Auxier Branch, dark and dim in summer after the open sandstone above. Briefly trace this tributary of the Red River before climbing west from its valley, meeting the

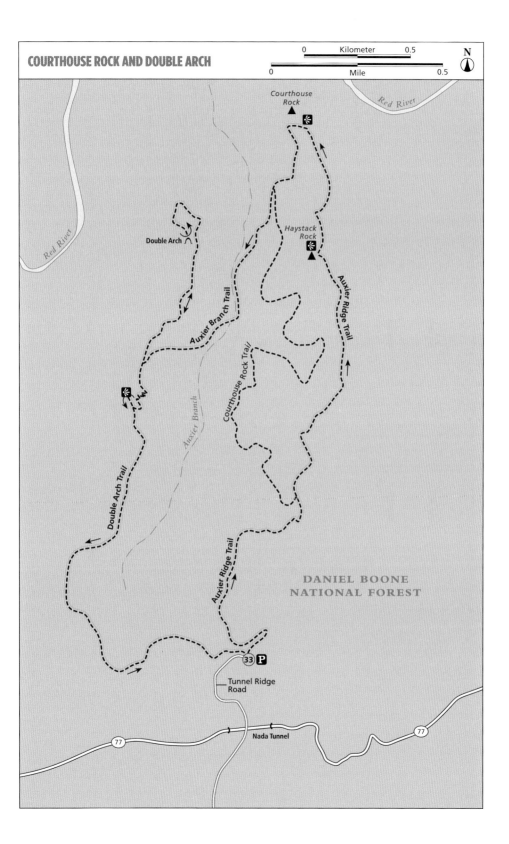

COURTHOUSE ROCK AND DOUBLE ARCH

Kilometer
0   0.5

Mile
0   0.5

N

Courthouse
Rock

Red River

Red River

Haystack
Rock

Double Arch

Auxier Branch Trail

Auxier Ridge Trail

Courthouse Rock Trail

Auxier Branch

Double Arch Trail

DANIEL BOONE
NATIONAL FOREST

Auxier Ridge Trail

33 P

Tunnel Ridge
Road

77   Nada Tunnel   77

Double Arch Trail in cool woods of tulip tree, hemlock, and magnolia, mounting above mosses and ferns. Next you'll pass a small stream then circle around the north side of Double Arch.

And then you reach Double Arch, one of my favorite places in the Red River Gorge. The span forms a 10-foot-high clearance and stretches about 20 feet wide. Above it you can see a parallel arch with a long, slender, almost envelope-like opening. The rockhouse formed by the arch is wide open on both sides, making it easy to identify from elsewhere in the gorge. Now trace the carved steps to the top of the sandstone pillar. Views extend in three directions. Courthouse Rock is visible among other stone icons, as well as the Red River Valley below. Wow!

After carefully descending, backtrack to the Auxier Branch Trail, then keep south on the Double Arch Trail. Climb to the ridgetop and reach a gated road, open only to forest personnel, that you join for the rest of the hike. Here a view down Rocky Branch to the Red River awaits. From here on, the walking is easy and level more than not. Depending on how tired you are, you may be tempted to explore user-created side trails spurring off the official road/trail. After circling around the headwaters of Auxier Branch, you are back at the trailhead, a fine hike completed.

MILES AND DIRECTIONS

0.0   Start on the Auxier Ridge Trail heading north then northeast, skirting an upthrust rock formation.

0.1   The path curves southwest nearly back to the trailhead before joining the ridgeline of Auxier Ridge, rising narrow in places.

0.5   Rise on carved sandstone steps.

0.9   The south end of the Courthouse Rock Trail leaves left. Stay straight with the Auxier Ridge Trail, savoring more distant looks from sandstone outcrops.

1.7   Reach the regal views from the open sandstone expanse looking directly on Haystack Rock in the near and points west in the distance.

2.1   Reach a view and the end of Auxier Ridge. Gaze north from the outcrop onto sheer Courthouse Rock. Descend elaborate steps and stairs toward Auxier Branch. Watch for user-created trails below the stairs.

2.4   Meet the other end of the Courthouse Rock Trail. Stay right with the Auxier Branch Trail, continuing an extended descent, crossing the branch then climbing back out.

3.1   Meet the Double Arch Trail near the base of a cliff line.

3.8   Come to Double Arch after circling a knob. Find the layered spans then climb atop the arch for a fine view. Backtrack to the Auxier Branch Trail.

4.5   Pass the intersection with the Auxier Branch Trail. Pick up a new trail. Shortly rise on the Double Arch Trail using switchbacks.

4.7   Gain the crest of the sandstone ridge and come to a gated road. Head to the westerly view to your right, then resume south on the Double Arch Trail, tracing the gated road.

6.0   Leave the doubletrack as Double Arch Trail becomes singletrack. Continue eastbound.

6.1   Arrive back at the trailhead.

34 **D BOON HUT AND GRAYS ARCH**

This vertically challenging trek begins with a twist on a popular Red River Gorge day hike. Start at worthy Grays Arch Picnic Area, then wind your way to a huge historic rockhouse known as D Boon Hut (the famed son of Kentucky may or may not have visited there), then loop past a pair of bluff overlooks. Next join the main route to Grays Arch, a photogenic curved span that draws the crowds. From there, loop along Rush Ridge's everywhere-you-look beauty, finding another pair of vistas before returning to the trailhead.

Start: Grays Arch Picnic Area
Distance: 4.6-mile loop
Difficulty: Moderate; does have significant elevation change
Elevation change: +/-1,641 feet
Maximum grade: 13% grade for 0.6 mile
Hiking time: About 2.5 hours
Seasons/schedule: Year-round
Fees and permits: Permit required if camping in the Red River Gorge between 10 p.m. and 6 a.m.
Dog friendly: Yes

Trail surface: Natural surface
Land status: National forest
Nearest town: Slade
Other trail users: None
Maps to consult: USFS Red River Gorge Brochure, Grays Arch Trail #205
Amenities available: Picnic area, restrooms at trailhead
Cell service: Good
Trail contacts: Daniel Boone National Forest, Cumberland Ranger District; (606) 776-5456; fs.usda.gov/dbnf

FINDING THE TRAILHEAD

From exit 33 on the Mountain Parkway near Slade, take KY 15 South for 3.3 miles. Turn left on Tunnel Ridge Road and continue for 0.9 mile to Grays Arch Picnic Area and the trailhead. Trailhead GPS: 37.807449 / -83.658037

THE HIKE

A hike with this many highlights is bound to be popular. Shoot for off times if you can to avoid the crowds. The addition of the trip to D Boon Hut lessens the crowds but adds climbs and descents to the adventure. And the hike wastes no time with this vertical variation, dropping into the hollow created by Martins Fork, past sandstone cliff lines so often found in this part of the Bluegrass State. The forest rises rich and lush along Martins Fork, with magnolia trees rising from thickets of rhododendron.

Then you meet a long cliff line, making your way to famed D Boon Hut. This rock shelter, now preserved with a metal fence, was mined for potassium nitrate, often called saltpeter. The element is essential for making gunpowder, some of which made its way to the War of 1812 and was also used during the Civil War, via Lexington, where powder mills transformed the saltpeter into gunpowder. To obtain the saltpeter crystals, miners first boiled sandstone fragments in water, reducing the fragments to sand. Next, cold water was poured through the sand, leaching out the niter. Finally, the cold water was

Grays Arch is a massive span.

allowed to evaporate, leaving crystals of nitrate. Parts of old wooden troughs and stone fireplaces stand behind the wire fence, left over from mining days.

Also here you will find interpretive information concerning Kentucky's "first son," Daniel Boone. The idea that ol' Dan'l used this shelter as a winter camp came from a 1959 find when a visitor discovered the inscription "D Boon" on a board of a hut standing beneath the rock shelter. This has not been verified, especially when considered against all the other locales in the Bluegrass State where Daniel Boone supposedly visited, hunted, and explored, carving his name. Additionally, a suspicious number of old family rifles passed down generation to generation were allegedly used by Boone. Whether the story is true or not, this impressive rock shelter has one of the most memorable names in the state.

The trek resumes down Martins Fork then meets the Rough Trail, where the Rough Trail abruptly climbs from Martins Fork, rising to sandstone ledges where you can look down the valley from which you came—and beyond. A little more climbing leads to the intersection with the Grays Arch Trail. The hike may become busier now as you stay with the Rough Trail under pines and oaks then descend into moister woods along a tributary of King Branch, where you first pass along a gigantic rock shelter then come to Grays Arch, making its majestic curve into the Kentucky sky. The highest point of the arch rises 50 feet above the forest floor while stretching 80 feet end to end.

The highlights—and challenges—aren't over yet. From here you descend to King Branch, reaching the hike's low point, then make an extended climb to Rush Ridge, back in the pines, maples, sourwoods, and oaks. The hike isn't perfectly level, but the

D Boon Hut was historically used for making saltpeter.

undulations are moderate. Additionally, a pair of overlooks from Rush Ridge serve to distract potentially fatigued hikers. The sandstone cliff lines of the Red River Gorge contrast the hilly woodlands. After keeping south on the ridgetop beyond the views, you come to Tunnel Ridge Road. A short walk returns you to the Grays Arch Picnic Area and the trailhead.

MILES AND DIRECTIONS

0.0 Start south from Grays Arch Picnic Area on the singletrack D Boon Hut Trail, near Tunnel Ridge Road. Descend an impressive series of steps coming along a massive curved rock shelter.

0.3 Span a small stream coursing below a cliff line.

0.4 Meet and join the signed trail leading left to D Boon Hut. Hike along a huge sandstone cliff line.

0.5 Reach the fenced historic stone shelter known as the D Boon Hut, alleged stopping spot of Daniel Boone but certainly a place mined for saltpeter in the 1800s. Return to the D Boon Hut Trail.

0.9 Bridge Martins Fork then meet the Rough Trail. Turn right here, climbing.

1.1 Reach an outcrop that opens to a vista down Martins Fork. Ahead, you can see Auxier Ridge from a second sandstone ledge.

2.0 Soak in a distant view of Grays Arch from the ridge above the natural bridge. This view may be obscured by summer foliage. Descend into a hollow.

2.1 Reach the spur trail to Grays Arch, shortly coming along an enormous rockhouse before reaching stately Grays Arch. Admire it from all angles, then backtrack, resuming the Rough Trail, descending northeast for King Branch.

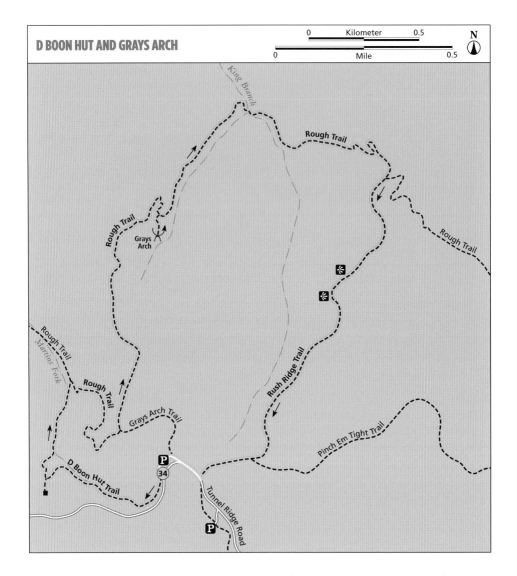

2.8 Cross King Branch then turn upstream. Just ahead, cross the stream a second and third time. You are now climbing along the left bank of the brook.

2.9 Turn up a side stream hollow of King Branch, rising on stair after stair after stair.

3.3 Level off on Rush Ridge, then come to a trail intersection. Here the Rough Trail dives left for Rush Branch, while our hike stays right with the Rush Ridge Trail. Cruise south along Rush Ridge.

3.7 Pass an overlook.

3.8 Pass a second overlook.

4.2 Dip to a gap on Rush Ridge. Climb.

4.4 Intersect the Pinch Em Tight Trail and stay right, ending the Rush Ridge Trail.

4.5 Come to Tunnel Ridge Road. Turn right and walk the road.

4.6 Arrive back at the picnic area and trailhead.

35 ROCK BRIDGE

There's a lot to see on this well-liked Red River Gorge trek, highlighted by the Rock Bridge, an arch spanning Swift Camp Creek. Leave the fine Rock Bridge Picnic Area, then visit a rockhouse before cruising along Rockbridge Fork to find 12-foot Creation Falls, a picturesque stream-wide pour-over. From there, you come to the Rock Bridge, doing what its name implies, straddling Swift Camp Creek. Continue down Swift Camp Creek, entering Clifty Wilderness, where you will find 25-foot Turtle Falls, a shower-like cataract dropping from a cliff line. Your return trip loops you past an overlook.

Start: Rock Bridge Picnic Area
Distance: 4.0-mile reverse balloon loop
Difficulty: Moderate
Elevation change: +/-744 feet
Maximum grade: 17% downhill grade for 0.3 mile
Hiking time: About 2.2 hours
Seasons/schedule: Year-round
Fees and permits: Permit required if camping in the Red River Gorge between 10 p.m. and 6 a.m.
Dog friendly: Yes

Trail surface: Old pavement at first, then natural surface in woodland
Land status: National forest
Nearest town: Campton
Other trail users: None
Maps to consult: USFS Red River Gorge Brochure, Rock Bridge Trail #207
Amenities available: Picnic area, restrooms at trailhead
Cell service: Better on ridgetop
Trail contacts: Daniel Boone National Forest, Cumberland Ranger District; (606) 776-5456; fs.usda.gov/dbnf

FINDING THE TRAILHEAD

From exit 40 on the Mountain Parkway near Pine Ridge, take KY 15 North for 1.3 miles. Turn right on KY 715 North and continue for 0.4 mile. Turn right on Rock Bridge Road and follow it for 3.3 miles to dead-end at the Rock Bridge Picnic Area. Trailhead GPS: 36.989868 / -82.984350

THE HIKE

This hike presents several highlights covering all the bases, whether you are geologically inclined and want to view Rock Bridge Arch as well as cliffs and rockhouses or a waterfall lover who can view a pair of comely cataracts. Creation Falls is a wide, classic pour-over with a long pool, while Turtle Falls is a narrow spiller showering over a cliff line. Rock Bridge Arch stands between the two cataracts. The 60-foot-long, 14-foot-high stone bridge stretches across Swift Camp Creek and is a sight to behold.

The Rock Bridge Trail, which this hike uses, is a very popular path in Kentucky's fabled Red River Gorge Geological Area, part of the Daniel Boone National Forest. A shaded picnic area can enhance your hike. The Rock Bridge Trail is a loop and thus has two points of egress from the parking area. For the best loop, start on the southwestern

Creation Falls

trailhead. It leaves Rock Bridge Picnic Area then descends to a cliff line and a high, imposing, dripping rockhouse before turning down a tributary of Rockbridge Fork, itself a tributary of Swift Camp Creek, itself tributary of the Red River. After sauntering through the woods along Rockbridge Fork, you will come to Creation Falls. This pour-over makes its 12-foot drop after running over a long rock slab. The upper part of the falls makes a vertical curtain drop then spreads in angled white froth before gathering in a dark linear pool. To reach the beach below the falls, make a bridgeless crossing of Rockbridge Fork above the falls then walk downstream. However, if you stay along the trail, a developed overlook will give you an easy alternate, dry-footed view of Creation Falls, purportedly named for nearby Rock Bridge Arch, since the stone span was formed by water erosion.

Beyond Creation Falls you will come to scenic Swift Camp Creek. In the valley, lush vegetation topped with regal trees rises amid outstanding rock outcrops, with Swift Camp Creek flowing over rock and sand in pools and shoals. And the spot where Rock Bridge crosses the creek will astound first-time arch viewers. The natural bridge spreads 60 feet completely across Swift Camp Creek, about 10 feet above the stream. Its bridge-like form completes the tableau.

The eye-pleasing hike leads onward to Turtle Falls, entering 12,646-acre Clifty Wilderness, encompassing much of the Red River Gorge Geological Area. Dip into intimate Bearpen Branch then continue up Swift Camp Creek to find Turtle Falls. Here, a

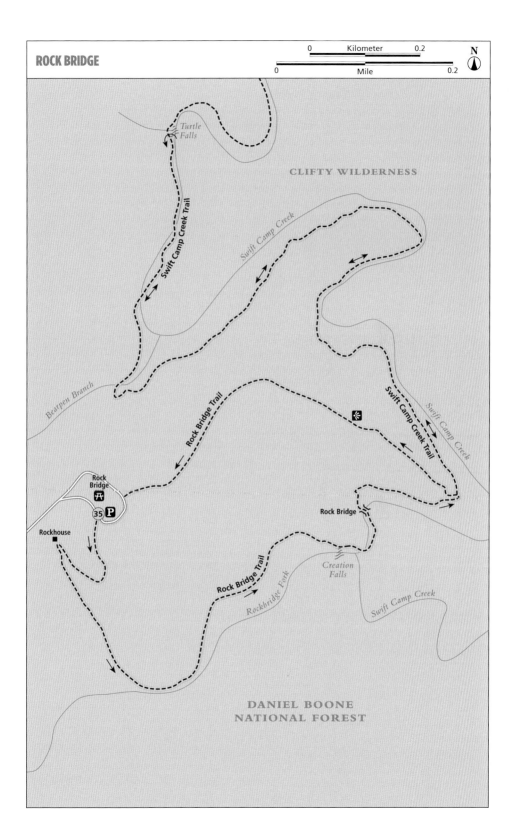

ROCK BRIDGE

Kilometer
0   0.2
Mile
0   0.2

N

CLIFTY WILDERNESS

Turtle
Falls

Swift Camp Creek Trail

Swift Camp Creek

Bearpen Branch

Rock Bridge Trail

Swift Camp Creek Trail

Swift Camp Creek

Rock
Bridge

35 P

Rock Bridge

Rockhouse

Rock Bridge Trail

Creation
Falls

Rockbridge Fork

Swift Camp Creek

DANIEL BOONE
NATIONAL FOREST

tributary of Swift Camp Creek makes a vertical nosedive from a cliff line into a colorful grotto beside Swift Camp Creek. The trail takes you directly beside the waterfall, offering a top-down view. Turtle Falls is also known as Turtleback Falls and Pooch Turtle Falls. The derivatives of the turtle moniker come from nearby Turtle Back Arch, found nearby via a user-created spur trail.

The tributary forming Turtle Falls flows across the trail, making the waterfall a cinch to find. However, accessing the base of the falls is anything but a cinch. Be careful. The view from the falls' base reveals this waterfall plummeting from a rock rim to splash into a sand floor. Iron-stained rock walls fashion an arresting framework for the pour-over. This spiller is best enjoyed from winter through spring. In summer and fall, its flow can be disappointing.

After backtracking from Turtle Falls, rejoin the loop of the Rock Bridge Trail. The path climbs from Swift Camp Creek along a steep and narrow piney ridgeline. A developed overlook stands above Swift Camp Creek. It could stand an occasional clearing to enhance the view of the Swift Camp Creek Valley. Climb a bit more on neat looking carved stone steps. The trail levels off before reaching hike's end on the north side of the picnic area.

MILES AND DIRECTIONS

0.0 Start from the south side of Rock Bridge Picnic Area on the Rock Bridge Trail, a path asphalted long ago. Leave upland hardwoods for moister woods.

0.1 Reach a high, imposing rockhouse with a very low-flow, part-time waterfall dripping from its heights. Beyond here, turn down a tributary of Rockbridge Fork, shaded by white pines.

0.3 Come alongside Rockbridge Fork; turn down its charming valley.

0.4 Come to 12-foot-high Creation Falls, a wide slide cascade found where Rockbridge Fork tumbles downstream of a long rock slab. Good views of the waterfall can be had from across the creek or just downtrail at a developed overlook. From here, turn north along Swift Camp Creek.

0.5 Arrive at Rock Bridge Arch. The 60-foot stone span stretches completely across Swift Camp Creek. Keep downstream. The path delivers views of Rock Bridge Arch from both sides.

0.9 Intersect and join the Swift Camp Creek Trail. You will return to this intersection later. For now, enter the Clifty Wilderness, undulating down the Swift Camp Creek gorge under pines aplenty along with other evergreens. The trail runs the gorge rim, allowing looks into Swift Camp Creek.

1.3 Make a 180-degree northwest-to-southeast bend as the trail mimics the curves of the creek.

1.9 Turn up Bearpen Branch. The trail leads through a mini-gorge, leaving you to briefly walk directly up the small creek. Turn back out to Swift Camp Creek's rim.

2.2 Reach the top of Turtle Falls as it spills into a stone alcove below. The slender 25-foot spiller is challenging to access for a bottom-up view, but it is done with regularity. Backtrack to the Rock Bridge Arch Trail.

3.5 Rejoin the Rock Bridge Trail to finish the loop. Climb away from Swift Camp Creek.

3.7 Come to a developed overlook above Swift Camp Creek. It may or may not be clear.

4.0 Arrive back at the trailhead.

36 CARTER CAVES CIRCUIT

This loop hike explores a host of highlights at famed Carter Caves State Park, one of Kentucky's best state parks. Leave the welcome center, circling above X Cave then wander wooded hollows and ridges to find Shangri La Arch. Next come to Smoky Valley Lake. Circle the impoundment then cross big Smoky Creek on a swinging bridge. From there, pass two large arches and a rock climbing site on this loop that takes you throughout this jewel of a preserve. A pair of backcountry campsites adds overnighting possibilities to the trek.

Start: Park welcome center
Distance: 7.9-mile loop
Difficulty: Moderate-difficult
Elevation change: +/-1,937 feet
Maximum grade: 17% downhill grade for 0.9 mile
Hiking time: About 4 hours
Seasons/schedule: Year-round
Fees and permits: No fees or permits required
Dog friendly: Yes
Trail surface: Forest natural surface
Land status: State park, small portion is state forest

Nearest town: Olive Hill
Other trail users: Short segments shared with mountain bikers and equestrians
Maps to consult: Carter Caves State Resort Park
Amenities available: Information, restrooms, gifts, maps at welcome center
Cell service: Okay
Trail contacts: Carter Caves State Resort Park; (606) 286-4411; parks.ky.gov/olive-hill/parks/resort/carter-caves-state-resort-park

FINDING THE TRAILHEAD

From exit 161 on I-64 near Counts Crossroads, take US 60 East for 1.5 miles. Turn left onto KY 182 and follow it for 2.7 miles. Turn left at the sign for Carter Caves State Park on Cave Branch Road and follow it for 1 mile to turn right into the welcome center and gift shop. Trailhead GPS: 38.377295 / -83.122922

THE HIKE

The caves beneath Kentucky's Carter County have been drawing visitors for a long, long time. Early settlers extracted raw materials from the caves, and for decades their exploration has been a source of recreation. Cave tours were being conducted long before the state park was established in the 1940s. Within the park there are twenty charted caves, several of them open for guided tours of all lengths and challenge levels, from easy, short walking tours to wild cave expeditions. Check the park website for the latest cave tour offerings. Although the underground sights are a primary attraction, the 1,900-acre park also offers 30 miles of hiking trails. One of the longest—and the one you follow on this hike—is the 4Cs (for Carter Caves Cross Country) Trail, which winds through the wooded backcountry of the park and a small section of adjacent Tygarts State Forest.

Eagles Nest backcountry campsite has a trail shelter.

After hiking the picturesque wooded loop—a definite trek through nature—you will be shocked to learn that the circuit completely encircles a golf course, a lodge, and cabins—the "resort" part of Carter Caves State Resort Park. As a whole, the trail system is well signed, blazed, and maintained. That is a good thing, because you will encounter a plethora of trail intersections as you follow the 4Cs Trail the entirety of the hike. Be apprised that at times the 4Cs Trail runs in conjunction with other paths. If you wish to use one of the two backcountry campsites along the route, you must obtain a permit ahead of time. Call the park office for permit instructions.

While on the adventure, be sure to appreciate this preserved slice of the Commonwealth with its rich woods, clear streams, regal cliff lines, and arches. The preserve is a living embodiment of why state parks should exist.

MILES AND DIRECTIONS

- **0.0** Start from the east side of the welcome center, heading toward X Cave. Follow steps uphill then quickly pass the barred entrance and stay right to reach an intersection. Here, the Horn Hollow Trail leaves right and straight. We split left with the 4Cs Trail, traveling directly over the X Cave entrance. Begin a pattern of winding in and out of wooded hollows.
- **0.4** Pass a cliff line and low rockhouse.
- **0.5** Cross a stream with a 10-foot faucet-style waterfall dropping off a nearby cliff line.

The author crosses Smoky Creek on a trail bridge.

0.8 Cross a normally dry streambed then turn downstream. Stay with the blazes as the path splits right, away from an old roadbed. You are now in Bat Cave State Nature Preserve.

1.3 Drop into a clearing and turn right on a grassy road. Enter Tygarts State Forest.

1.6 Stay left with the 4Cs Trail as the multiuse Kiser Hollow Trail keeps straight. Climb.

1.9 Reach gravel Cave Branch Road. Walk right a few feet then split left into woods.

2.2 The Kiser Hollow Trail splits left. Keep straight (south) toward Smoky Valley Lake.

2.5 Cross the Kiser Hollow Trail again. Continue descending.

3.0 Reach and descend a set of stairs then walk under the stone passage of Shangri La Arch, a cave-like passage littered with rockfall. Below here, a stream is normally running.

3.1 Come to a trail intersection and Smoky Valley Lake. Split right as a left takes you to the park boat ramp. Cruise the shoreline of the lake in sycamores along the marshy upper part of the impoundment, running parallel to a large cliff line to your right.

3.6 Cross the stream coming out of Kiser Hollow.

3.7 Come along the Eagles Nest backcountry campsite, with a three-sided metal shelter as well as regular campsites. Ahead, cross the multiuse Collins Passage Trail the first of numerous times. Stay with the 4Cs Trail.

3.9 Cross clear and pretty Smoky Creek on a swinging bridge. Climb, crossing the Collins Passage Trail twice more.

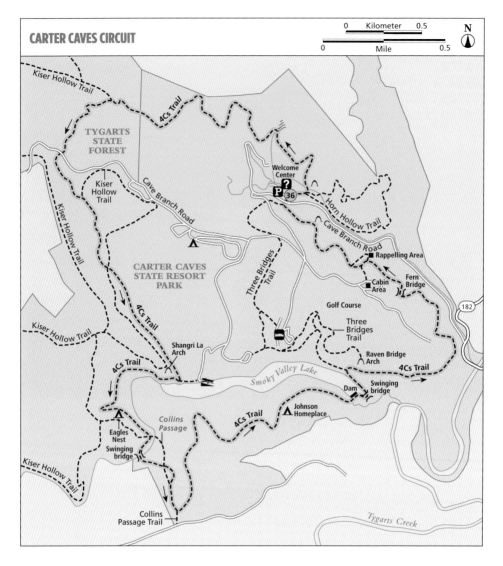

Kiser Hollow Trail

4Cs Trail

TYGARTS STATE FOREST

Kiser Hollow Trail

Welcome Center

P 36

Horn Hollow Trail

Cave Branch Road

Kiser Hollow Trail

Cave Branch Road

Rappelling Area

CARTER CAVES STATE RESORT PARK

Three Bridges Trail

Cabin Area

Fern Bridge

182

4Cs Trail

Kiser Hollow Trail

Golf Course

Three Bridges Trail

4Cs Trail

Shangri La Arch

Raven Bridge Arch

4Cs Trail

Swinging bridge

Smoky Valley Lake

Dam

4Cs Trail

Johnson Homeplace

Collins Passage

4Cs Trail

Eagles Nest

Swinging bridge

Kiser Hollow Trail

Collins Passage Trail

Tygarts Creek

4.3   Leave left for good from the Collins Passage Trail, passing a small farm pond. Trace an old farm road and watch as the 4Cs Trail splits right from the road.

5.2   Come to the signed Johnson Place backcountry campsite after passing a trickling spring branch that serves as the water source for the campsite/homesite. A small-ish rock shelter provides some respite from the elements. Note the stone blocks of the former dwelling. The site offers a fire ring and tent sites. Keep east, well above Smoky Valley Lake, then sharply descend to come along a lake dam spillway. Stay with the blazes as the trail works around the spillway then crosses the dam.

5.8   Cross the main dam spillway on a swinging bridge. Climb left then skirt along a cliff line. Note the small column arches at the base of this cliff line.

6.0   Meet the Three Bridges Trail. Split right and climb.

Smoky Valley Lake in autumn

6.1 Meet the Raven Bridge Trail. Head left on it a short distance to view the classic arch of Raven Bridge. Backtrack and continue with the 4Cs Trail eastbound in woods, rolling through a land rife with sinkholes.

6.6 Turn north as you come near but well above CR 182. Cruise along some imperial cliff lines, in and out of steep hollows. Cave Branch Road is well below you.

7.0 Turn into the hollow of Fern Bridge, a massive arch close to the main cliff line from which it has split away. The trail picks its way through extensive rockfall and delicate vegetation, a truly beautiful area, dripping with water in summer and icicles in winter. Ahead, curve below park cabins.

7.3 Pass a spur trail left to the park cabins then a spur trail right to the designated rappelling area. Stay straight with the 4Cs Trail, keeping along the top of a wooded cliff line.

7.6 Walk by a small barred cave entrance just to the left of the trail.

7.9 Walk beside the entrance to Saltpetre Cave then cross Cave Branch Road and arrive back at the welcome center.

37 **LICK FALLS**

Make a loop hike featuring three cataracts, including the star of the show—60-foot Lick Falls. Set at fine Grayson Lake State Park, you will ramble through rolling woods before first reaching Lick Falls, dashing in segments through a mini-gorge to make a final plummet from a stone ledge directly into Grayson Lake. From there, work your way along the lakeshore, where you will find 15-foot Buckeye Branch Falls tumbling into the impoundment from a more modest rim. Your third and final spiller is Bowling Branch Cascade, a long slide that also slips into pretty Grayson Lake.

Start: Near campground entrance station
Distance: 3.0-mile loop
Difficulty: Moderate
Elevation change: +/-655 feet
Maximum grade: 5% downhill grade for 0.4 mile
Hiking time: About 1.4 hours
Seasons/schedule: Year-round; winter and spring for bolder falls
Fees and permits: No fees or permits required
Dog friendly: Yes

Trail surface: Forest natural surface
Land status: State park
Nearest town: Grayson
Other trail users: None
Maps to consult: Grayson Lake State Park
Amenities available: Picnic area at trailhead
Cell service: Good
Trail contacts: Grayson Lake State Park; (606) 474-9727; parks.ky.gov/olive-hill/parks/recreation/grayson-lake-state-park

FINDING THE TRAILHEAD

From exit 172 on I-64 at Grayson, take KY 7 South for 7 miles. Turn right onto Grayson Lake State Park Road (you will also see a sign for the park golf course). Follow the main park road and follow the signs to the park campground. If the campground is open, pass the campground entrance station and take the first acute right just beyond the entrance station to park near the basketball court. If the campground is closed and gated, park just outside the campground entrance station then walk a short distance to the trailhead. Trailhead GPS: 38.201528 / -83.029233

THE HIKE

Although Cumberland Falls gets the most waterfall accolades among Kentucky state parks, Grayson Lake ought to get at least an honorable mention. This eastern Kentucky preserve offers fine scenery and a few waterfalls of its own. Grayson Lake State Park boasts three scenic spillers, one of which is deservedly well known—Lick Falls, a 60-foot diving wall of white that pirouettes into Grayson Lake. The bottom segment of the falls is most often seen by boaters tooling around Grayson Lake. Hikers get to see the upper part of the falls, which boaters cannot see, but they cannot fully enjoy the bottom-up

Autumn view of Grayson Lake

view from the lake due to the sheer sandstone cliffs from which Lick Falls makes its final tumble.

In addition to thrilling Lick Falls, you also get to view lesser-heralded Buckeye Branch Falls. This seasonal cataract makes a 15-foot drop off a stone ledge into a secluded cove of Grayson Lake. The final waterfall—Bowling Branch Cascade—delivers yet another type of pour-over as it makes a widening slide toward the impoundment before releasing in a final vertical downgrade.

The hike to the waterfalls is fun and scenic too. The blazed, well-marked, and well-maintained Lick Falls Loop leaves the park campground and wanders west through woods, crossing streams between hills before sidling alongside Lick Branch. Then you come down the creek and reach the upper part of Lick Falls as it cuts through rock in splashy phases before its final plunge from the gorge rim. Fortunately, we can enjoy the upper falls; unfortunately, landlubbers cannot get the face-on view no matter where they go or how much they lean out from the cliff line by the falls, so don't try. However, when cruising along the cliff line down from Lick Creek Falls—if the streams are high—you will hear and see another waterfall spilling 40 feet into the same cove across the gorge. Enjoy this wet-weather falls and the upper part of Lick Falls, then move on.

And you will enjoy what lies ahead. Here the Lick Falls Overlook Trail wanders along the rim of the gorge above Lake Grayson, allowing for numerous and nearly continuous winter views of the impoundment and the hills that rise above, as well as the sandstone walls that seem to go on for miles along the shore. In winter and spring you will hear

Find Bowling Branch Cascade near hike's end.

other waterfalls making their dives into the still water of the impoundment. In autumn, all the cataracts can be mere trickles.

Ahead you will find Buckeye Branch Falls, the most seasonal of the three spillers on this hike. Since it is below the trail, expect to scramble to the pour-over. Then you are walking once more on the edge of the gorge above the lake, simply an enjoyable endeavor. After that, the trail takes you directly above Bowling Branch Cascade; it is easy to view and maneuver around this pour-over for a complete look.

The final part of the hike leads away from the lake and back to the trailhead. While here, consider enhancing your hiking adventure with boating, paddling, fishing, camping, or picnicking. It would be cool to view these waterfalls by both land and water.

MILES AND DIRECTIONS

0.0   Start from the signed trailhead near the park campground entrance station and basketball court and take the Lick Falls Loop westerly into woods, with open terrain on either side of the wooded strip.

0.1   Reach a trail intersection. Here, stay with the Lick Falls Loop as it keeps straight. Your return route comes in from the left and an old country road goes right. The blazes lead you to Bowling Branch; cross it on a wooden hiker bridge. Hike among oaks and other hardwoods. Watch for an old stone fence from the days when this was a farm.

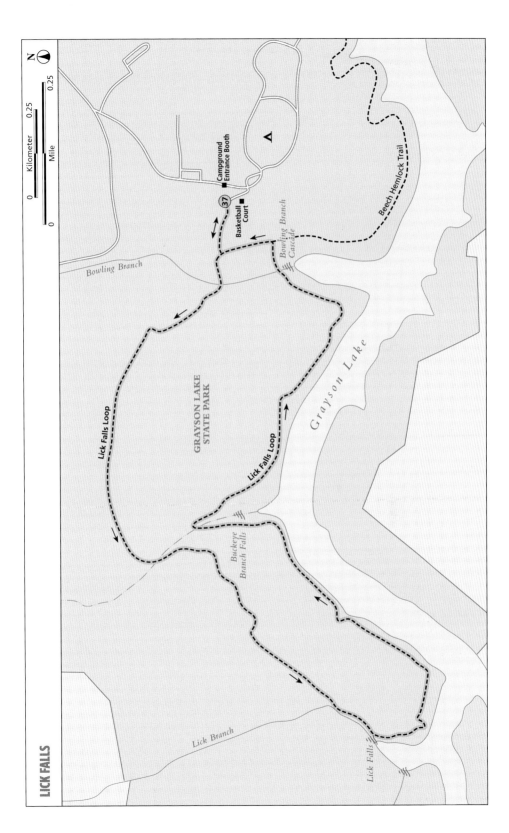

LICK FALLS

0.2 Cross a golf cart path. This segment of the hike is near holes 7 and 8 of the park golf course. Ahead, roll through hills.

0.7 Pass through former farmland still growing over with brush and younger trees.

0.8 Cross small Buckeye Branch.

1.3 Come to Lick Creek after descending on an eroded track. The old roadbed you have picked up fords Lick Creek, but the official Lick Falls Overlook Trail stays on the left bank as a singletrack path, traversing through mountain laurel and rhododendron.

1.4 Reach the upper part of Lick Falls. Here the cataract makes an initial slide over smooth rock then fans out, sliding again to a plunge pool below. It then makes another run over smooth rock before the final rush into Grayson Lake. The trail then keeps along the rim of the gorge and opens onto the main body of long, narrow Grayson Lake. Watery views open.

2.1 Hike above Buckeye Branch Falls. To get the best look at the pour-over, circle Buckeye Branch and approach the spiller from the other side. You will still have to descend to get a face-on view of Buckeye Branch Falls. Turn back out to the main body of the lake.

2.7 Reach the hiker bridge crossing Bowling Branch. Bowling Branch Cascade makes a slide fall below the bridge into Grayson Lake. You can get a face-on look without much difficulty. Ascend from Bowling Branch.

2.8 Reach a trail intersection. Here the Beech Hemlock Trail leaves right while we go left, still making the loop.

2.9 Complete the loop portion of the hike after crossing a golf cart path. Turn right, backtracking toward the campground.

3.0 Arrive back at the trailhead.

38 DAWKINS LINE RAIL TRAIL

Take a stroll—or an extended hike—on the Bluegrass State's longest rail trail, now an officially designated Kentucky state park. The Dawkins Line Rail Trail traces a former railroad grade through rural and remote Johnson County. On this sampler hike, you can get a fine taste of life in these parts while traveling near homesteads, by clear streams, and over bridges where coal and transportation trains once ran.

Start: Swamp Branch trailhead
Distance: 5.2 miles out and back
Difficulty: Easy-moderate due to slight elevation change
Elevation change: +/-140 feet
Maximum grade: 3% grade for 0.3 mile
Hiking time: About 2.5 hours
Seasons/schedule: Year-round
Fees and permits: No fees or permits required
Dog friendly: Yes
Trail surface: Mostly pea gravel

Land status: State park
Nearest town: Salyersville
Other trail users: Bicyclers, equestrians
Maps to consult: Dawkins Line Rail Trail
Amenities available: None
Cell service: Decent
Trail contacts: Dawkins Line Rail Trail; (502) 564-2172; parks.ky.gov/swamp-branch/parks/recreation/dawkins-line-rail-trail

FINDING THE TRAILHEAD

From Salyersville near Ramey Memorial Park, take US 460 East for 9.5 miles. Turn right onto KY 825 (Swamp Branch Road) and stay with it for 5.1 miles. Turn right onto the signed gravel road to the trailhead, located at the end of the gravel road running parallel to KY 825 and the rail trail. Trailhead GPS: 37.737702 / -82.906780

THE HIKE

Over the past few decades, rail trails have certainly caught on throughout the United States, and Kentucky is no exception. The Dawkins Line Rail Trail stretches for 36 miles end to end, the longest rail trail in the Bluegrass State. And since the path is an official Kentucky state park, it is well managed and here to stay. The stretch recommended below travels from the Swamp Branch trailhead along several streams in a quiet segment of Johnson County, deep in the hills and hollows of eastern Kentucky. Hopefully this segment will spur you to try other sections of the path. The rail trail's eastern terminus leaves from Johnson County's Hagerhill, crossing numerous streams between wooded hills into Magoffin County and the exciting Gun Creek Tunnel to cross the upper Licking River. From there the rail trail winds west to the Tip Top Tunnel (under restoration). The last segment enters Breathitt County and turns south to end near the hamlet of Evanston. Several official trailhead accesses have been established along the way.

Crossing one of the trestles on this fine rail trail

You will find it a fine scenic as well as cultural experience. When traveling the trail, you will see homes and farms representing this part of the state, as well as the natural beauty contained within—from translucent brooks to biodiverse woods to bucolic small farms raising everything from goats to geese, hay to vegetables, and pumpkins to parsnips.

Rail trails such as this go through evolutionary stages and affect trailside communities along the way. First, a railroad line is abandoned, leaving most places feeling like a link to the rest of the world is lost, as is the economic value once brought by the train and its transportation capabilities. Then a government entity views the rail line as a potential trail and obtains the right-of-way. Already resenting the loss of the rail line, some folks think the rail trail is a waste. Furthermore, the trail will bring strangers into their backyards. However, as the trail becomes established and visitors come to their counties and spend money, they begin to see the value of the rail trails. Over time, the rail trail becomes a point of local pride and a positive economic force.

In the early 1900s the Dawkins Lumber Company laid out a railroad to transport the timber they were cutting in eastern Kentucky's upper Licking River and Big Sandy River watersheds. Known as the Dawkins Line, the railroad coursed through the timbered hills. However, the stock market crash of 1929 rippled all the way to these remote hinterlands, shutting down the timbering and the rail line itself. As economic fortunes turned for the better, the Dawkins Line was purchased, restarted, and even expanded

Flowers grace the edge of the Dawkins Line Rail Trail.

westerly into Breathitt County. However, like many short rail lines in remote areas, it became unprofitable. The last train ran over the tracks in 2004, and was then abandoned. The state purchased the Dawkins Line right-of-way. Gravel was laid over the bed, bridges repaired, and trailheads created. The Dawkins Line Rail Trail was opened in 2013, starting with around 13 miles of path. Since then it has been expanded to what we see today. Over time the Dawkins Line will continue to follow the evolutionary stages of a rail trail, sure as day follows night. Give it a shot.

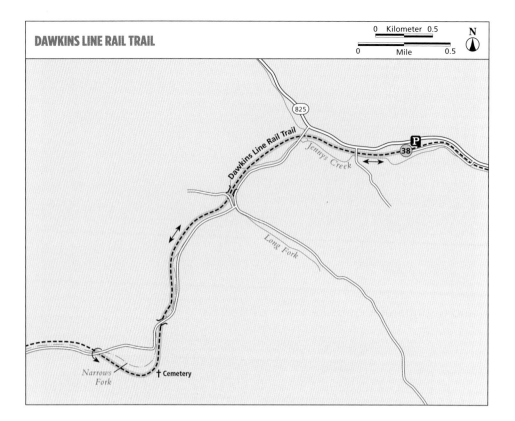

MILES AND DIRECTIONS

0.0 Start from the Swamp Brach trailhead parking area and walk west on the gravel Dawkins Line Rail Trail, bordered by fields and cedar, walnut, and tulip trees. Jennys Creek flows in the thickets to your left.

0.3 Cross a road leading to a homestead. Continue west, traveling behind homes facing KY 825 as well as small farms. Some local residents have planted landscaping beside the trail on their property. The trail is partly shaded but mostly open overhead.

0.6 Bridge Greenrock Creek then cross Riceville Road.

0.9 Bridge Jennys Creek.

1.1 Bridge Jennys Creek again then turn up Narrows Fork, a tributary of Jennys Creek, heading southwest on a gentle incline.

1.3 Pass the concrete D10 marker, a mileage post from the days when the Dawkins Line was active. Hike astride cut bluffs where the hillside was blasted to make room for the railroad. Woods crowd the trail as the hollow narrows, creating a shady canopy.

2.0 Cross well above Narrows Fork and what remains of KY 1867. Leave houses behind and enter deep woods.

2.2 Curve past the small Collins Cemetery to the left of the trail. Ahead, find a contemplation bench.

2.3 Pass the concrete D11 marker.

2.6 Reach a large high bridge well above Narrows Fork. This is a good place to turn around and retrace your steps.

5.2 Arrive back at the Swamp Branch trailhead.

39 PINE MOUNTAIN STATE SCENIC TRAIL

This one-way backpacking adventure runs atop rugged and remote Pine Mountain. Start at US 119 near Whitesburg. The first several miles are exclusively in Kentucky before meeting Virginia at Stateline Knob then runs along the state line. Enjoy geological features such as Eagle Arch and Lemon Squeezer and the Rock Fortress, as well as views from High Rock, Mars Rock, and Twin Cliffs. End at Pound Gap, although long-distance backpackers can stretch their overnight adventure in both directions with the latest expansions of the Pine Mountain Trail. The path is well marked and maintained. Trail shelters and designated campsites make overnighting easier.

Start: US 119 trailhead

Distance: 16.5 miles point to point

Difficulty: Difficult due to elevation change

Elevation change: +4,774 feet,-5,056 feet

Maximum grade: 15% downhill grade for 0.7 mile

Hiking time: About 10.5 hours

Seasons/schedule: Year-round; winter could be rough

Fees and permits: No fees or permits required

Dog friendly: Yes

Trail surface: Forested natural surface, open rock slabs

Land status: State park, national forest

Nearest town: Whitesburg

Other trail users: None

Maps to consult: Pine Mountain Trail Highland Section, Clinch District, Jefferson National Forest

Amenities available: Restroom at US 119 at trailhead; store at US 23 trailhead

Cell service: Pretty decent

Trail contacts: Pine Mountain State Scenic Trail; pinemountaintrail.com

FINDING THE TRAILHEAD

From US 23 in Pound, Virginia, take US 23 North for 4.5 miles, passing through Pound Gap, where you can leave a shuttle car at the parking area on the southwest side of the gap near a convenience store. (Look for the trailhead kiosk and make sure to ask permission at the store for where to park.) To reach the US 119 trailhead, also known as the Little Shepherd trailhead, continue north on US 23 for 1.5 miles into Kentucky. Turn left, joining US 119 South. Follow US 119 South for 11 miles to Whitesburg, Kentucky, and a traffic light. Turn left here, staying with US 119 South, and continue for 4.7 miles more to the crest of Pine Mountain and the trailhead parking area, on your right. Trailhead GPS: US 119 trailhead: 37.076057 / -82.810262; US 23 trailhead: 37.154512 / -82.631181

The view from Mars Rock

THE HIKE

The Pine Mountain Trail (PMT) is a growing pathway ultimately slated to run 140 miles from Cumberland Gap National Park to Breaks Interstate Park. More than 50 miles of the end-to-end path are currently open, including the latest section linking Kingdom Come State Park to the US 119 trailhead, where this hike starts. Pine Mountain harbors one of the largest stretches of unfragmented forest in the Bluegrass State and, with its wild nature, scenic highlights, and public lands, is an ideal venue for a long-distance path. This path has been designated a Kentucky State Scenic Trail.

This particular stretch of the PMT is known as the Highland Section. I recommend it as a two-night backpack, allowing you time to explore the sights as well as tackle the ups and downs along the ridge-running pathway. Water is available at decent intervals along the way. This point-to-point adventure requires either two cars or a shuttle. The Pine Mountain Trail's governing body offers shuttles for a reasonable fee, part of which goes to maintain the pathway. Please schedule your shuttle through the Pine Mountain Trail website at least 48 hours in advance.

The PMT is signed with fluorescent-yellow metal blazes. After leaving US 119 you will soon come to the Flamingo trail shelter, where you can stay if you want an early first day. Roll along the ridge, passing a communications tower, dipping to a creeklet, then ascending to the ridge crest. Ahead you will pass Americorps Cliff, with its view to the west, then come to Eagle Arch. Look for the span below the trail, extending nearly straight for almost 40 feet rather than being curved, as with most arches.

Ahead, the PMT borders Bad Branch Nature Preserve then descends past a spring and runs atop naked rock, a common occurrence on the PMT. South-facing woods are heavy with pine, oak, and mountain laurel; hollows and north-facing areas sprout rhododendron and magnolia and tulip trees. Geological wonders are never far away. You find one at the Lemon Squeezer, where a boulder garden crowds the path. You may have to twist a bit to get through with a fully loaded backpack.

After dipping to a tributary of Bad Branch, the PMT overcomes a knob to intersect the Bad Branch Trail. Ahead meet the High Rock Loop and make your way to High Rock, an open angled rock slab with incredible views in all directions. Continue past more views amid the rocks and pines. Intersect the other end of the High Rock Loop then open onto Mars Rock, another angled ledge with an otherworldly view. The pock-marked stone recalls the fourth planet from the sun.

Continue undulating, mostly atop the ridge but also along cliff lines, where you pass Slip and Slide Rock then top out on Mayking Knob, where iron bars help you climb bare rock. Next comes the Adena Shelter, built the same as the Flamingo shelter. The wood refuge offers a fine place to camp, with partial views into Virginia.

Beyond the Adena shelter, the PMT widens to doubletrack and begins several miles without a singular feature, yet it's rife with everywhere-you-look beauty. Ahead, the Indian Grave campsite is set in a small bowl atop Pine Mountain, with a spur trail leading south to a spring. Pass the actual Indian Grave Gap at 11.1 miles. The PMT rolls over wooded knobs and gaps, keeping a northeasterly course, then climbs past the signed Rock Fortress—looking like what its name implies. The trail resumes singletrack and passes the Twin Cliffs, a double vista, with one view into Virginia and another into Kentucky.

The PMT reaches a good spring just after Twin Cliffs. Next comes a gap and the Jack Sautter campsite, with designated tent sites and a 0.2-mile walk to a spring and the Old Meade Place, site of an ecologically significant bog. After cutting under a major power line, you make the big drop toward Pound Gap.

Descend past the historic Red Fox Trail, an old road that passed through Pound Gap. In 1892 a family of five was robbed and murdered near here in what was dubbed the "Killing Rock Massacre." The book, play, and movie *Trail of the Lonesome Pine* is based on the episode. You can already hear the vehicles on US 23 and are shortly at the trailhead at Pound Gap, a segment of the Pine Mountain Trail completed.

MILES AND DIRECTIONS

0.0 Start from the US 119 trailhead above Whitesburg and join wooden steps climbing to a cell tower access road. Head left on the tower road.

0.4 The PMT passes around a pole gate, leaving the access road and winds along the mountainside.

0.6 Reach the Flamingo trail shelter. The wood refuge has a two-story bunk area, capable of housing eight sleepers, and offers a covered picnic table and staging area. A fire ring, bear-resistant food storage pole, and outhouse complete the camp. Water is accessed a bit downtrail at a concrete spring box.

0.9 Reach a communication tower. The town of Whitesburg lies below.

PINE MOUNTAIN STATE SCENIC TRAIL

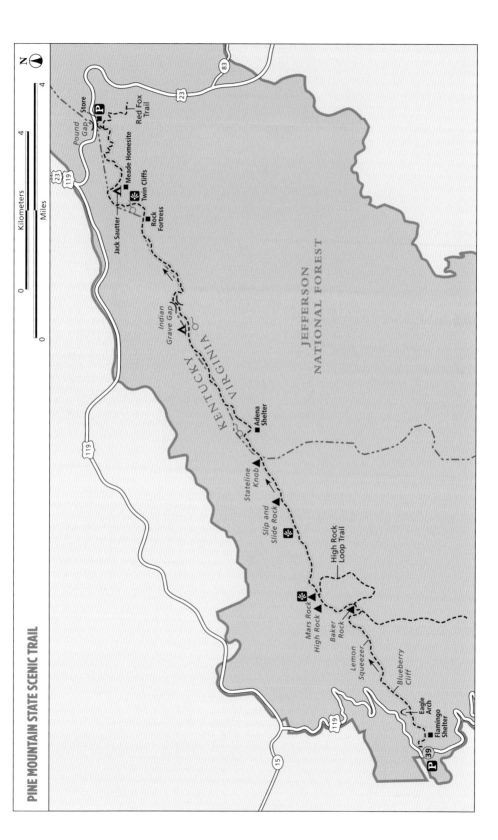

A highland view from the crest of Pine Mountain

1.1 Come to nearly straight Eagle Arch after passing the westerly view from Americorps Cliff.

1.7 Reach a spur and northwesterly view from Blueberry Cliff. Ahead, the PMT dips to cross a streambed in a hollow before regaining the ridge crest.

2.7 Squeak through Lemon Squeezer, where big boulders crowd the trail, then cross a tributary of Bad Branch.

3.6 The Bad Branch Trail leaves right. Stay left and descend to soon pass Baker Rock and its overhang.

3.8 Meet the High Rock Loop. Stay left with the Pine Mountain Trail, ascending beside an attractive tributary of Bad Branch.

4.3 Reach signed Ran Polly Gap. Keep climbing, often over naked rock bordered in pines.

4.6 Open onto High Rock, with its large surface of stone and a brow pointing west, with scattered trees rising from crevices in the rock. Grab first-rate views west to nearly unbroken forests. Reenter woods.

4.8 Reach an intersection. Here the High Rock Loop splits right. Stay left with the Pine Mountain Trail and open onto sloped and pocked Mars Rock, with 180-degree views to the west. Continue along the crest then slide to the base of a cliff line.

6.2 Soak in a southerly panorama of Black Mountain amid stunted pines pocking a rock slab.

6.7 Reach Slip and Slide Rock.

7.5 Come to Stateline Knob. From here on, the PMT runs the Kentucky-Virginia state line.

8.1 Pass beside a spring then rise to the Adena trail shelter, 0.3 mile ahead.

10.5 Reach the Indian Grave Gap campsite with a spur to a spring.

11.1 Dip to Indian Grave Gap; climb then undulate along Pine Mountain.

13.4 Cruise past the signed Rock Fortress. Circle a knob.

13.7 Reach the spur right to the Twin Cliffs Overlook, dotted with pines rising from the rock slab. Pass a spring shortly beyond the spur to the lookout.

14.8 Reach the small Jack Sautter campsite in a gap. A spur goes down to the Old Meade Place and water.

15.5 Hike under a big power line cut. Descend steadily ahead.

16.5 Arrive at the Pound Gap trailhead shortly after passing the Red Fox Trail.

40 BAD BRANCH FALLS AND HIGH ROCK LOOP

This highly recommended hike explores one of Kentucky's most beautiful state nature preserves. First, climb past cascades and pools aplenty in a pristine highland gorge cut into Pine Mountain to reach 60-foot Bad Branch Falls. From there continue up to the rugged crest of Pine Mountain to join the expanding Pine Mountain Trail. Grab an outstanding view from High Rock, then cruise the mountain crest to explore Mars Rock, with its strange formations and distant vistas. Descend along upper Bad Branch, completing a loop. Finally, backtrack to the trailhead.

Start: Bad Branch trailhead
Distance: 7.5-mile balloon loop with spur
Difficulty: Difficult due to elevation change
Elevation change: +/-2,108 feet
Maximum grade: 18% grade for 0.5 mile
Hiking time: About 5.5 hours
Seasons/schedule: Year-round
Fees and permits: No fees or permits required
Dog friendly: Yes
Trail surface: Forested natural surface, some open rock slabs

Land status: State park
Nearest town: Whitesburg
Other trail users: None
Maps to consult: Clinch River District Jefferson National Forest, Bad Branch State Nature Preserve
Amenities available: Restrooms, visitor center at trailhead
Cell service: Okay on ridgetop; bad elsewhere
Trail contacts: Office of Kentucky Nature Preserves; (502) 573-2886; eec.ky.gov

FINDING THE TRAILHEAD

From Whitesburg, take KY 15 South for 1.4 miles. Turn right onto US 119 South and continue for 7 miles. Turn left onto KY 932 East and continue for 1.7 miles to reach the Bad Branch State Nature Preserve parking area, on your left. Trailhead GPS: 37.067475 / -82.772056

THE HIKE

Bad Branch is deserving of its status as a Kentucky state nature preserve. Upon entering the scenic stream valley at the southern foot of Pine Mountain, natural splendor is immediately evident. A clear sparkling stream dashes over multicolor stones bordered by sandy banks over which rises a regal forest of hemlock, yellow birch, and Fraser magnolia. This part of the state harbors Kentucky's highest elevations and also more closely recalls the Southern Appalachians rather than the Cumberland Plateau to the west. Bad Branch certainly has its share of geological wonders, among them the stone palace from which Bad Branch makes it dive, as well as the incredible boulder field lying below the

Bad Branch Falls

waterfall. High Rock and Mars Rock, the mountaintop highlights, are massive angled stone protrusions aiming for the sky that open up the heavens above and the lands below.

Established in 1985, Bad Branch Nature Preserve was originally 485 acres, protecting the core of the stream gorge, including Bad Branch Falls. Later the preserve was expanded to more than 2,700 acres, including the south side and crest of Pine Mountain, where you find High Rock and Mars Rock. The preserve hosts over thirty species of rare flora and fauna. One more superlative: Bad Branch is a designated Kentucky Wild River.

Looking out from High Rock

Allow ample time for the hike, which entails more than 2,000 feet of climbing. The trail can be rocky in places, slowing the trek. From the trailhead, you will enter the Bad Branch gorge in deep forest of hemlocks and yellow birch. Span the clear, clean stream twice on hiker bridges. Bad Branch, a tributary of the Poor Fork of the Cumberland River, is known for its exceptional water quality. However, the hemlocks of Bad Branch are threatened by the hemlock woolly adelgid, a non-native insect. Many of the 20,000-plus hemlocks at Bad Branch State Nature Preserve are being treated for the insect through soil injection of insecticide specific to the adelgid.

Beyond these two crossings, you continue up the wildflower-rich valley featuring painted trillium. Water song echoes up the trail as lesser slides and chutes fall over boulders. Then you reach the spur to Bad Branch Falls. Wind your way up to a sandstone wall over which Bad Branch recklessly dives 60 feet, dashing to rocks then working its way down an incredible boulder jumble. Your first view of Bad Branch Falls will be sidelong, but you can maneuver to a front-on view of the cataract as well as getting to its base.

After backtracking to the main trail, begin a steady climb to the crest of Pine Mountain on a much less used tread, only to drop to a tributary of Bad Branch. A final assault, much of it over naked stone, leads you up to High Rock and a view west over the Cumberland Plateau and beyond, with Whitesburg in the immediate valley below. Roll the mountain crest then find unmistakable Mars Rock, with its pocked surface evoking the red planet. More views extend from Mars Rock. From there, trace upper Bad Branch as it gains volume before climbing back to the crest of Pine Mountain then making an extended backtrack descent to the trailhead.

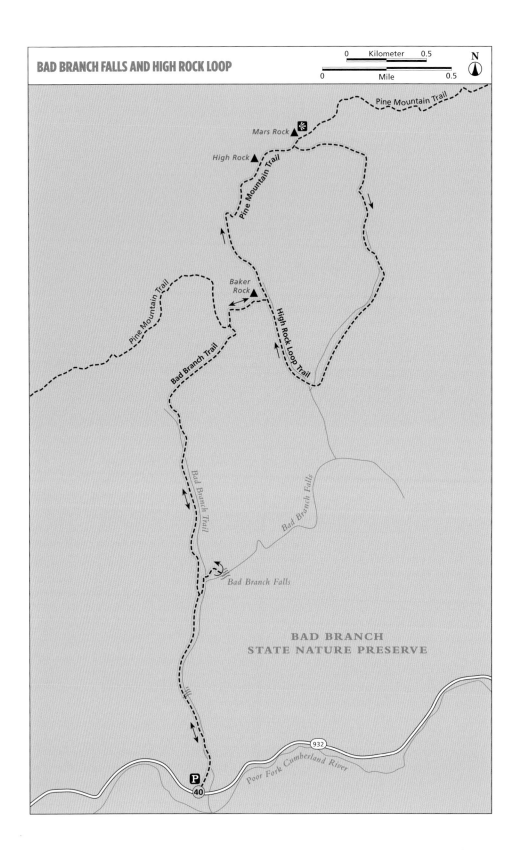

BAD BRANCH FALLS AND HIGH ROCK LOOP

0 — Kilometer — 0.5

0 — Mile — 0.5

N

Pine Mountain Trail

Mars Rock

High Rock

Pine Mountain Trail

Baker Rock

Pine Mountain Trail

Bad Branch Trail

High Rock Loop Trail

Bad Branch Trail

Bad Branch Falls

Bad Branch Falls

BAD BRANCH
STATE NATURE PRESERVE

932

Poor Fork Cumberland River

P

40

Option: Hike to Bad Branch Falls only for a 2.0-mile out-and-back experience.

MILES AND DIRECTIONS

0.0 Start from the Bad Branch parking area and walk past a trail sign on the singletrack Bad Branch Trail. Bad Branch flows off to your right. Pass an informational kiosk.

0.1 Cross Bad Branch on a trail bridge, entering a big flat roofed with hemlocks. Quickly bridge the stream a second time. You are now ascending the left bank of the stream under yellow birch aplenty.

0.4 Look down to admire a two-tiered slide cascade dropping perhaps 15 feet over 100 feet of creek. Look for other lesser shoals. Bluffs form in the valley.

0.6 Step over a tributary of Bad Branch flowing across the trail. Just ahead, you can look across the creek at a multi-tiered 100-foot waterfall across the creek. When the leaves are on, this spiller will be hard to see, and at lower flows it will be nothing but a trickle. However, in winter, when the water is up, it is a sight to behold. A huge bluff develops on the far side of the vale.

0.8 Reach a signed trail intersection. Here the Bad Branch Trail goes straight for High Rock, atop the crest of Pine Mountain along the Pine Mountain Trail, while we turn right toward Bad Branch Falls. Descend to rock hop a tributary of Bad Branch then climb among huge mossy rocks toward a sandstone cliff.

1.0 Come to Bad Branch Falls after ascending wooden steps and walking along the base of a cliff. Here you come to sidelong view of the 60-foot cataract somersaulting off a ledge then bashing its way down into a long and implausible boulder jumble. Be very careful when exploring here; do *not* climb to the top of the falls under any circumstances. Backtrack.

1.2 Rejoin the path to High Rock and Pine Mountain. Climb sharply at first along a tributary of Bad Branch.

1.7 Cross to the right-hand bank of the stream. Keep ascending to tunnel under rhododendron thickets.

2.4 Meet and join the Pine Mountain Trail. Head right, immediately descending to soon pass Baker Rock with its big overhang.

2.6 Reach the High Rock Loop. Stay left with the Pine Mountain Trail, climbing on another pretty tributary of Bad Branch.

3.0 Reach signed Ran Polly Gap. Keep climbing, often over naked rock bordered in pines.

3.4 Open onto High Rock, with its large surface of stone and a brow pointing west, opening onto rumpled wooded hills broken by little sign of civilization, save for Whitesburg immediately below. Scan High Rock for trees growing from crevices. Reenter woods.

3.5 Reach an intersection. Here the High Rock Loop splits right, but first briefly stay left with the Pine Mountain Trail and open onto sloped and pocked Mars Rock with its 180-degree views to the west. Return and begin descending back into woods on the High Rock Loop. Sidle alongside uppermost Bad Branch, gurgling clear over sand and rock, ensconced in rhododendron. Watch for big boulders and rockhouses as you descend a pleasant old roadbed.

4.8 Reach a signed intersection. Here an unofficial trail traces the old road down Bad Branch. The High Rock Loop splits right, crosses Bad Branch, works through a wooded flat, then turns up another tributary of Bad Branch. Ascend an irregular rock path before joining an old woods track.

5.3 Complete the High Rock Loop. Backtrack on the Pine Mountain Trail.

5.5 Head left, backtracking on the Bad Branch Trail.

7.5 Arrive back at the Bad Branch parking area.

41 KINGDOM COME HIGHLIGHT HIKE

Make a fun loop at this remote high-elevation state park atop Pine Mountain. Start at the picturesque park lake, then walk to the base of Raven Rock to find a huge rockhouse. From there, rise to Raven Rock, gaining southerly views across the Poor Fork valley. Climb to the crest of Pine Mountain for still more vistas, this time north into the greater Kentucky River valley as far as the sky allows. The lesser used Nature Haven Trail returns you to the park lake and the trailhead.

Start: Visitor center
Distance: 3.0-mile loop with 2 spurs
Difficulty: Easy due to distance but does have elevation changes
Elevation change: +/-810 feet
Maximum grade: 14% downhill grade for 0.4 mile
Hiking time: About 1.8 hours
Seasons/schedule: Year-round
Fees and permits: No fees or permits required
Dog friendly: Yes
Trail surface: Forested natural surface; some open rock slabs

Land status: State park
Nearest town: Cumberland
Other trail users: Vehicles on portion of Little Shepherd Trail
Maps to consult: Kingdom Come State Park
Amenities available: Restrooms, visitor center at trailhead
Cell service: Okay on ridgetop; bad elsewhere
Trail contacts: Kingdom Come State Park, (606) 589-4138; parks.ky.gov/cumberland/parks/recreation/kingdom-come-state-park

FINDING THE TRAILHEAD

From Whitesburg on US 119, take the first Cumberland exit and drive toward Cumberland a short distance to Park Road, on the right. Take Park Road up Pine Mountain for 1.3 miles and turn left at the sign for the lake and hiking trails. The trailhead is next to the lake at the end of the parking lot. *Alternate directions:* From Harlan, take US 119 North to Cumberland, then turn left on Park Road to the park visitor center. Trailhead GPS: 36.989868 / -82.984350

THE HIKE

Every square foot of Kingdom Come State Park stays above 2,000 feet, making it the highest-elevation state park in Kentucky. It is also the black bear capital of the Bluegrass State—you may even see one on your hike. The park's name comes from the title of a novel popular in the early 1900s, *The Little Shepherd of Kingdom Come.* The author, John Fox Jr. (1863–1919), was a Kentuckian, and the book deals with Kentucky mountain life and the Civil War.

Raven Rock is the focal point of a series of short nature trails that wind through the preserve. Our highlight hike will touch many of them. Raven Rock is a 290-foot-high

Looking north into the upper Kentucky River Valley

sandstone slope near the top of Pine Mountain that affords an excellent view from its upper edge. The rock tilts at a 45-degree angle toward the south, across the Poor Fork Cumberland River valley toward the ridge of Benham Spur. To the southeast stands 4,145-foot Black Mountain, the highest point in the Bluegrass State.

The hike starts at the park's small but scenic lake, 3.5 acres in size, next to the visitor center, where you can pick up a trail map—and a souvenir. During the warm season, paddleboats can be rented too. The impoundment is open to fishing for trout, catfish, bass, and bream; a Kentucky fishing license is required. You walk around the pond on foot, ambling beside some quaint stone walls circling the east side of the water. In a matter of minutes you are heading up the Laurel Trail, in thick woods along a small stream. Pass by a rockhouse across the creek before coming to the cool trail to another rockhouse that doubles as a park amphitheater. Here you bend under giant boulders, passing through dark passageways near the slope of lower Raven Rock to reach the expansive stone den that doubles as a park amphitheater—dim and dark, but dry.

After backtracking, the switchbacking Powerline Trail leads you up to Raven Rock, where the massive stone slab opens vistas to Black Mountain, Kentucky's highest point. You will also note the scarred trees, evidence of past fires, a natural occurrence on this south-facing xeric habitat of greenbrier, mountain laurel, bracken fern, and sourwood. Views continue even after you cross the most open part of the rock slab.

Raven Rock

The next part of the hike navigates several trail intersections that ultimately lead to the Little Shepherd Trail, the paved road running atop this part of Pine Mountain, along with the now-extended Pine Mountain Trail. At the paved road you will find a restroom and a picnic area. Now take a little road walk west and quickly come to the 12 O' Clock Trail, a short spur footpath leading to a fantastic panorama north across the Cumberland Plateau into ol' Kentuck' as far as the horizon allows. Climb past the power line–marred vista from Holcomb Overlook then the fantastic Bullock Overlook, where you are perched on a deck extending from the mountain crest.

It's all downhill from Bullock Overlook. You soon are on the richly vegetated Nature Haven Trail, winding down a ferny hollow then along a piney south-facing slope, passing another rockhouse along the way. Finally, you reach an alternate parking area near the park lake. After a final turn along the pond, you are back at the visitor center, to ponder just which Kingdom Come State Park souvenir you are going to purchase.

MILES AND DIRECTIONS

0.0 Start from the visitor center parking lot. Facing the pond, head right, circling the east side of the impoundment, passing along rock walls. Curve along the lake's edge, turning westerly.

0.1 Head north on the Laurel Trail, across a narrow gravel road running parallel to the shore. Pass a rockhouse along the way, across the small stream.

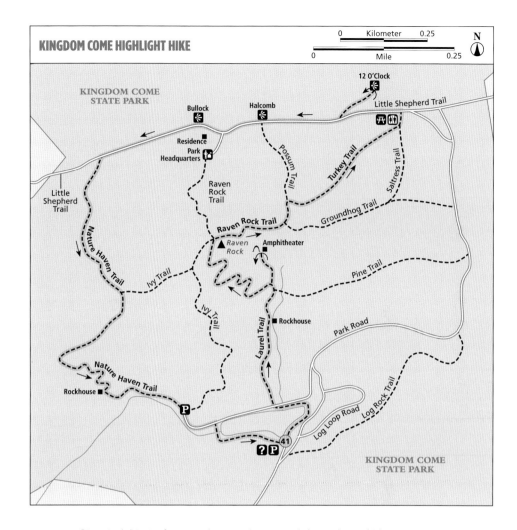

0.3 Stay straight at a four-way intersection toward the park amphitheater, passing a spring then climbing steps along the lower part of Raven Rock. Squeeze under gargantuan boulders then reach the big shelter, a natural amphitheater, alongside Raven Rock. Backtrack then join the Powerline Trail, switchbacking through woods, with the slope of Raven Rock to your right.

0.8 Reach an intersection. Head right on the Raven Rock Trail, crossing the top of the open rock face with fulfilling views stretching south toward Black Mountain. Scrubby shortleaf pines flank the stone clearing. The Poor Fork of the Cumberland River flows in the hollow below.

0.9 Come to a three-way intersection. Head left (northbound) on the Possum Trail in full woods. Quickly come to the intersection with the Turkey Trail. Split right with the Turkey Trail, gently working uphill.

1.2 Meet the Saltress Trail. Head left on the Saltress Trail and emerge at the Little Shepherd Trail—a road. Here are a restroom and picnic area. Head left on the paved Little Shepherd Trail.

1.3 Split right on the 12 O'clock Trail. Climb in hardwoods and pines along a narrow ridge then open onto a stone deck with a fantastic vista to the north across

Kentucky woodlands. Backtrack to the Little Shepherd Trail. Head west along the road, quickly passing the Halcomb Overlook.

1.8 Stay right with the Little Shepherd Trail as a paved road goes left to park headquarters. Ahead, come to the Bullock Overlook, located near a ranger residence. Walk out on the deck and behold a first-rate panorama of rolling ridges to the north as far as the eye can see. Continue west on the Little Shepherd Trail.

2.0 Split left on the mossy Nature Haven Trail. Dip into a thickly wooded, ferny hollow. Cross a streamlet, steadily descending.

2.3 Stay right with the Nature Haven Trail as the Ivy Trail splits left.

2.4 The path steepens. Pass the abandoned Scout Overlook and keep on a sharp slope where views open of the town of Cumberland below.

2.8 Level off, enter an alternate parking area and junction with the Ivy Trail, then emerge at the park lake. Circle right, around the impoundment.

3.0 Arrive back at the visitor center parking area and trailhead.

42 CHAINED ROCK

This hike at fine Pine Mountain State Resort Park leads you past Powderhorn Arch then through a mini-gorge of a highland creek. From there, top out on Pine Mountain then work your way to Chained Rock, where you can climb an incredible open rock slope with eye-popping vistas of Chained Rock in the near and Pineville, the Cumberland River Valley, and adjacent mountains rising beyond. While at the state park, consider adding the easy trek to Honeymoon Falls.

Start: Laurel Cove shelter
Distance: 2.8 miles out and back
Difficulty: Moderate; does have solid climb
Elevation change: +/-959 feet
Maximum grade: 26% grade for 0.2 mile
Hiking time: About 1.8 hours
Seasons/schedule: Year-round; clear days for views
Fees and permits: No fees or permits required
Dog friendly: Yes, but parts of the trail are naked rock.

Trail surface: Natural surface; some open, sloped rock
Land status: State forest
Nearest town: Pineville
Other trail users: None
Maps to consult: Pine Mountain State Resort Park
Amenities available: Picnic shelter, restrooms at trailhead
Cell service: Good
Trail contacts: Pine Mountain State Resort Park; (606) 337-3066; parks. ky.gov/pineville/parks/resort/pine-mountain-state-resort-park

FINDING THE TRAILHEAD

From the intersection of KY 66 and US 25E in Pineville, take US 25E south for 1 mile. Turn right onto State Park Road (there is sign here for Chained Rock Overlook and Laurel Cove Amphitheater) and follow it for 0.4 mile. Veer right, still on State Park Road, and follow it for 0.3 mile. Turn right toward the Laurel Cove picnic shelter, just as State Park Road makes a hard left, and follow it to dead-end at the Laurel Cove picnic shelter, not the amphitheater. Trailhead GPS: 36.743579 / -83.705771

THE HIKE

At the edge of a cliff face on Pine Mountain above the town of Pineville, a huge rock appears to perch precariously. For years local lore had it that only a chain tethering the rock to the mountainside kept the little town below from being flattened. There was, of course, nothing to the story. There was no chain, and the rock wasn't about to go anywhere. According to state park officials, the rock is actually connected to the cliff but, due to erosion and weathering, appears to be separated.

In 1933, apparently inspired by an out-of-state couple passing through Pineville who were completely taken in by the story, the local Kiwanis Club formed a committee to turn fiction into fact. In an act of truly superhuman proportions, citizens, with help

Walking under Powderhorn Arch

from the Civilian Conservation Corps, hauled a big chain up the mountain by mule and anchored the chain to the rock on one end and the cliff face on the other. It was a master stroke of community promotion, gaining Pineville attention in hundreds of newspapers across the country.

Today this 101-foot-long, 1.5-ton chain is still in place, and Chained Rock makes a unique destination for a hike up Pine Mountain. Kids will love it. The outcropping makes a great lookout too, with views south to Cumberland Mountain, east along Pine Mountain Ridge, and north down into Pineville.

Pine Mountain was Kentucky's first state park, and it's certainly one of its prettiest. This hike follows delightful Laurel Cove Trail most of the way to Chained Rock. Well used and easy to follow, it is billed as the park's longest and hardest trail. While the hike's inbound leg is mostly uphill, the grades are not severe.

From the Laurel Cove trailhead near the pavilion, you ascend initially northeast and then northwest and, after a short level stretch, reach Powderhorn Arch. The trail actually travels under the sandstone span, so you can't miss the slender, 8-foot-high natural bridge with a 20-foot span. Next you turn into an intimate creek valley where water has cut a mini-chasm through which you hike, repeatedly bridging the small creek. In places the watercourse rushes straight down the mountain, forming low-flow slide chutes, all flanked by stone and framed in beautiful stands of rhododendron.

Chained Rock

You will top out at an intersection with Chained Rock to your right. (A left turn at this intersection takes you 0.5 mile to scenic Chained Rock Road, with an additional view.) Our hike descends stone steps then works along the base of a massive open outcrop. Chained Rock—and its chain—stand ahead.

After coming to Chained Rock you split left and work your way up the massive open outcrop. The best views are from the outcrop to which the chain of Chained Rock is

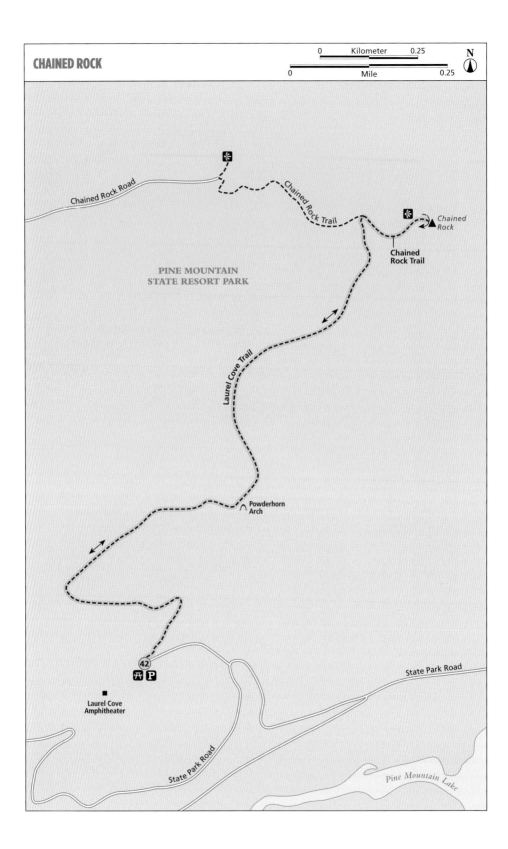

0   Kilometer   0.25

0   Mile   0.25

N

Chained Rock Road

Chained Rock Trail

Chained Rock

Chained
Rock Trail

PINE MOUNTAIN
STATE RESORT PARK

Laurel Cove Trail

Powderhorn
Arch

42

Laurel Cove
Amphitheater

State Park Road

State Park Road

Pine Mountain Lake

Gazing down on Pineville from Chained Rock

attached. There is no set route up the outcropping, and you should watch children carefully. As for the chain, it's made of steel, each link weighing 4.5 pounds.

It's a simple backtrack to the parking lot.

Option: If you desire another trek at Pine Mountain State Resort State Park, try Honeymoon Falls. The waterfall is only 0.3 mile from its trailhead, located about 0.5 mile from the state park lodge. You will cross the creek of Honeymoon Falls a total of five times on the way up, experiencing the Catch-22 of waterfall hiking: When a stream is up, the waterfalls will be bold, but that also means the creek crossings will be more difficult. This particular stream is small and so should not present much difficulty. You will find Honeymoon Falls tucked away in a little rock grotto, uniformly pouring from a stone cleft straight down from an overhung rockhouse, diving 18 feet down to a pebble and rock–strewn base below. You can admire the discharging water from multiple angles.

MILES AND DIRECTIONS

0.0 Start from the Laurel Cove picnic shelter and leave northeast, away from the shelter on the signed Laurel Cove Trail. Resist the urge to head west on a well-used path toward the Laurel Cove amphitheater. Begin climbing the south slope of Pine Mountain on a singletrack path making switchbacks under sourwood, cucumber magnolia, and pine.

0.6 Reach a big outcrop; climb over it then walk under Powderhorn Arch.

0.7 Come to an unnamed creek flowing off Pine Mountain. Alternately cross it on natural stone bridges, rock hops, and even wood bridges, climbing all the while. Hike alongside a long slide cascade. Parts of the trail use carved stone steps.

0.9 Pass under a low rockhouse. Ahead, squeeze through a narrow passage with rock walls on both sides of what is remaining of the stream.

1.3 Come to an intersection after passing another rockhouse on your left. The Chained Rock Trail leads left to Chained Rock Road and an alternate view. (This is the primary access for visitors coming to Chained Rock.) We split right at the intersection on the Chained Rock Trail toward Chained Rock, descending on stone steps.

1.4 Come to Chained Rock and a massive outcrop. Climb the outcrop for stellar views of Pineville and beyond. Retrace your steps.

2.8 Arrive back at the Laurel Cove picnic shelter trailhead.

43 CUMBERLAND GAP HIKE

This trek at Cumberland Gap National Historical Park traces the route used by man and beast for millennia, working their way west into what became Kentucky. Made famous by Daniel Boone, the passage through Cumberland Gap follows the "Wilderness Road," now restored to its original appearance. You will walk a foot trail, tracing Daniel's steps to and through the actual Cumberland Gap, marked by a memorial. Next, climb to Tri-State Peak, where Kentucky, Tennessee, and Virginia meet. After that, follow the Wilderness Road, looping back through Cumberland Gap. Your return trip leads you to Cumberland Furnace, an iron-making operation, as well as Gap Cave, which also figures in the history of this mountainous, history-laden land of three states.

Start: Daniel Boone Visitor Information Center trailhead
Distance: 5.5-mile balloon loop with spurs
Difficulty: Moderate
Elevation change: +/-1,180 feet
Maximum grade: 10% grade for 1.1 miles
Hiking time: About 3 hours
Seasons/schedule: Year-round
Fees and permits: No fees or permits required
Dog friendly: Yes

Trail surface: Some gravel; mostly forested natural surface
Land status: National park
Nearest town: Middlesboro
Other trail users: None
Maps to consult: Cumberland Gap National Historical Park
Amenities available: Picnic tables, restrooms at trailhead
Cell service: Good
Trail contacts: Cumberland Gap National Historical Park; (606) 248-2817; nps.gov/cuga

FINDING THE TRAILHEAD

From Middlesboro, Kentucky, take US 25E south for 2.3 miles to the US 58 East ramp, passing through the Cumberland Gap Tunnel. Join US 58 East and follow it for 0.4 mile. Turn left on TN 825, toward the town of Cumberland Gap, Tennessee. Follow this road for 0.2 mile, entering Virginia, then turn right to reach the Daniel Boone Visitor Information Center trailhead. Trailhead GPS: 36.601674 / -83.660056

THE HIKE

Cumberland Gap is a natural passage in the mountain barrier dividing Kentucky from Virginia. Once fought over by Shawnee and Cherokee, the gap was used to connect the rich—and disputed—hunting grounds of Kentucky with points south. The Native American trail through the gap even had a name: Warriors Path. After European colonists arrived, the mountain barrier of the Appalachians kept colonists at bay, but it was the Cumberland Gap through which they eventually spilled westward. First came Dr.

Hiking to the one and only Cumberland Gap

Thomas Walker in 1750, in search of lands for the Loyal Land Company. He entered what became Kentucky on the Warriors Path, naming the Cumberland River before returning east. He was followed through the years by long hunters, the most famous of which was Daniel Boone. Employed by a different land speculator—Judge Thomas Henderson—Boone made a foray from his home in the Yadkin Valley of North Carolina, beyond the Cumberland Gap, returning with a haul of furs.

Hiking away from Gap Cave on a colorful fall day

This Kentucky region intrigued him, and in 1775 Boone hacked out a rough road from the Holston River's Long Island in Tennessee (near present-day Kingsport) to and through the Cumberland Gap and on to the Kentucky River. This became the famous Wilderness Road, eventually through which came thousands, eventually establishing Kentucky as the fifteenth state in the Union, in 1792.

Cumberland Gap remained an important passageway between East and West. During the Civil War, both North and South vied for control of the passage. Although it changed hands during the conflict, there were no major battles fought here, though Civil War fort sites remain.

After the Civil War, the natural resources of the region brought attention back to the area where Virginia, Kentucky, and Tennessee come together. An iron forge was established just below the gap. Coal mining rose to prominence, resulting in the founding of Middlesboro, Kentucky, just north of Cumberland Gap. The gap became a rutty, mired mess. Eventually an auto highway (US 25) was run through the passage, altering its historical appearance. By the 1930s, a movement was afoot to establish a national park here, resulting in today's Cumberland Gap National Historical Park. The highway has since been removed from the passage (US 25 now tunnels its way through Cumberland Mountain) and Cumberland Gap restored to its original appearance.

Today you can absorb loads of history at the elaborate trailhead and walk the Wilderness Road to and through the gap. Explore the iron forge just below the gap in a scenic

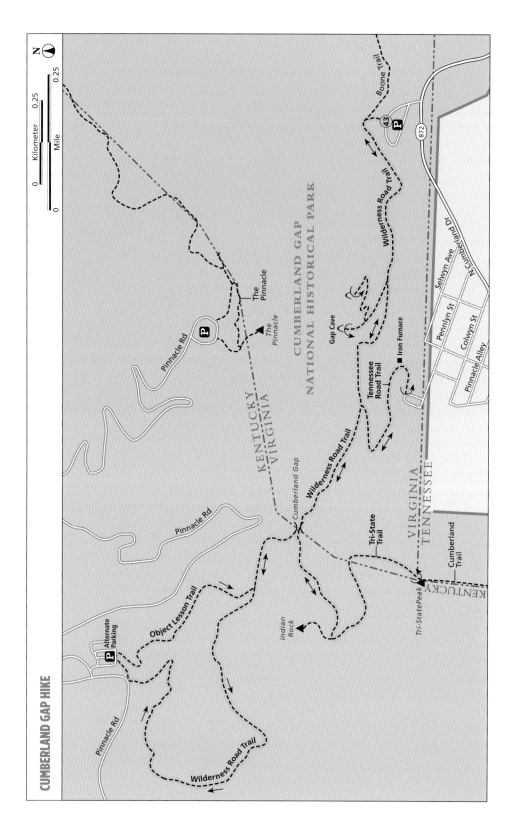

setting along Gap Creek. Climb to Tri-State Peak and stand in three states at once. Visit Gap Cave and its nearby alternate entrance (cave exploration allowed only on park tours). This cave provided shelter and water for passersby and later became a popular cave tour destination when illuminated with electric lights in 1934. Tours were expanded when a tunnel was dug linking other caves to Gap Cave. The grotto was damaged and vandalized, but it has since been restored to its natural state with restoration of the gap.

Enlightening interpretive information is scattered throughout the hike. While here, be mindful of those who came before—the buffalo that created the trail, the Native Americans that followed, the long hunters, the future Kentuckians, the Civil War soldiers, the coal miners, the iron forgers, the tourists of the twentieth century, the national park visitors of the twenty-first century—and now you. It is truly a walk along the footsteps of history.

MILES AND DIRECTIONS

0.0   Start at the Daniel Boone Visitor Information Center and walk under the breezeway. Go left with the Wilderness Road Trail as the Boone Trail splits right. Walk a wide track westerly in mixed woods.

0.1   Enter a restored segment of the Cumberland Gap. The area of old US 25E is now grassy and growing up with trees. The trail continues westerly. The hamlet of Cumberland Gap, Tennessee, lies below.

0.4   A spur path leads right to Gap Cave. For now, stay straight on the Wilderness Road Trail.

0.5   Cross Gap Creek on a log bridge. The stream flows out of Gap Cave. This stream was mentioned in the journals of Dr. Thomas Walker, who passed through here in 1750. The stream also provided drinking water for Civil War soldiers stationed at Cumberland Gap, as well as the throngs who passed through this break in Cumberland Mountain.

0.6   The Tennessee Road Trail leaves left to the iron forge and the town of Cumberland Gap, Tennessee. Stay straight with the Wilderness Road Trail. Mountains rise all around you.

0.9   Reach the actual Cumberland Gap after a short steep section. The gap was dug out when the highway ran through but is now at its original elevation. At this point the Wilderness Road descends into Kentucky. Turn left, joining the Tri-State Trail up wood-and-earth steps to reach the stone pyramid, commemorating passages through the gap. Continue up the Tri-State Trail, passing a spur to Fort Foote and Indian Rock.

1.5   Reach Tri-State Peak, marked by a gazebo and plaques for Kentucky, Tennessee, and Virginia, as well as the northern terminus of the Cumberland Trail, extending into Tennessee all the way to Lookout Mountain near Chattanooga. Views open into Middlesboro and beyond. Backtrack.

2.1   Continue into Kentucky on the Wilderness Road Trail after returning to Cumberland Gap. Traverse preserved sections of the original path used by early Kentuckians, steadily descending, and pass the intersection with the Object Lesson Trail.

2.6   Bottom out then curve along a slope, passing near the railroad tunnel that goes from Virginia into Kentucky beneath the actual Cumberland Gap.

2.9   Reach the large Thomas Walker parking area off Pinnacle Road. Head right, joining the Object Lesson Trail, which follows an early road-building project that was meant to be an object lesson for the value of road investment. Gently climb in evergreens toward Cumberland Gap.

3.4 Return to Cumberland Gap. Stay with the Wilderness Road Trail, descending back into Virginia.

3.7 Join the Tennessee Road Trail, switchbacking downhill through woods toward the Cumberland iron furnace.

4.0 Reach the furnace on your left. Steps lead to the interior of the former forge that made iron. Backtrack to the Wilderness Trail and resume toward the trailhead.

4.5 Turn left on the Gap Cave Trail. You are following the route of old US 25E. Ahead, the trail splits right to an alternate cave entrance/exit. Keep straight for Gap Cave.

4.6 Reach Gap Cave. Today, ranger-led, lantern-lit cave tours are run by the National Park Service. Backtrack, then walk up to the other cave entrance/exit. This arched cave entrance is also barred. (Gap Cave has six known entrances.) Explore the other entrance nearby then backtrack to the Wilderness Road Trail. Trace the Wilderness Trail easterly back toward the trailhead.

5.5 Arrive back at the trailhead.

44 HENSLEY SETTLEMENT

This hike at Cumberland Gap National Historical Park climbs Cumberland Mountain on the old Chadwell Gap Trail to reach a preserved mountaintop community. Once the home of Sherman Hensley and his descendants, the remote habitation existed in isolation for five decades. Today, a strenuous, 2,000-plus-foot climb leads to the secluded and gorgeous locale where two dozen buildings, from homes to the schoolhouse to outbuildings, await your visit. It is truly a fascinating trip back in time.

Start: Chadwell Gap trailhead
Distance: 9.6-mile balloon loop
Difficulty: Difficult due to elevation change and mileage
Elevation change: +/-2,436 feet
Maximum grade: 25% grade for 0.6 mile
Hiking time: About 7 hours, including touring Hensley Settlement
Seasons/schedule: Mar through Oct
Fees and permits: No fees or permits required unless backpacking
Dog friendly: Yes

Trail surface: Mostly forested natural surface
Land status: National park
Nearest town: Middlesboro
Other trail users: None
Maps to consult: Cumberland Gap National Historical Park
Amenities available: Picnic tables, restrooms at Hensley Settlement
Cell service: Okay; limited atop Hensley Settlement
Trail contacts: Cumberland Gap National Historical Park; (606) 248-2817; nps.gov/cuga

FINDING THE TRAILHEAD

From Middlesboro, Kentucky, take US 25E south for 2.3 miles to the US 58 East ramp, passing through the Cumberland Gap Tunnel. Join US 58 East and follow it for 9.7 miles. Turn left on Caylor Road (VA 690). (The right turn will be Doc Hurst Road.) Follow Caylor Road for 1.7 miles then veer right onto VA 688. Stay with VA 688 for 0.7 mile to reach the Chadwell Gap trailhead, on your left. Trailhead GPS: 36.653905 / -83.496615

THE HIKE

The Hensley Settlement protects and preserves lifeways long abandoned in the Southern Appalachian Mountains. This former community is set 3,300 feet high in a perched mountaintop valley where the headwaters of Shillalah Creek flow between Brushy Mountain to the north and Cumberland Mountain to the south. It remains a remote and scenic parcel of ol' Kentuck', the place where Sherman Hensley, back in 1904, decided to retreat from the lower reaches of Harlan County, Kentucky, and make his home in the back of beyond here along the Kentucky-Virginia state line. Sherman brought his wife and built on the pasturage and woodland, set apart from the rest of the world.

One of the many preserved homesteads at the Hensley Settlement

Relatives of Hensley joined the settlement, and a bona fide community was established. Despite the inroads of such things as indoor plumbing and electric lighting had made in the Southern Appalachians, the Hensley Settlement remained cast in the nineteenth century, inadvertently preserving a self-sufficient, simple subsistence life that—despite its primitive conditions—seems unpretentious, almost romantic, compared to today's rush-rush digital world.

By 1908 enough children were in the settlement to establish a simple school. The place of learning went through several incarnations. Today you can see the clapboard schoolhouse, with its wooden desks and cast-iron stove for heat. The settlement continued to expand, ultimately reaching more than one hundred residents in the mid-1920s. Residents grew their own food, raised their own animals, and used horses, wagons, or foot power for transportation. The residents did leave regularly to trade their products such as corn and corn juice—read: moonshine—down in Caylor, Virginia, using the Chadwell Gap Trail to make their runs, following roughly the same route we use to access the settlement today.

Ultimately, the lure of civilization and money that could be made down the mountain drew its residents from the settlement. By 1949 only its founder, Sherman Hensley, remained. Two years later, at age 71, Hensley left the mountain himself. The buildings fell into disrepair, the forest began reclaiming once-productive fields, and the Hensley Settlement was no more.

Another preserved homestead at the Hensley Settlement

After the establishment of Cumberland Gap National Historical Park in 1959, plans were made to restore the Hensley Settlement as a historical window to the past. In the 1960s the Job Corps restored many structures. They continue to be maintained to this day.

This hike traces portions of the historic Chadwell Gap Trail. At hike's end, the path steeply makes its way astride foreboding rock ramparts, attaining the crest of Cumberland Mountain. Here join the Ridge Trail, then come to the Hensley Settlement.

The hike then leaves the settlement, crosses Shillalah Creek, then visits Indian Rock, an impressive rock shelter. You are soon back on the Ridge Trail, backtracking toward the trailhead. Allow plenty of time to explore as well as execute the actual hike.

Option: The trail passes a pair of backcountry campsites and comes near yet another camp that also offers a cabin for overnighting, making a backcountry camping adventure possible in conjunction with this hike.

MILES AND DIRECTIONS

- **0.0** Start at the Chadwell Gap Trail, heading uphill through woods.
- **0.5** The trail curves left into a tulip tree–filled hollow. Keep westerly, undulating in hills and hollows.
- **1.1** Reach the old Chadwell Gap Trail. Turn right here on the wide track. Briefly descend, then cross a hollow. Look right for a spur trail leading to a rocked-in spring.

HENSLEY SETTLEMENT

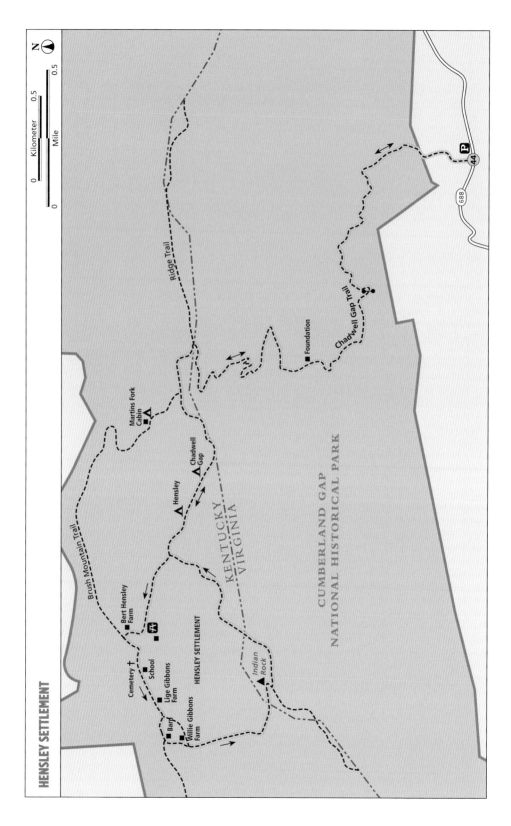

Sherman Hensley and other travelers on the Chadwell Gap Trail surely used this water source while heading up and down the mountain.

1.5 Curve close to a rocky drainage on your left, then quickly turn away from it.

1.6 Pass a concrete building foundation on your right. Continue climbing as the slope steepens. Note the rock bluffs atop the ridge.

1.9 Take a hard switchback to the left. The trail steepens.

2.1 Make a series of short switchbacks in extremely rocky, bouldery, bluff-filled torturous terrain. The slope steepens, rhododendron appears, and views open south of the mountain.

2.6 Come just below the actual Chadwell Gap, but veer right, walking beneath a huge rock bluff. Keep up a lung-busting climb.

2.7 Reach the crest of Cumberland Mountain and the Ridge Trail. The mountain crest delineates the Kentucky-Virginia state line. Turn left on the Ridge Trail. Pass the actual Chadwell Gap, then descend past a tall rock rampart to your left.

3.0 Intersect the Martins Fork Trail. It leaves right to its namesake stream and a small rustic cabin and campsite. Keep straight on the Ridge Trail, walking the state line. Skirt massive rock pillars.

3.4 Meet the spur trail to the Chadwell Gap campsite just after leveling off. Keep straight on the Ridge Trail. The trail remains mostly level as you enter what is described on USGS topo maps as Hensley Flats.

3.5 Pass the Hensley Camp campsite on your right. Keep straight on the wide Ridge Trail.

3.7 Reach a signed trail junction. The Ridge Trail splits left and will be your return route. For now, keep straight on the unnamed trail leading to the Hensley Settlement.

3.9 Come to the Hensley Settlement, which opens dead ahead. A sand road/trail leads to your right past a maintenance area. Keep straight, entering open meadows and a picnic area while staying along a fence line.

4.1 Pass the Bert Hensley Farm on your right. Here, a road spurs right. Stay left, working through a mix of field and woods.

4.2 Pass the Hensley Cemetery on your right, then the schoolhouse on your left. Look in the window at the desks and wood stove. Walk through bucolic meadows where deer are often seen.

4.4 A road leads left down to the Lige Gibbons Farm, a beautifully intact wooden structure. Continue walking along the fence line.

4.5 Pass a barn to your right, then curve left. Here, the Shillalah Creek Trail leads right. Explore many small outbuildings, part of the greater Willie Gibbons Farm.

4.6 Pass the Gibbons Farm chimney, then leave the open fields of the settlement and join a path entering forest. Gently descend southbound.

4.8 Rock-hop Shillalah Creek. Leave the creek and enter a wide flat with rock ramparts to your left.

5.2 Come underneath Indian Rock, a huge dry rock shelter used by Native Americans. Abruptly descend to meet the Ridge Trail. Turn left on the Ridge Trail and come along the mountain edge. Southward views open through the trees.

5.8 Look for the remains of a pigpen and other wooden structures just before stepping over the upper reaches of Shillalah Creek. Walk uphill, passing a clearing on your left with a crumbled chimney in it.

5.9 Complete the loop portion of the hike. Turn right here, staying with the Ridge Trail. From here it is 3.7 miles back to the trailhead. Backtrack past the campsites to turn right on the Chadwell Gap Trail and carefully descend.

9.6 Arrive back at the Chadwell Gap trailhead.

45 **WHITE ROCKS SAND CAVE HIKE**

This hike to two incredible Kentucky wonders actually starts in Virginia at Cumberland National Historical Park, shared by Kentucky, Virginia, and Tennessee. This trek first scales Cumberland Mountain, forming the state-line border between Kentucky and Virginia, then wanders the highlands, climbing first to the White Rocks, an outcrop with phenomenal views. Next, head to extraordinary Sand Cave, a huge rockhouse enclosing a sea of grains that will impress. Nearby, Sand Cave Branch plummets 25 feet off the red-rock rampart adjacent to Sand Cave onto a bed of sand. From Sand Cave take the upper Ewing Trail before backtracking to the trailhead.

Start: Ewing Civic Park trailhead
Distance: 8.4-mile balloon loop
Difficulty: Difficult due to elevation change
Elevation change: **+/-**2,476 feet
Maximum grade: 13% grade for 1 mile
Hiking time: About 5.5 hours
Seasons/schedule: Year-round
Fees and permits: No fees or permits required unless backpacking
Dog friendly: Yes
Trail surface: Forested natural surface
Land status: National park

Nearest town: Ewing, Virginia
Other trail users: Equestrians on parts of hike
Maps to consult: Cumberland Gap National Historical Park
Amenities available: Picnic area, picnic shelter, restroom at trailhead
Cell service: Good while facing Virginia
Trail contacts: Cumberland Gap National Historical Park; (606) 248-2817; nps.gov/cuga

FINDING THE TRAILHEAD

From Middlesboro, Kentucky, take US 25E south for 2.3 miles to the US 58 East ramp, passing through the Cumberland Gap Tunnel. Join US 58 East and follow it for 14 miles. Turn left on VA 724 (Sand Cave Road) in Ewing and continue for 1 mile to dead-end at Ewing Civic Park. Trailhead GPS: 36.652130 / -83.435506

THE HIKE

I think the vista from White Rocks is one of the finest in the Southeast. Rising majestically from the ridge of Cumberland Mountain, the wide outcrop not only provides first rate panoramas but is also a sight from the lowlands below. From White Rocks, you will visit Sand Cave and Sand Cave Falls. More of a rockhouse than an actual cave, Sand Cave stretches 1.25 acres in size, according to the National Park Service, and has an opening 250 feet wide. The floor of the rockhouse is covered deep in more sand than you can imagine occurs naturally, a result of cave erosion. A commonly repeated legend (also

Peering into Kentucky from White Rocks

repeated here) is that Sand Cave has twenty-one different colors of sand. In pre–national park days, Sand Cave was accessible by auto. It became a popular gathering spot, especially in the heat of summer. Not only would the air temperature be cooler here at 3,000 feet, but the rear of the rock shelter would be cooler still. Sand Cave was also known for its good acoustics, and group sing-alongs would be held in the colossal rockhouse.

Today, the only way to get to the rockhouse is by trail, and after you see Sand Cave Falls and Sand Cave, you will be singing its praises both inside and outside the rock shelter—often argued to be the single largest rock shelter in Kentucky, which is saying a lot. I'll personally add that it is the most memorable rockhouse I've seen in the Bluegrass State. You can turn this hike into an overnight adventure, as the trek passes near a designated backcountry campsite.

The hike leaves Ewing Civic Park on a hiker-only path bordered by scads of mountain laurel. Cruise up a tributary of Roaring Branch, crossing it twice to meet the equestrian trail leading up from lower Ewing Park. Next, the wide path angles its way up the slope of Cumberland Mountain, easing the ascent as it crosses tributaries of Indian Creek using numerous switchbacks. The Ewing Trail ascends below White Rocks, but then you join the hiker-only Ewing Spur Trail, executing still more upward switchbacks for a total climb of 1,700 feet to reach the Kentucky-Virginia state line.

At this point, the trek picks up the also wide Ridge Trail. First you will head east on the Ridge Trail to large and spectacular White Rocks, elevation 3,369 feet. Here, on

Sand Cave is the largest rock shelter in all of Kentucky.

this open outcrop, you can see into Kentucky, Virginia, and Tennessee, all the way to the Great Smoky Mountains. After backtracking from White Rocks, trace the Ridge Trail west, passing the spur to the White Rocks backcountry campsite. A park service permit is required to overnight at this rocky, mountainside camp. The hike fully enters Kentucky and travels through thick woods, rife with rhododendron. You will cross the uppermost reaches of Sand Cave Branch—the stream forming Sand Cave Falls—before picking up the side trail to Sand Cave and Sand Cave Falls. This hiker-only path descends by switchbacks through evergreen thickets. Wood and concrete steps aid your passage toward Sand Cave. Step over a gravelly streambed then come to Sand Cave. You will be impressed with the size and beauty of this geological wonder that redefines "rockhouse." Sand Cave Falls spills from the east side of the cave edge, making a noisy drop as it pours over a slightly overhung ledge then splashes 25 feet later into a shallow grainy pool. In late summer and autumn, Sand Cave Branch can shrink to a trickle up here at 3,020 feet. Next you backtrack to the Ridge Trail and climb westerly to meet the upper part of the Ewing Trail. The wide track leads you east back into Virginia, completing a highland loop, followed by a 2.4-mile backtrack descent to the trailhead at Ewing Civic Park.

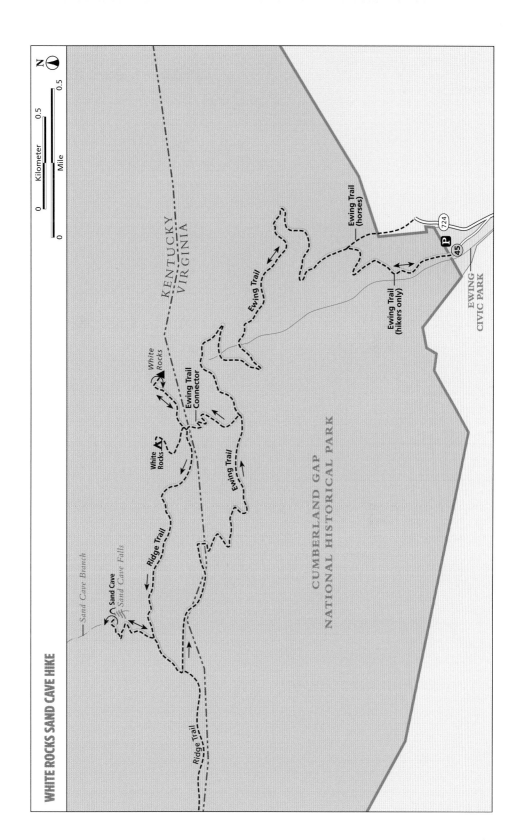

WHITE ROCKS SAND CAVE HIKE

Sand Cave Branch

Sand Cave
Sand Cave Falls

Ridge Trail

White Rocks

White Rocks

Ridge Trail

Ewing Trail Connector

Ewing Trail

Ewing Trail

KENTUCKY
VIRGINIA

Ewing Trail

CUMBERLAND GAP
NATIONAL HISTORICAL PARK

Ewing Trail (hikers only)

Ewing Trail (horses)

724

45

EWING
CIVIC PARK

N

Kilometer
0   0.5

0   0.5
Mile

A view into the Volunteer State from White Rocks

MILES AND DIRECTIONS

0.0 Start on the Ewing Trail, leaving from near the pavilion at the uppermost part of Ewing Civic Park. This trail is hiker only. Ascend along an unnamed tributary of Roaring Creek, crossing it twice.

0.5 Intersect the equestrian trail coming up from the lower end of Ewing Civic Park. Continue working up the slope of Cumberland Mountain. The path is wider.

0.9 Cross the upper reaches of a tributary of Roaring Creek, known to run dry in summer and fall. Ahead, make a big switchback to the left, recrossing additional intermittent streamlets.

1.8 Make a big switchback to the right. Keep ascending.

2.4 Reach a trail intersection on the south slope of Cumberland Mountain. Here the Ewing Trail goes left; we stay with the Ewing Trail Connector, aiming for the top of the state-line ridge. Ascend by switchbacks.

2.8 Reach the top of Cumberland Mountain and the intersection with the Ridge Trail, the spur trail to White Rocks campsite, and the spur trail to White Rocks. Head right (easterly) with the Ridge Trail on the state line, curving into Kentucky to climb the outcrop.

3.1 Open onto the outcrop of White Rocks. Eye-popping views range north into Kentucky and south into Virginia and Tennessee. Buzzards will often be found riding the thermals here. Backtrack, staying west on the Ridge Trail, drifting onto the Kentucky side of Cumberland Mountain.

4.0 Cross the upper reach of Sand Cave Branch, the stream of Sand Cave Falls.

4.2 Turn right onto the hiker-only Sand Cave Trail. Descend through evergreens.

4.4 Reach Sand Cave and Sand Cave Falls. Explore both the 25-foot cataract and the immense shelter. Backtrack.

4.6 Return to the four-way intersection with the Ridge Trail. Head right (westerly), climbing in hardwoods.

4.8 Intersect the upper end of the Ewing Trail. Head left on the Ewing Trail, curving easterly. Rise to the state line then descend easterly by switchbacks into Virginia.

6.0 Complete the loop portion of the hike. Here, stay straight with the Ewing Trail, backtracking toward the Ewing Civic Park trailhead.

8.4 Arrive back at the trailhead.

HIKE INDEX